Dictionary of
MULTICULTURAL PSYCHOLOGY

Dictionary of
MULTICULTURAL PSYCHOLOGY
Issues, Terms, and Concepts

LENA E. HALL
Nova Southeastern University

SAGE Publications
International Educational and Professional Publisher
Thousand Oaks ■ London ■ New Delhi

For information:

Sage Publications, Inc.
2455 Teller Road
Thousand Oaks, California 91320
E-mail: order@sagepub.com

Sage Publications Ltd.
1 Oliver's Yard
55 City Road
London EC1Y 1SP
United Kingdom

Sage Publications India Pvt. Ltd.
B-42, Panchsheel Enclave
Post Box 4109
New Delhi 110 017 India

Library of Congress Cataloging-in-Publication Data

Hall, Lena E.
Dictionary of multicultural psychology: issues, terms, and concepts / Lena E. Hall.
   p. cm.
Includes bibliographical references.
ISBN 0-7619-2822-7 (cloth)—ISBN 0-7619-2823-5 (pbk.)
   1. Ethnopsychology—Dictionaries. 2. Multiculturalism—Psychological aspects—Dictionaries. I. Title.
GN502.H336 2005
155.8′2—dc22

                              2004011262

Printed on acid-free paper in the United States of America.

05 06 07 08 09 10 9 8 7 6 5 4 3 2 1

Acquisitions Editor:	Jim Brace-Thompson
Editorial Assistant:	Karen Ehrmann
Production Editor:	Tracy Alpern
Copy Editor:	Dan Hays
Proof reader:	Sally Scott
Typesetter:	C&M Digitals (P) Ltd.
Cover Designer:	Edgar Abarca

Contents

Preface

The production of this dictionary was motivated by more than 11 years of teaching multicultural psychology. Students often become so excited by the topic that they constantly ask for more information than can be provided due to the limited term schedule. The dictionary serves two purposes. First, it allows students to broaden their knowledge on topics introduced in the class. Each entry gives the meaning of the term or concept. Second, in addition to the definitions, there are reference sources so that students can do further reading on the topic. Professors are free to use the dictionary entries as a starting point in class by initiating discussion on individual entries followed by discussion of research findings by students, prompted by the included references. Thus, this dictionary goes well beyond meaning definitions and can provide a wealth of resources for the multicultural student.

The compilation of the dictionary was done with the enthusiastic help of many of the students and faculty involved with the teaching of multicultural psychology or the clinical practice with culturally diverse clients. Needless to say, some of the entries were more difficult to access than others. Some students simply could not find any references for some of the terms, and some terms could be accessed only from other dictionary sources.

The definitions of the terms are concise. Although this has resulted in a less voluminous document, it is an advantage for multicultural students who may prefer exploring entries on a more in-depth level on their own rather than rely solely on the entries. Also, professors can be more creative in the use of the dictionary in terms of the research and written assignments that can be developed for each entry.

Acknowledgments

I thank Sage Publications Senior Editor Jim Brace-Thompson, who was very supportive throughout this process and helped motivate me to complete this task. I also thank Guda Gayle-Evans, PhD, of the University of South Florida and Michael Reiter, PhD, of Nova Southeastern University, who contributed terms that they either coined or found in their work on multicultural issues. I acknowledge several multicultural psychology students who also eagerly researched terms for this work. Among this group, the most significant contributors were Beverley Jean-Jacques and Gari Senderhoff. Others include Alex Hache, Rashmeen Nimal, Diane Alves, Katya Delgado, Thomas Brown, Sabrina Tassy, Mary Brylski, Michael Palamino, Corinth Calvo, Krystal Lamb, Peter Davis, Michelle Alvarez, Angela Conner, Graham Rasanen, Tanya Echavarria, Bijou Stoc, Laura Reyes, Janin Guerra, Elizabeth Resnick, Lori Pantaleao, Holly Tomecko, Christina Thorpe, Katie Wintle, Micaela Mercado, Maria Usberghi, Melanie Denny, Jennifer Fedak, Ed Vargas, Diane Klein, Angela Heron, Tara Swasy, Marsha Gray, Alison Allen, David Hollingsworth, and Jessica Davis.

Sage Publications acknowledges the contributions of reviewers Philip S. Wong, Long Island University; Christy Barongan, Washington and Lee University; William H. George, University of Washington; Chi-Ah Chun, California State University, Long Beach; Joseph G. Ponterotto, Fordham University; and Gordon C. Nagayama Hall, University of Oregon; in addition to other reviewers.

Abnormal There are several approaches to this definition (Bulhan, 1985): (a) the statistical approach wherein a behavior is considered normal if it is the behavior of the majority; (b) the subjective distress as reported by the individual; (c) the medical disease approach with a focus on the biochemistry of the individual; (d) the "cultural relativist" approach, which posits that some disorders are specific to a culture, with varying definitions and expression of symptoms; and (e) the ideal state approach, which fosters the idea that everyone is expected to behave within the context of that ideal state. Anyone who is unable to do so is considered "abnormal." Marsella (1982) and Chin, De La Cancela, and Jenkins (1993) concluded that rather than searching for universal norms to define normality, such definitions should be viewed from a cultural perspective. Self-disclosure has been used as a measure of mental health. According to Sue and Sue (1990), this orientation is characteristic of the Anglo American counseling and therapy process. The fact that many minorities are reluctant to initially self-disclose would place them in a position to be judged as mentally unhealthy.

References

Bulhan, H. A. (1985). *Franz Fanon and the psychology of oppression*. New York: Plenum.

Chin, J. A., De La Cancela, V., & Jenkins, Y. (1993). *Diversity in psychotherapy: The politics of race, ethnicity, and gender*. Westport, CT: Praeger.

Marsella, A. J. (1982). Culture and mental health: An overview. In A. J. Marsella & G. M. White (Eds.), *Cultural conception of mental health and therapy* (pp. 359–388). Boston: Reidel.

Sue, D. W., & Sue, D. (1990). *Counseling the culturally different* (2nd ed.). New York: John Wiley.

Aborigine Aborigines are the first inhabitants of a region as contrasted with invading or colonizing people. A term such as *aboriginality* is derived from aborigine and is used to define the original group of people who occupied Australia before the invasion by Europeans (Coolwell, 1993). Aboriginal cultures are also found in America and Africa. The terms *native* and *indigenous* are used synonymously with

1

aborigine, which derives from the Latin word meaning original inhabitants. There are approximately 400,000 Aboriginal people, which represents approximately 2% of Australia's population. Where the ancestors of the Aborigines came from is still debated, but increasing evidence indicates Southeast Asia. It is also assumed that there were a series of migrations over centuries (Bell, 1963). The physical characteristics of Aborigines are distinctive. Most are dark skinned, and there are regional variations in their hair color (Bell, 1963). In 1788, the Europeans arrived and destroyed Aboriginal societies ("Aborigines, Australian," 2003). They remained unified, however, due to their strong spiritual beliefs, storytelling, art, and colonial history. They believe that their ancestors metamorphosed into nature, and they are spiritually alive (Siasoco, 2000). They maintain systems of totemism, which is the belief that there is a relationship between people and species of animals or plants ("Australian Aborigines," 2003). In addition, they believe in the concept of dreaming, which is the creative period when spirits shaped the land and established life ("Aborigines, Australian," 2003). In the Northern Territory, art included baskets, sculptures, and rock paintings. Yellow ochre, charcoal, and gypsum were used for painting. The subject matter of Aboriginal art is confined to hand stencils, animals, plants, human beings, and geometric designs (Bell, 1963). Their most famous instrument is the didgeridoo, which is used at ritual ceremonies ("Aborigines, Australian," 2003). There was trade throughout the continent, and they lived by hunting and gathering ("Australian Aborigines," 2003). In addition, religion and economics played an important role in their lives. Everyone belonged to a local descent group, which collected food and performed other activities. The tribes were connected by kinship. The kin terms indicated marriage eligibility, responsibilities, and reasons for avoidance of people ("Aborigines, Australian," 2003). The rules of marriage, residence, and descent determine how they interact ("Australian Aborigines," 2003). By the late 1880s, most Aborigines had joined White rural and urban communities because of forced assimilation. In the 1990s, they were given rights, which included government legislation, autonomy, increased wages, and welfare benefits. Since 1967, Aborigines have obtained legal reform, sovereignty issues, land rights, compensation for land lost, and self-governance ("Aborigines, Australian," 2003). In 1976, the Aboriginal Land Rights Act was passed. In 1993, the Native Title Act gave Aboriginal title to the land ("Aborigines, Australian," 2003). In 1999, the Australian government issued an expression of regret for past mistreatment of the Aborigines. The government opposed issuing a national apology, however, because it may have encouraged a movement toward compensation ("Australian Aborigines," 2003). In 2002, approximately 460,000 Aboriginal and Torres Strait Islander people were identified. Less than 100,000 are of homogeneous ancestry, and the rest are mixed Aboriginal and European. Examples of Aboriginal groups are the Yir-yoroni, Wurora, Wailbri, Tiwi, Murngin, Kamilaroi, Gunwinggu, Gurindji, Bidjandjadjara, and Aranda. Most Aborigines live in fixed settlements. The Aboriginal and Torres Strait Islander Commission provides housing, health, and educational facilities. Aborigines engage in cattle raising, tourism, and mining ("Aborigines, Australian," 2003).

References

Aborigines, Australian. (2003). In *Grolier encyclopedia*. Danbury, CT: Grolier.

Australian Aborigines. (2003). In *Columbia encyclopedia* (4th ed.). New York: Alacritude.

Bell, J. H. (1963). The culture of the aborigines. In A. L. McLeod (Ed.), *The pattern of Australian culture* (pp. 441–468). Ithaca, NY: Cornell University Press.

Coolwell, W. (1993). *My kind of people: Achievement, identity and aboriginality.* St. Lucia, Queensland: University of Queensland Press.

Siasoco, R. V. (2000). History and culture of Australia's indigenous peoples. In *Columbia encyclopedia*. New York: Columbia University Press.

Accents   Accents are the way in which people pronounce words in a particular area or country. Specifically, accents are characteristic pronunciations that determine both "the regional or social background of the speaker" and "the phonetic habits of the speaker's native language carried over to his or her use of another language" (*Webster's Third International Dictionary*, 1993, p. 7). The word *accent* is derived from the Latin word *accentus*. Goetz (1991) notes that

accents are distinctive manners of oral expression; the inflection, tone, or choice of words associated with a particular situation, event, emotion, or attitude or taken to be unique in or highly characteristic of an individual. They are speech habits typical of natives or residents of a region or of any other group, rhythmically significant stress on the syllables of a verse usually at approximately regular intervals (p. 24)

which stands out in an utterance in comparison to the other syllables in the word or sentence. Accents are complex signs of difference in which several semiotic principles converge. They are constructs that classify people as do race, nationality, and kinship, each assuming a natural boundary (Urciuoli, 1998). As such, accents become enactments of identity (LePage & Tabouret-Keller, 1985). Accents may index underpinnings of language prejudice. For example, English-dominant students come to view Spanish language elements (accents) as signs of contamination, internalizing Anglo teachers' perceptions of Spanish-speaking peoples' nonstandard English as deviant and their code switching as a sign that they have no real language (Walsh, 1991).

References

Goetz, P. W. (Ed.). (1991). *The new encyclopedia Britannica* (Vol. 1 Micropedia). Chicago: Encyclopedia Britannica.

LePage, R. B., & Tabouret-Keller, A. (1985). *Acts of identity: Creole based approaches to language and ethnicity.* Cambridge, UK: Cambridge University Press.

Urciuoli, B. (1998). *Exposing prejudice: Puerto Rican experiences of language, race and class.* Boulder, CO: Westview.

Walsh, C. (1991). *Pedagogy and the struggle for voice: Issues of language, power and schooling for the Puerto Rican*. New York: Bergin & Garvin.

Webster's third international dictionary. (1993). Springfield, MA: Merriam-Webster.

Acculturation   Berry, Poortinga, Segall, and Dasen (1992) refer to acculturation as the cultural and psychological change brought about due to contact with peoples of different cultures. Baron (1991) conceptualized the process of acculturation as both multidimensional and multidirectional, whereby immigrant groups incorporate observable and unobservable characteristics of the dominant culture. Observable characteristics include dress, language usage, eating habits, and celebrations. Unobservable characteristics include beliefs, values, attitudes, and feelings. Graves (1967) coined the term *psychological acculturation* to refer to the change that an individual experiences as a result of going through the process of acculturation. According to Berry et al., at this individual level changes in identity, values, and attitudes occur. Acculturative changes at the group level include political, economic, and demographic changes. Individual and group acculturation do not necessarily occur at the same rate and at the same time (Olmeda, 1979). Berry et al. believe that although the population level sets the stage for individual change, individual differences in the psychological characteristics of the individual affect the acculturative process. American Indian psychologist La Fromboise and colleagues (La Fromboise, Coleman, & Gerton, 1993) proposed models of acculturation that are applicable to ethnic minorities in the United States, including assimilation, which involves absorption into the dominant culture; acculturation, which involves competence in a second culture without complete acceptance; fusion, which is a combination of cultures to form a new culture; alternation, which is bicultural competence; and multicultural, which involves a model of acculturation involving distinct cultural identities that are maintained within a single multicultural social structure (see Assimilation).

References

Baron, A. (1991). *Explorations in Chicano psychology*. New York: Praeger.

Berry, J. W., Poortinga, Y. H., Segall, M. H., & Dasen, P. R. (1992). *Cross-cultural psychology: Research and applications.* Cambridge, UK: Cambridge University Press.

Graves, T. D. (1967). Psychological acculturation in a tri-ethnic community. *Southwestern Journal of Anthropology, 23,* 337–350.

La Fromboise, T. D., Coleman, H. L. K., & Gerton, J. (1993). Psychological impact of biculturalism: Evidence and theory. *Psychological Bulletin, 114,* 395–412.

Olmeda, E. (1979). Acculturation: A psychometric perspective. *American Psychologist, 34,* 1061–1070.

Acculturative stress   This is the kind of stress that one experiences as a result of the acculturation process (see Acculturation). This stress may be experienced as mild to severe. Symptoms may be as innocuous as mild anxiety or as significant as delusional paranoia. Other symptoms of varying severity include depression, feelings of loneliness and isolation, and psychosomatic symptoms (Berry, 1975). Acculturative stress will vary from individual to individual depending on the psychological makeup of the person, the age of the individual, the support from the host culture, the support from other group members in the host culture, and the presence or absence of prejudice and discrimination. Less stress will be experienced if the individual has marketable skills, is familiar with the language and lifestyle of the host culture, and is younger and married (Berry, Poortinga, Segall, & Dasen, 1992).

References

Berry, J. W. (1975). Ecology, cultural adaptation, and psychological differentiation: Traditional patterning and acculturative stress. In R. Brislin, S. Bochner, & W. Lonner (Eds.), *Cultural perspectives in learning* (pp. 207–228). Beverley Hills, CA: Sage.

Berry, J. W., Poortinga, Y. H., Segall, M. H., & Dasen, P. R. (1992). *Cross-cultural psychology: Research and applications.* Cambridge, UK: Cambridge University Press.

Adaptation   Originally, the concept of adaptation related to biology in which there is population change through natural selection. Adaptation in social sciences refers to the changes that occur during the lifetime of an organism in response to environmental demands (Berry, Poortinga, Segall, & Dasen, 1992). When used in reference to multicultural issues, this term implies the social and psychological adjustment of individuals or cultural groups to the new cultural environment in which they now reside (Adelman, 1988). Immersion into a new culture challenges one's view of the self and the world as individuals are confronted with different sets of values, customs, and beliefs (Cross, 1995). According to Mio, Trimble, Arrendondo, Cheatham, and Sue (1999), successful cultural adaptation is the mutual respect for, and by, the surrounding cultures. The arriving individuals or groups do not abandon their values, beliefs, and customs but engage in a mutual exchange of norms with their environment. Eventually, both will be altered, thus enhancing the process of cultural adaptation. See Cultural Adaptation.

References

Adelman, M. B. (1988). Cross-cultural adjustment: A theoretical perspective on social support. *International Journal of Intercultural Relations, 12,* 183–204.

Berry, J. W., Poortinga, Y. H., Segall, M. H., & Dasen, P. R. (1992). *Cross-cultural psychology: Research and applications.* Cambridge, UK: Cambridge University Press.

Cross, S. E. (1995). Self-construals, coping and stress in cross-cultural adaptation. *Journal of Cross-Cultural Psychology, 26,* 673–697.

Mio, J. S., Trimble, J. E., Arrendondo, P., Cheatham, H. E., & Sue, D. (1999). *Key words in multicultural interventions: A dictionary.* Westport, CT: Greenwood.

African American   This term identifies a citizen of the United States with lineage that can be traced to Africa, south of the Sahara. This history is linked to the transatlantic slave trade and does not include White South Africans and Black people from the Caribbean or Africa who have obtained citizenship through the immigration naturalization process. Children of these parents who are born in the United States are usually identified as African Americans. The term *African American* almost exclusively replaced the term *Black* in reaction to the notion postulated by Jesse Jackson, a spokesperson for the group. He asserted that the term *Black* is "baseless," whereas African American has "cultural integrity" (Edelin, 1989, p. 76). Not withstanding some opposition to the name change, this term is still used predominantly to identify Americans of African ancestry. The American Psychological Association (1994) noted that terms such as *Negro* and *Afro-American* are archaic and inappropriate for publication, but the terms *Black* and *African American* are acceptable.

References

American Psychological Association. (1994). *The publication manual of the American Psychological Association* (4th ed.). Washington, DC: Author.

Edelin, R. (1989). African American or Black: What's in a name? *Ebony, 44,* 76–80.

Afrocenticity   This term is used to denote a worldview that encompasses and focuses on the history and culture of Africa as the focal point of consciousness of self and reality. According to Grant and Ladsen-Billings (1997), Afrocentrism "addresses the interpretation or reinterpretation of reality from perspectives that maintain and perpetuate African life and culture" (p. 11). According to Early (1995), Afrocentrism is "an intellectual movement, a political view, a historically traceable evolution, a religious orthodoxy" (p. 235). According to Drake (1970), the Bible gave African Americans the vindication needed to reject the evaluation of inferiority and not warranting of respect. Black people turned to the Bible to prove that they are powerful and worthy of recognition. From this Biblical root came the tradition of scholarship that reached its maturity in the 1890s. Greater development and prominence were reached during the Harlem Renaissance of the 1920s, with a new emergence in the 1960s Black Power movement (Semmes, 1992). The development of the word Afrocentric was a product of the 1960s and 1970s ferment, but Afrocentric nomenclature should not be misperceived as a recent phenomenon. It should also not be perceived as "simply the inclusion of African rhetoric in a linguistic sense, or the symbolic prominent expression of traditional African cultures" but as being tied to "its early vindicationist expressions" (Semmes, 1992, p. 20). It also has a knowledge base that includes extensive methodological tools and includes a broad spectrum of disciplines (Semmes, 1992).

References

Drake, S. C. (1970). *The redemption of Africa and Black religion.* Chicago: Third World Press.

Early, G. (1995). Understanding Afrocentrism: Why Blacks dream of a world without Whites. In J. A. Kromkowski (Ed.), *Race and ethnic relations* (6th ed.). Guilford, CT: Dushkin.

Grant, C. A., & Ladsen-Billings, G. (1997). *Dictionary of multicultural education.* Phoenix, AZ: Oryx.

Semmes, C. E. (1992). *Cultural hegemony and African American development.* Westport, CT: Praeger.

Allocentrism   This term may be used synonymously with the term *collectivism.* This is the value that embraces concern for the group to which one belongs. Triandis (1988) distinguished between the group-level value, which he termed *collectivism* (see Collectivism), and this same value expressed at the individual level, which he defined as *allocentrism.*

Reference

Triandis, H. C. (1988). Collectivism vs individualism: A reconceptualization of a basic conception of cross-cultural social psychology. In C. Bagley & G. K. Verma (Eds.), *Personality, cognition, and values* (pp. 60–95). London: Macmillan.

Amae   This is a Japanese term that implies indulgent dependency in the context of the mother-child bond. According to Doi (1996), this term does not have a European language equivalent. Tillich (1957) views the closest Western equivalents as the Greek concepts of Eros and agape. Eros connotes the child's immature need to be loved, whereas agape is derived from the mother's need to give unconditional love. In the Japanese culture, amae is distinctive to the production and reproduction of Japanese culture (Doi, 1973). According to Vogel (1996), amae is experienced by the child as "feeling of dependency or a desire to be loved," whereas the mother experiences satisfaction from her overindulgence and overprotectiveness.

References

Doi, T. (1973). *The anatomy of dependence.* Tokyo: Kodansha.

Doi, T. (1996). Foreword. In D. W. Shwalb & B. J. Shwalb (Eds.), *Japanese childrearing: Two generations of scholarship* (pp. 15–17). New York: Guilford.

Tillich, P. (1957). *Dynamics of faith.* New York: Harper.

Vogel, S. (1996). Urban middleclass family life, 1958–1956: A personal and evolving perspective. In D. W. Shwalb & B. J. Shwalb (Eds.), *Japanese childrearing: Two generations of scholarship* (pp. 172–201). New York: Guilford.

Amerasians   This term is applied to the offspring of the union of Americans and Asians. It was first used by Buck (1930) to refer to a specific classification of children of intergroup mating. Spickard (1989) applied the term to the offspring of Japanese "war brides" and U.S. military personnel from World War II. After the Vietnam War in 1975, the term came to be applied to people having Vietnamese mothers and American fathers. Today the term is generally applied to all people who are the progeny of Asians (Vietnamese, Koreans, Phillipinos, Thai, and Taiwanese) and Americans (Valverde, 1992).

References

Buck, P. (1930). *East wind, west wind.* New York: John Day.

Spickard, P. R. (1989). *Mixed blood: Intermarriage and ethnic identity in twentieth century America.* Madison: University of Wisconsin Press.

Valverde, K. L. C. (1992). From dust to gold: The Vietnamese Amerasian experience. In M. P. R. Root (Ed.), *Racially mixed people in America* (pp. 144–161). Newbury Park, CA: Sage.

American Indian   Recently termed Native American, an American Indian has been defined by the Bureau of Indian Affairs (BIA; 1988) as one who is a registered or enrolled member of a tribe or whose blood quantum is one fourth or more, genealogically derived, and can legally demonstrate this to the BIA. The definition of who is an Indian has spurred a number of controversies. Pavar (1992) recognizes a person as an American Indian only if that person has more than half Indian blood and the Indian community recognizes him or her as an Indian. Svennson (1973, p. 9) posits that "Indianness is a state of being, a cast of mind, a relationship to the Universe. It is indefinable." American Indians comprise more than 500 tribes of indigenous people living in the Unites States. According to the 1990 U.S. census, there are approximately 1.8 million Indians in the United States, although the majority live west of the Mississippi River, with 40% of the total population living in Arizona, California, New Mexico, Oklahoma, and Washington. More than half reside in urban areas, and approximately one fourth live on the 52 million acres of land identified as reservations (Stock, 1987). American Indians comprise less than 1% of the population. The exact number is difficult to ascertain due to the fact that although some are full-blooded, others are biracial, triracial, or multiracial with mixed blood of Blacks, Whites, Hispanics, and many other populations. These individuals may choose to identify with any of these other groups rather than register with the BIA as American Indians. It is estimated that 10 to 20 million Americans have some Indian blood (Taylor, 1984). According to the BIA, there are approximately 150 tribal languages spoken in the 505 federally recognized, and the 365 state recognized, tribal groups.

References

Bureau of Indian Affairs. (1988). *American Indians today.* Washington, DC: Author.

Pavar, S. L. (1992). *The rights of Indians and tribes: The ACLU guide to Indian and tribal rights.* Carbondale: Southern Illinois Press.

Stock, L. (1987). Native Americans: A brief profile. *Journal of Visual Impairment and Blindness, 81,* 152.

Svennson, F. (1973). *The ethnics in American politics: American Indians.* Minneapolis, MN: Burgess.

Taylor, T. W. (1984). *Bureau of Indian Affairs.* Boulder, CO: Westview.

Amish The Amish are a religious group of people who live in settlements in 22 states in the United States and in Ontario, Canada. The oldest group of Old Order Amish, approximately 16,000 to 18,000 people, live in Lancaster County, Pennsylvania. The Amish have their roots in the Mennonite community. Both were part of the early Anabaptist movement in Europe, which took place at the time of the Reformation. The Anabaptists believed that only adults who had confessed their faith should be baptized, and that they should remain separate from the larger society. Many early Anabaptists were put to death as heretics by both Catholics and Baptists, and many others fled to the mountains of Switzerland and southern Germany. Here began the Amish tradition of holding their worship services in homes rather than churches. Because they hold their services in private homes, these Old Order Amish are also known as House Amish, distinguishing them from the New, Church, and Beachy Amish. These more modern Amish have fewer reservations about the use of labor-saving technology and associating with the non-Amish population (Hostetler, 1980). The Old Order Amish culture is based on two verses of the scripture: "Be not conformed to this word: but be ye transformed by the renewing of your mind, that ye may prove what is that is good, and acceptable and perfect, will of God" (Romans 12:2) and "Be ye not unequally yoked together with unbelievers: for what fellowship hath righteousness with unrighteousness? And what communion hath light with darkness?" (11 Corinthians 6:14). The Amish maintain their own culture and values. They endeavor to exclude the outside world except for the purchases of essential necessities. They observe strict rules of behavior, dress, language usage, education, and religion. They value the extended family and community involvement (Good, 1985).

References

Good, M. (1985). *Who are the Amish?* Intercourse, PA: Good Books.

Hostetler, J. A. (1980). *Amish society.* Baltimore: Johns Hopkins University Press.

Amok *Amok* is a culture-bound syndrome that involves wild aggressive behavior of limited duration in which there are attempts to kill or injure a person. It has been identified in Southeast Asia (Malaya, Indonesia, and Thailand). Amok is a Malay term that means "to engage furiously in battle" (Westmeyer, 1973). "Running amok" is a common English expression meaning "in a murderous frenzied manner" (*Merriam-Webster Dictionary*, 1974). According to Gaw (2001), the individuals afflicted with amok are usually young or middle-aged men living away from home who have recently experienced a loss or otherwise "lost face." This is one way of expressing aggression in a culture that otherwise would not condone such behaviors. Gaw found that illnesses associated with amok are schizophrenia, depression, psychosis and dissociative disorders, epilepsy, and infections such as malaria and syphilis.

References

Gaw, A. C. (2001). *Concise guide to cross-cultural psychiatry.* Washington, DC: American Psychiatric Publishing.

Merriam-Webster dictionary. (1974). New York: Simon & Schuster.

Westmeyer, J. (1973). On epidemicity of Amok violence. *Archives of General Psychiatry, 28,* 873–876.

Anglo-American   There are several similar definitions of an Anglo-American. An Anglo-American is an American of English origin, in contrast to the non-English races in or on the borders of the United States; an inhabitant or citizen of the United States who was, or whose ancestors were, born in England; and belonging to both England and America (*Oxford English Dictionary*, 1989). The shortened term *Anglo* is used to distinguish Americans of any European heritage from Americans of color and white Hispanics. The term *Anglo* originated from the Latin root, *Anglo.* The evolution of its usage was derived from the term *Anglo-Saxon,* which once referred to Germans (Angles, Saxons, and Jutes) who settled in Britain in the fifth and sixth centuries but now includes descendants of England, Scotland, and Ireland (Higham, 1975). The four largest English-speaking democracies of the Anglo-American society are Australia, Canada, Great Britain, and the United States. They are generally regarded as similar societies, although there are variations in area; population; and the degree of ethnic, racial, and linguistic homogeneity. These nations also differ in their formal political institutions (*American Heritage Dictionary*, 2000). The similarity that these Anglo cultures share is their rugged individualism. The individual is the primary unit, and the individual bears primary responsibility for his or her actions. Independence and autonomy are highly valued and rewarded. There is an emphasis on the scientific method, and thinking tends to be objective, rational, and linear. Holidays are based on Christian religion and White history, and music and art are based on the European culture. Women's beauty is associated with being blonde, blue eyed, tall, and young, and men's attractiveness is based on athletic ability, power, and economic status (Katz, 1985). See Caucasian.

References

American heritage dictionary of the English language (4th ed.). (2000). Boston: Houghton Mifflin.

Higham, J. (1975). *Send these to me.* New York: Athaneum.

Katz, J. H. (1985). *The counseling psychologist.* Beverley Hills, CA: Sage.

Oxford English dictionary (2nd ed.). (1989). Oxford, UK: Clarendon.

Arab American   Arab Americans are residents of the United States who trace their ancestry to Arab countries of the Middle East. The term *Arab* refers to a variety of peoples who share a general culture, language, and history rather than a specific racial group. Arab Americans are an extremely varied group with roots in numerous countries in which the Arabic language is spoken (Fayad, 1999). The communities of Arab Americans consist of descendants of the Arab American immigrants who came to the United States in the 19th century in addition to recent groups. For more than 75 years, the American public did not acknowledge their existence (Abraham, 1983). It was during the 1970s Middle East crisis that attentioned focused on Arab Americans (Abraham, 1983). One third of all Arab Americans live in metropolitan areas, such as Detroit, Michigan, Los Angeles, and New York City. On a national scale, Arabic-speaking immigrants constitute less than 3% of the total immigrant population in the United States. Lebanese Christians were the first to immigrate in the 1900s. A steady flow of Arab immigrants continued to migrate into the United States until 1924 (Gall, 1988). Arab immigrants were considered traders in their work, and explicit discrimination and prejudice existed among Americans (Gall, 1998). Numerous Americans mistakenly assume Arabs are defined as Muslims, followers of Islam. Ten percent are Christians, however. Arab Americans are emotionally attached to their culture and food and are devoted to Arab values, such as strong family ties and preservation of female chastity and fidelity (Abraham, 1983). With the exception of those who have assimilated, Arab Americans object to American courtship rituals such as dating. Arab American Christians and Muslims generally equate dating with premarital sex. Arranged marriages occasionally occur among recent immigrants.

Divorce, once a rarity in Arab society, has become more frequent among Arab Americans (Peterborough, 2002). A well-known practice among Arab Americans is prohibition against eating pork. Arab Americans seek to participate in mainstream U.S. society while retaining their distinctive cultural heritage and language. Arab Americans must also cope with the anti-Arab and anti-Muslim stereotypes that pervade U.S. popular culture (Abraham, 1983). During the 1980s, Arabs and other people from the Middle East were associated with terrorism. Although prejudice declined in the early 1990s, Arabs and Arab Americans remain mistakenly suspected as terrorists. With few exceptions, Arab Americans are law-abiding residents and citizens of the United States.

References

Abraham, S. (1983). *Arabs in the New World: Studies on Arab American communities.* Detroit, MI: Wayne State University, Center for Urban Studies.

Fayad, M. (1999, Fall). Arab and Arab American women in the mainstream in the United States. *Arab Studies Quarterly, 21*(4), 1–2.

Gall, T. (Ed.). (1998). *Worldmark encyclopedia of cultures and daily life* (Vol. 2). Columbus, OH: Eastwood.

Peterborough, M. (2002). Arab American. In *Gale encyclopedia of multicultural America cobblestone* (Vol. 23, p. 46). Detroit, MI: Gale.

Arranged marriage   Arranged marriage is a marriage that occurs when the pair originates from a person other than the future spouses (Levinson, 1994). Often, parents or relatives of the soon-to-be couple, friends of the families, or professional go-betweens take the initiative in negotiating the marriage (Levinson, 1994). In class-stratified societies, arranged marriages were sometimes reserved for the upper classes or important personages (Levinson, 1994). Today, in large areas of Africa, Asia, and the Middle East, a substantial percentage of marriages are arranged (Batabyal, 2001). When marriages are arranged, there are vast differences across cultures as to the extent to which the future bride and groom have a say in the person they will marry (Levinson, 1994). Among the Burusho of India, the parents supposedly negotiate a marriage without consulting the children, but often prospective brides and grooms have grown up together and know each other well. In addition, the feelings of the children are taken into account when the matches are being made (Levinson, 1994). Arranged marriage rituals have evolved over time. At one time in India, prospective couples would not have met prior to marriage. Today, they commonly get together with their families' permission (Mackinnon, 2002). In northern India, among Hindu families with high educational levels, parents frequently act as matchmakers by selecting appropriate possible spouses and arranging meetings for their children of marriageable age. Lack of consent from the bride, groom, or either set of parents results in the breaking of the arrangement (Carstensen & Yalom, 2002). In many Asian cultures, the male and female traditionally had no say in the selection of a spouse (Levinson, 1994). The ritual has changed over time. In Japan, 25% to 30% of all marriages are arranged. People of higher standing and age than the prospective couple typically organize the marriages. Both the future bride and groom maintain the power to veto the match, however (Applbaum, 1995).

References

Applbaum, K. D. (1995). Marriage with the proper stranger: Arranged marriage in metropolitan Japan. *Ethnology, 34*(1), 37–55.

Batabyal, A. A. (2001, April). On the likelihood of finding the right partner in an arranged marriage. *Journal of Socio-Economics, 30*, 3.

Carstensen, L. L., & Yalom, M. (2002). *Inside the American couple: New thinking/new challenges.* Los Angeles: University of California Press.

Levinson, D. (1994). *Encyclopedias of the human experience; Marriage, family, and relationships: A cross-cultural encyclopedia.* Denver, CO: ABC-CLIO.

Mackinnon, I. (2002, September). Love is a game. In *Newsweek international* (pp. 3–5). Farmington Hills, MI: Gale Group.

Asian American   People of Asian descent living in the United States, including but not limited to people of Chinese, Japanese, Korean, Vietnamese, Cambodian, Filipino, and Nepalese heritage, are called Asian Americans. People from India are sometimes referred to South Asians and those from Pakistan as West Asians. There are differences within the specific Asian group in terms of the level of acculturation, primary language spoken, and the generalized status in the country. For example, the primary language in the Chinese group may be Cantonese, Mandarin, or English. Filipinos comprise the largest Asian American immigrant group. McWilliams (1964) reported that Filipinos' arrival in the United States in large numbers began in 1908 when 141 workers were recruited by the Hawaii Sugar Plantations Association. By the 1930s, there were 108,206 Filipinos in the United States. Most were farmers who worked on farms on the West Coast. They exchanged their labor as commodity with the sugar planters. They were subjected to racism and discrimination. Between 1945 and 1960, there was a second wave of immigrants. They immersed themselves in U.S. society, and more than 7,000 Filipinos joined the U.S. armed forces during World War II. Following political upheavals and a depressed economy in the Philippines, there was a third wave of immigrants after 1965 that is still under way. Today, there are more than 2.1 million Filipinos in the United States. Most of the new immigrants are nurses, scientists, and technicians of all types. San Juan (1991) reports that in the United States, the public can rarely discern Filipinos from other Asians or even Latinos. When mention is made of Asian Americans, the public usually thinks of Chinese or Japanese. According to Nee and Sanders (1995), Filipinos as a group receive the lowest income among Asians and tend to be underemployed. The Chinese are the second largest Asian American group. They arrived abundantly in the 1840s after a crop disaster in China. Many of the Chinese immigrants worked in gold mines. Others worked on the railroads. Approximately 20% lived in New York. The Chinese experienced discrimination and prejudice soon after their arrival, resulting in the Exclusion Act in 1882–1944. This act prevented males from bringing their wives into the country, and even today, among the older Chinese, there are more males than females. Today, there has been an increase in Chinese immigration. There are more than 20,000 immigrants each year. They are becoming more an immigrant group than an American-born group. According to Hsu (1981), Chinese immigrants are changing. He reported that prior to the late 1970s, almost all Chinese immigrants came from Hong Kong and Taiwan, but since then many have come from the People's Republic of China. Many arrive as students and legal residents, but a large number also enter the country illegally. They often enter port cities, such as New York and San Francisco. Due to the large number of recent immigrants, the percentage of Chinese in unskilled, low-paying jobs has increased. Many aggregate in Chinatowns in New York and California. Chinese are perceived as "the model minority." They are considered successful, even though a large percentage of them live in poverty. They are often described as the "forgotten minority." Twenty percent of Chinese live in overcrowded conditions. The Japanese comprise the third largest Asian American group in the United States. Seventy-two percent live in Hawaii and California. The rate of immigration is low compared to that of the Chinese. Immigration averages 5,000 per year. Japanese will be increasingly characterized as American born. Japanese immigration was highest in the 1890s. They filled the demand for cheap labor to replace the Chinese. Many of these Japanese were from the working class. They worked as agricultural laborers as well as on the railroads and in canneries. Japanese immigrants were perceived as more desirable than the Chinese because they brought their families with them. They experienced prejudice and discrimination, however. In 1906, the San Francisco Board of Education issued an order segregating Japanese children from White schoolchildren. Negative feelings against the Japanese culminated in the allocation of more than 110,000 to detention camps during World War II. Today, Japanese are considered the "model minority." Many tend to be underemployed.

References

Hsu, F .L. K. (1981). *Americans and Chinese: Passage to difference* (3rd ed.). Honolulu: University Press of Hawaii.

McWilliams, C. (1964). *Brothers under the skin*. Boston: Little, Brown.

Nee, V., & Sanders, J. (1995). The road to parity: Determinants of the socio-economic achievements of the Asian Americans. *Ethnic Racial Studies, 8*(1), 77–83.

San Juan, E., Jr. (1991). Mapping the boundaries: The Filipino writer in the U.S.A. *Journal of Ethnic Studies, 19*, 117–131.

Assimilation   Assimilation is the process whereby individuals or groups of differing ethnic heritage are absorbed into the dominant culture of society ("Assimilation," 2003). Associated with assimilation is acculturation, the process of change in artifacts, customs, and beliefs that results from the contact of societies with different cultural traditions ("Assimilation," 2003). Each person, depending on the culture, may choose to view assimilation in his or her own way. Due to the demand of assimilation on many cultures soon after arrival, the true definition has been distorted and is commonly misunderstood (Salins, 1997). It is believed that for immigrants to properly assimilate, all native traditions, beliefs, and behaviors must be abandoned. This is commonly referred to as "up or out": Either immigrants bring themselves up to native cultural standards or they are doomed to live out of the charmed circle of the national culture. For some, most likely those who are ethnocentric, the up or out motto is very important. Others, however, view assimilation on a symbiotic level. Assimilations occur in a culture-friendly way when creating a "melting pot." The term *melting pot* was originally coined in the 1908 play, "The Melting Pot," which was based on the United States. Unfortunately, assimilation does not necessarily exist on generous and blissful terms. Many believe that the whole melting pot never existed, and such a term was a useless metaphor (Salins, 1997). As a result, several people have attempted to create other catchy phrases. Wallace (1997) wrote, "It is sometimes easy to forget that culture comes in many more flavors than just ethnic, racial, and national" (p. 140). Therefore, it may be preferable that each person creates his or her own idea of assimilation. Former mayor of New York City, David Dinkins, simply stated "gorgeous mosaic," whereas former congresswoman Shirley Chisholm characterized the United States' ethnic groups as being ingredients in a "salad bowl." Some have even said that the United States is like a kaleidoscope (Salins, 1997). Nevertheless, it is absolutely imperative to keep in mind that as individuals, each person is influenced in a different way. No one is going to become exactly how one may want him or her to be. For this reason, it is questionable whether assimilation is even necessary (Wallace, 1997).

References

Assimilation. (2003). In *Encyclopedia Britannica*. New York: Encyclopedia Britannica.

Salins, P. D. (1997). *Assimilation, American style*. New York: Basic Books.

Wallace, W. L. (1997). *The future of ethnicity, race and nationality*. Westport, CT: Praeger.

Ataque de nervios   "Attack of nerves" is a culture-specific illness among Puerto Ricans and other Latinos. According to Latinos, it is an out-of-conscious state resulting from evil spirits. According to Guarnaccio (1993), ataque de nervios is a culturally sanctioned response to stressful experiences associated with grief, such as funerals, threat, accidents, and family conflicts. This response is more likely to be experienced by women older than age 45 with less than a high school education and among the lower socioeconomic class (Gaw, 2001). The afflicted individual experiences trembling, heart palpitations, a sense of heat in the chest rising into the head, fainting, seizure-like activities, accompanied by uncontrollable shouting. Consciousness quickly returns without memory of the episode (Guarnaccio, 1993).

References

Gaw, A. C. (2001). *Concise guide to cross-cultural psychiatry*. Washington, DC: American Psychiatric Publishing.

Guarnaccio, P. J. (1993). Ataque de nervios in Puerto Rico: Culture bound syndromes or popular illness? *Medical Anthropology, 15*, 1657–1669.

Attachment   This term originally referred to the type of relationship that exists exclusively between infants and their mothers (Gerwitz & Kurtines, 1991). In 1958, John Bowlby first introduced the attachment theory in an article titled "The Nature of a Child's Tie to His Mother," which was followed by his trilogy, *Attachment and Loss* (Ainsworth, Blehar, Wall, & Waters, 1978). Bowlby's inspiration to produce the behavioral theory derived from Mary Ainsworth's unresolved research and his interest in Harry Harlow's studies of maternal deprivation on the rhesus monkey (Bowlby, 1988). Initially, attachment behavior is activated whenever young children feel distressed and insecure and need to get into close proximity with their main caregiver. It is not just a case of the attachment figure being physically present, however. Children have to believe that their attachment figure is available psychologically and physically. Thus, attachment figures that are emotionally unavailable and unresponsive are just as likely to cause anxiety and distress as those who are physically absent (Brandon, Hinings, Howe, & Schofield, 1999). Internal factors within the central nervous system and external reasons are other causes of activation of this behavioral system (Ainsworth et al., 1978). The theory has two principal components: (a) a normative component, which attempts to explain modal, species-typical patterns of behavior and stages of development through which nearly all human beings pass, and (b) an individual difference component, which attempts to explain stable, systematic deviations from the modal behavioral patterns and stages (Rholes & Simpson, 1998). When attachment behavior is activated, the child is unable to engage in other useful developmental experiences, such as exploration, play, and dealing with others for reasons other than protection. As a result, there is a said connection between attachment and exploration (Brandon et al., 1999). The attachment theory not only applies to infants and children but also explains patterns of behavior in adolescents and adults (Bowlby, 1988). Studies have indicated that a great deal of cultural variability occurs in what is viewed as the ideal form of attachment between children and caregivers. The number of cultures in which stable, multiple caregivers are essential for raising well-adjusted children has cast doubt on the long-held belief that a mother-child relationship is the hallmark of raising a well-adjusted child (Rothbaum, Weisz, Pott, Miyaki, & Morelli, 2000).

References

Ainsworth, M. D., Blehar, M. C., Wall, S., & Waters, E. (1978). *Patterns of attachment: A psychological study of the strange situation.* Hillsdale, NJ: Lawrence Erlbaum.

Bowlby, J. (1988). *A secure base: Parent-child attachment and healthy human development.* New York: Basic Books.

Brandon, M., Hinings, D., Howe, D., & Schofield, G. (1999). *Attachment theory, child maltreatment, and family support: A practice and assessment model.* Hillsdale, NJ: Lawrence Erlbaum.

Gewirtz, J. L., & Kurtines, W. M. (1991). *Intersections with attachment.* Hillsdale, NJ: Lawrence Erlbaum.

Rholes, W. S., & Simpson, J. A. (1998). *Attachment theory and close relationships.* New York: Guilford.

Rothbaum, F., Weisz, J., Pott, M., Miyaki, K., & Morelli, G. (2000). Attachment and culture: Security in the United States and Japan. *American Psychologist, 55,* 1093–1104.

Avenga   This term is used to describe a constellation of specific forms of culture-specific disorders (see Culture-Specific Syndromes), all of which include a vivid imaginary companionship with a single external spirit. Originating in the rural areas of the Tongan culture, its incidence is increasing as people move to urban areas (Puloka, 1997).

Reference

Puloka, M. H. (1997). A commonsense perspective on the Tongan folk healing. *International Journal of Mental Health, 26*(3), 69–93.

B

Bicultural   Of or relating to two distinct cultures in one nation or geographic region. It is the blending of traditions with the experience of living in the United States. It is two distinct cultural traditions—having or combining two cultures (Kim, 2001). In addition to this definition, bicultural is often used to define the offspring of parents from two different cultures. Biculture may also imply the offspring of two different races, and the term *bicultural* is often used interchangeably with *biracial*. The offspring of two different races may not necessarily imply two different cultures, however. A black Cuban and a white Cuban are culturally similar, whereas the offspring of an African American and a European would be both biracial and bicultural. Bicultural identity integration (BII) is used to describe the proposed differences in the moderate cultural frame switching. An example of BII is a bicultural person perceiving his or her cultural identity as compatible or complementary, whereas others may describe their identity as contradictory and oppositional. Bicultural individuals are not always comfortable in their bicultural role. The role sometimes involves difficult decisions and conflicts that keep the individuals in a state of turmoil when attempting to resolve problems of culture and ethnic loyalty (Keefe & Padilla, 1987). Ethnic minorities use four acculturation strategies to manage their culture identities: assimilation, integration (or biculturalism), marginalization, and separation (Berry, 1990). Assimilated individuals identify with only one culture—their own culture or the mainstream culture. Integrated individuals identify with both cultures. Marginalized individuals do not identify with either group. "Bicultural" identity orientation contributes to greater adaptation between Eastern European immigrants in the United States. There is less likelihood of the development of biculturalism when there are close links among the separated groups, lack of out-group communication activities, and various psychological and social skills among structurally isolated ethnic minorities. These have been identified and documented among reservation Indians (Darder, 1995).

References

Berry, J. W. (1990). Cultural variations in cognitive style. In S. Wapner (Ed.), *Bio-psycho-social factors in cognitive style*. Hillsdale, NJ: Lawrence Erlbaum.

Darder, A. (1995). *Culture and difference: Critical perspectives on the bicultural experiences in the United States*. Westport, CT: Greenwood.

Keefe, S. E., & Padilla, A. M. (1987). *Chicano ethnicity.* Albuquerque: University of New Mexico.

Kim, Y. Y. (2001). *Becoming intercultural: An integrative theory of communication and cross-cultural adaptation.* London: Sage.

Bidialecticism   This is a phenomenon noticed when individuals are capable of communicating in two dialects. The individual makes a decision to use the dialect appropriate to the situation. For example, an African American in a professional setting will choose to speak in Standard English (see Standard English). The same individual will switch to Black English (see Black English) when conversing with another African American. The use of Black English in this circumstance serves the purpose of establishing camaraderie. A Black professional may also switch to the Black dialect when working with parents and clients who are Black. This switch serves the purpose of emphasizing that the professional understands the problems these individuals are experiencing (Gollnick & Chinn, 2002).

Reference

Gollnick, D., & Chinn, P. (2002). *Multicultural education in a pluralistic society* (6th ed). Columbus, OH: Merrill.

Bilis and cholera (also referred to as muina)   This is a culture-specific syndrome whose underlying cause is assumed to be anger and rage. The group most likely to experience these symptoms is Latinos, who view anger as a powerful emotion that can have direct effects on the body. They believe that these effects can exacerbate existing symptoms. They also believe that the major effect of anger is to disturb the core body balance between hot and cold valences in the body between the material and spiritual aspects (Gaw, 2001). Symptoms of bilis and cholera include acute nervous tension, headache, trembling, screaming, stomach disturbances, and, in more extreme cases, loss of consciousness. Chronic fatigue may also be a consequence of this episode.

Reference

Gaw, A. C. (2001). *Concise guide to cross-cultural psychiatry.* Washington, DC: American Psychiatric Publishing.

Biracial   One definition of biracial is "consisting of, or combining two races." There is no straightforward, easy, legal definition of biracial. When most people envision biracial children, they think of a child with one Black parent and one White parent, but this is only one example of a biracial child. There are children with one Native American parent and one Latino parent. There are children with one Italian parent and one Indian parent. They do not have the benefit of fitting in to the well-defined categories of Caucasoid, Negroid, and Mongoloid. Biracial is correct only if the individual is truly a product of two races. Golfer Tiger Woods and the media helped bring the subject to the forefront with his 1997 Masters win. He has taken his description of himself to another level. Woods, who is one fourth Black, one-fourth Thai, one-fourth Chinese, one-eighth White, and one-eighth American Indian, has penned the term *Cablinasian* to describe himself. Some members of the African American community believe that he should stop pretending he is not African American. To avoid this conflict, some biracial individuals compartmentalize their identities into public and private components, labeling themselves as African American to others but identifying themselves as mixed (Brown, 1995). According to the U.S. Bureau of the Census, a person with both a Black and a White parent is, in fact, Black. Most young persons who fit this description, however, describe themselves as biracial, both Black and White. Most young Americans, whatever their racial background, agree. Since the Voting Rights Act of 1965 signaled the culmination of the civil rights movement and the repeal of the antimiscegenation laws in the United States, there has been an increase in births of persons of biracial heritage. This has challenged the long-standing beliefs regarding the biological, social, and moral meaning of race (Root, 1992). This followed a transformation in the racial self-definition of Americans with both an African American and a White parent. Korgen (1998) describes how the transformation has its roots in the historical and cultural transitions in U.S. society since the civil rights era. Korgen's groundbreaking book, *From Black to Biracial*, will help all Americans understand the societal implications of the increasingly multiracial nature of the U.S. population. From affirmative action to the controversy regarding the 2000 U.S. census, the repercussions of the transformation in racial identity related here affect all race-based aspects of society (Wallace, 1998). It is estimated that the number of biracial individuals in the United States is between 1 million and 10 million. In April 2000, the U.S. Census Bureau added 126 racial combinations, for the first time in history giving biracial and multiracial individuals the option to self-identify with multiple heritage groups. As biracial people become empowered to claim their right to accurately label their heritage, and the numbers of biracial individuals and families continue to increase, society is compelled to broaden its definition of race. Biracial people are accustomed to being asked the question, "What are you?" Many theorists have argued that biracial people inherently live in between two worlds, unable to enjoy the benefits of full membership within one group (American Prospect, 1998).

References

American Prospect. (1998). *Half and half: Writers on growing up biracial and bicultural.* New York: Pantheon.

Brown, U. (1995). African American/European American interracial young adults: Quest for racial identity. *American Journal of Orthopsychiatry, 65,* 125–130.

Korgen, K. O. (1998). *From Black to biracial: Transforming racial identity among Americans.* Westport, CT: Greenwood/Praeger.

Root, M. P. P. (Ed.). (1992). *Racially mixed people in America.* Newbury Park, CA: Sage.

U.S. Bureau of the Census. (2000). *Current population reports.* Washington, DC: Government Printing Office.

Wallace, K. (1998). *Beyond Black.* Baltimore: University of Maryland Press.

Black English   Black English can easily be defined as "the nonstandard English spoken by Black people in the inner city." Black English is commonly associated with low-income Blacks (Cronnel, 1984). In abbreviated form, it is recognized as BEV (Black English Vernacular) or BE (Black English) (Labov, 1972). There are three major derivations: the Anglicist, the Creolist, and the synchronic. Anglicists believe that BEV originated from South England immigrants who settled along the eastern seaboard and south during colonial times. The Creolist supposed that Black English is "derived from a prototype Creole" and has been an ongoing movement toward Standard English that has lasted for more than 400 years. The synchronic position does not seek BEV establishment through historical derivation. Essentially, they believe that Black English just came out of nowhere (Harrison & Trabosso, 1976). Black English is characterized by the presence of a number of phonological and grammatical features. For example, -*s* or–*es* may be absent from words. Instead of "she looks," a person using BEV is accustomed to saying "she look." BEV users also have trouble with verbs in a sense that they may say "Mark be talking" rather than using proper grammar by saying "Mark is talking" (Cronnel, 1984). Those speaking Standard English, non-BEV, have actually adopted many Black English words or sayings. Familiar examples are "cool," "jive," "rap," "bad," and "that's where it's at" (Harrison & Trabosso, 1976). Unfortunately, it is also a proven fact that Black English does hold negative consequences to its name. Many elementary schoolchildren raised in Black English environments have been shown to have difficulty progressing in school (Cronnel, 1984). As a result, a great deal of federal aid has been provided to conduct research on the prevention of Black English entering classrooms (Labov, 1972). See Ebonics.

References

Cronnel, B. (1984). Black-English influences in the writing of third- and sixth-grade Black students. *Journal of Educational Research, 77*(4), 233–236.

Harrison, D. S., & Trabosso, T. (1976). *Black English: A seminar.* Hillsdale, NJ: Lawrence Erlbaum.

Labov, W. (1972). *Language in the inner city.* Philadelphia: University of Pennsylvania Press.

Black identity development   Prejudice and discrimination can produce simple conflicts to the extreme of genocide. In the United States, the only minority group that has "effectively and systematically" been enslaved is African Americans (Korgen, 1998). Throughout the years of enslavement, and the worst periods of racial oppression, there is evidence of Black people in the United States striving to reject imposed inferiority and progress toward a more positive, refined regard for oneself (Arrendondo, Cheatham, Mio, Sue, & Trimble, 1999). According to Sheets and Hollins (1999), coming to terms with the evolution of one's social identity is not a challenge in and of itself, but many African Americans find it necessary to reinvent themselves through Black identity development. It was the 1960s Black Power Movement that generated Black identity development. This movement brought together the thoughts of Black sociologists and psychologists in an attempt to recognize and explain African American adaptation and to disregard and disprove any preexisting theories that equated Blackness with mental impairment (Arrendondo et al., 1999). The civil rights movement affected not only the self-conception of certain Black individuals but also the identity of the whole generation of Black Americans (Korgen, 1998). To fully analyze Black identity, one must explore five variables: buffering, bonding, bridging, code switching, and individualism. *Nigrescence* is the five- or six-stage process that results in a radical change of a person's racial identity. These stages are classified into developmental divisions throughout a life span: infancy and childhood, preadolescence, adolescence, late adolescence, early adulthood, and adult nigrescence, which is an identity refinement during adulthood. These stages are not a required process for every Black person. Furthermore, not every Black person is raised to have a Black identity. Therefore, non-Blacks must develop a sensitivity to know when the absence of a Black identity is a discrepancy or when it is an indication that something other than race is central to a person's sense of joy and everyday living (Sheets & Hollins, 1999). People perceive themselves and their roles in society according to how they are viewed by people with whom they interact. It is through communication with others that people understand who they are and how they fit into society (Korgen, 1998). Several other Black identity development models have been developed, including the racial/cultural identity development model by Atkinson, Morten, and Sue (1989). According to this model, minorities develop through five stages: conformity, in which the attitude toward the self and others in the group is depreciating; dissonance, when there is conflict between self depreciating and appreciating; resistance and immersion; introspection; and integrative awareness. The three final states are concerned with and ultimately result in appreciation of self and others in the group and selective appreciation for those of the dominant group.

References

Arrendondo, P., Cheatham, H., Mio, J., Sue, D., & Trimble, J. E. (1999). *Key words in multicultural interventions: A dictionary.* Westport, CT: Greenwood.

Atkinson, D. R., Morten, G., & Sue, D. W. (1989). *Counseling American minorities: A cross-cultural perspective* (3rd ed.). Dubuque, IA: William C. Brown.

Korgen, K. O. (1998). *From Black to biracial: Transforming racial identity among Americans.* Westport, CT: Greenwood/Praeger.

Sheets, R. H., & Hollins, E. (1999). *Racial and ethnic identity in school practices: Aspects of human development.* Hillsdale, NJ: Lawrence Erlbaum.

Boat people   After the fall of Saigon in the summer of 1975, hundreds of thousands of people began fleeing the country "for fear of political persecution." They were all secretly escaping the country in small, rickety, and not seaworthy wooden boats across the Gulf of Thailand or the South China Sea. Most were completely unsuited to the open sea, giving rise to the term *boat people*. Some even escaped by foot through the Cambodian jungle (Anonymous, 1997). Large numbers ended up in detention camps in Hong Kong. Others arrived in Thailand, Malaysia, the Philippines, Indonesia, and Singapore. A total of 2.5 million refugees left Vietnam, Laos, and Cambodia. The number of people leaving Vietnam to escape poverty rather than because of human rights abuses increased dramatically in the late 1980s, with many coming from North rather than South Vietnam. The attitude among the international community changed. The West viewed the first wave of boat people in the 1970s as heroes escaping communism. With the worldwide fall of communism came the second wave of boat people, who were considered illegal immigrants (Anonymous, 1997). Today, more than 1.6 million Vietnamese have settled in new countries. All Vietnamese boat people have their own horrible experiences of their perilous escape to freedom. From the start, most boat people headed for southern Thailand, the nearest landfall. The pattern changed, however, when Thai pirates (they are actually small groups of Thai fishermen) regularly began to attack and rob refugee boats, often raping and killing the occupants. By mid-1977, most boat people were avoiding Thailand and instead heading for Malaysia, despite the additional mileage and longer time at sea. Most were blown off course or had engine trouble. As a result, they ended up in the Philippines, Brunei, and East Malaysian states (Anonymous, 1997). Canadians opened their hearts and individually sponsored tens of thousands of refugees (Davis, 1997). The term *boat people* has also been used to describe political and economic refugees from other areas, such as Haiti, who fled for these reasons.

References

Anonymous. (1997, July). The last boat people leave Hong Kong. *Refugee News*, 1–3.

Davis, C. (1997). *The greater Vancouver book: An urban encyclopedia*. Vancouver, BC: Linkman.

Boriquen   This term is used for Native Indians who inhabited the territory of Puerto Rico called the island Boriken or Borinquen, which means "the great land of the valiant and noble Lord" or "land of the great lords." Today, this word—used in various modifications—is still popularly used to designate the people and island of Puerto Rico. The Taíno Indians, who came from South America, inhabited the major portion of the island when the Spaniards arrived. The Taíno Indians lived in small villages and were organized in clans led by a *Cacique* or chief. They were a peaceful people who, with a limited knowledge of agriculture, lived on such domesticated tropical crops as pineapples, cassava, and sweet potatoes supplemented by seafood. They did carving in wood stone and clay, and they produced shell work and gold work (Gonzalez Y Perez, 2000). This term can be used interchangeably with Puerto Rican. Some Puerto Ricans call themselves *Boricuas* as a means to show their cultural pride and reaffirm their indigenous heritage in honor of the Taínos, who called the island Borinquen. Usage of the term *Boricua* has increased in popularity in recent years (Anonymous, 2001). African people were brought to the islands as slaves, and the Spanish who conquered the island interbred and intermarried with the Taínos (Novas, 1994). Puerto Ricans (in North America) comprise the second largest group of Hispanics. This culture is also the most socially and economically deprived (Parillo, 2000).

References

Anonymous. (2001). *The Tainos*. Washington, DC: National Association of Hispanic Journalists.

Gonzalez Y Perez, M. E. (2000). *Puerto Ricans in the United States*. Westport, CT: Greenwood.

Novas, H. (1994). *Everything you need to know about Latino history*. Middlesex, UK: Penguin.

Parillo, V. (2000). *Strangers to these shores: Race and ethnic relations in the United States* (6th ed.). Boston: Allyn & Bacon.

Boufee delirante   This syndrome is observed in West Africa and Haiti. It is a French term that refers to a sudden outburst of agitated and aggressive behavior, marked by confusion and psychomotor excitement. It may sometimes be accompanied by visual and auditory hallucinations or paranoid ideation (Gaw, 2001).

Reference

Gaw, A. C. (2001). *Concise guide to cross-cultural psychiatry*. Washington, DC: American Psychiatric Publishing.

Brain fag   This term was initially used in West Africa. It is often experienced by Nigerian males but is now widespread among south Saharan Africans. It was first described by Prince (1985) to refer to a condition experienced by high school or university students in response to the challenges of schooling. Symptoms include difficulties in concentrating, remembering, and thinking. Students often state that their brains are "fatigued." Other symptoms include pain in the head and around the neck. There is also the experience of pressure or tightness, blurring vision, eye pain, heat, or the sensation of burning. "Brain fatigue" or "too much thinking" has been reported by many cultures (Gaw, 2001; Simons et al., 2002). It was first named by Nigerian students suffering from a variety of somatic symptoms in class, especially vision disturbance when reading. Brain fag symptoms have occurred in many African students, independent of intelligence, when exposed to acculturative stress in Western education systems emphasizing theoretical book learning, which is quite different from the time-honored ways of acquiring knowledge in traditional African societies (Prince, 1985). In theory, culture-bound syndromes are those folk illnesses in which alterations of behavior and experience figure prominently. In actuality, however, many are not syndromes at all. Instead, they are local ways of explaining any of a wide assortment of misfortunes (Simons, 2001). See Culture-Bound Syndromes.

References

Gaw, A. C. (2001). *Concise guide to cross-cultural psychiatry*. Washington, DC: American Psychiatric Publishing.

Prince, R. (1985). The concept of culture-bound syndromes: Anorexia nervosa and brain fag. *Society for Science and Medicine, 21*, 197–203.

Simons, R. (2001). Introduction to culture bound syndromes. *Psychiatric Times, 18*, 11.

Simons, R., Murray, V., McLoyd, V., Lin, K., Cutrona, C., & Conger, R. (2002). Discrimination, crime, ethnic identity and parenting as correlates of depressive symptoms among African American children: A multilevel analysis. *Development and Psychopathology, 14*, 371–393.

Buddhism Buddhism is an Eastern form of spirituality. It is also called mystical religion. Conze (2002) notes, "Buddhism is also known as a part of the common human heritage of wisdom, by which men have succeeded in overcoming this world, and gaining immortality, or a deathless life" (p. 2). Buddhism derives from the word Buddha, which is the God of this religion. The core of the Buddhist movement consisted of monks. The monks lived either in communities or as hermits in solitude. The entire "brotherhood" of monks and hermits is called the Samgha. They are the only Buddhists in the proper sense of the word. There is another term for Buddhism, *popular Buddhism*, but in essence core Buddhism was and is a movement of monastic ascetics. As Buddhism grew from a sect into a widespread religion, the lay followers became increasingly important. Today, Buddhism is one of the world's greatest religions. Buddhism has spread throughout the world, and it is the fourth largest religion in the world, exceeded in numbers only by Christianity, Islam, and Hinduism. The Buddha, Siddhartha Gautama, founded this religion in northern India. He was born in approximately 563 B.C. in Lumbini, which is in modern-day Nepal. At the age of 29, he left his wife, children, and political involvements to seek truth. It was an accepted practice at the time for some men to leave their families and lead the life of an ascetic. He studied Brahmanism but ultimately rejected it. In 535 B.C., he attained enlightenment and assumed the title Buddha ("one who has awakened") (Ch'en, 1968). Buddhism contains a diversity of practices and flexibility of beliefs that make it unique among religions. Traditionally, there have been three groups: Theravada, meaning "tradition of the elders"; Mahayana, meaning "great vehicle"; and Vajrayana, denoted as "diamond vehicle" (Cusak, 2001). Mahayana Buddhism (sometimes called Northern Buddhism) is largely found in China, Japan, Korea, Tibet, and Mongolia. Modern Buddhism has emerged as a truly international movement. It started as an attempt to produce a single form of Buddhism, without local accretions, that all Buddhists could embrace. The Vajrayana group practices Tibetan Buddhism, which developed separately from Theravada and Mahayana Buddhism because of the isolation of Tibet. Vajrayana is also found in Mongolia and Nepal. Theravada Buddhism (sometimes called Southern Buddhism; occasionally spelled Therevada) has been the dominant school of Buddhism in most of Southeast Asia since the 13th century, with the establishment of the monarchies in Laos, Sri Lanka, and Thailand (Conze, 2002). The great number of Western converts throughout the 20th century has resulted in a new group, the Western Buddhists. This group makes use of elements from all the groups and has developed its own distinctive practices (Cusak, 2001).

References

Ch'en, K. K. (1968). *Buddhism.* New York: Barons.

Conze, E. (2002). *Buddhism and its essence and development.* New York: Harper & Row.

Cusak, C. (2001). *The essence of Buddhism: How to bring spiritual meaning into everyday life.* New York: Barnes & Noble.

C

Caste system   A caste system is a separation of society structured on variations in wealth, inherited status or privilege, and profession or occupation. It is a system of "rigid social stratification characterized by heredity status, endogamy, and social barriers sanctioned by custom, law, or religion" (*Merriam-Webster's Collegiate Dictionary*, 1998, p. 173). Groups of people engaged in particular occupations or with particular characteristics are ranked hierarchically (Barfield, 1997). India represents one of the most famous caste societies (Barfield, 1997). The Hindu caste system possibly has its roots in the culture of the Indus Valley civilization. The current form of the system, however, derives from the Indo-Aryans, who were a conquering people in approximately the 15th century B.C. Most likely, the Indo-Aryans were divided into three castes: the royalty and warrior nobility, the priests, and the freemen (Pearson, 1985). Over time, the structure of the caste system in India has changed. In the most recent structure, there are four great *varnas:* the twice-born Brahman priests, Kshatriya warriors, Vaisiya merchants, and the once-born Sudra peasants (Barfield, 1997). In this society, those excluded from the caste system are known as the untouchables and are the people who fill the most polluting occupations (Barfield, 1997). Academic definitions of a caste system are not solidified and fall into two categories. The first is "structurally functional, and views caste as a category or type, comparable in many respects to hierarchical organizations" (Barfield, 1997, p. 123). Therefore, Indian caste is similar to social structures in which rank is attributed, such as past U.S. racial grading (Barfield, 1997). The second definition "understands Indian caste as a total symbolic world, unique, self-contained, and not comparable to other systems" (Barfield, 1997, p. 127). In any definition, a caste system works on the notion that all living beings are differentiated into classes, each of which is believed to possess a defining substance (Barfield, 1997). In a caste system, the ethnic and social distinctions have transformed into "functional" distinctions (Weber, 1999). The caste structure transforms the horizontal and separate coexistences of ethnically divided communities into one vertical social system of superior and subordinates (Weber, 1999).

References

Barfield, T. (1997). *The dictionary of anthropology.* Malden, MA: Blackwell.

Merriam-Webster's Collegiate Dictionary. (1998). Springfield, MA: Merriam-Webster.

Pearson, R. (1985). *Anthropological glossary.* Malabar, FL: Krieger.

Weber, M. (1999). *Essays in economic sociology.* Princeton, NJ: Princeton University Press.

Caucasian   The word "White" is sometimes used synonymously with Caucasian. Sometimes it means non-Hispanic Whites, or the term may specifically refer to Anglo-Americans (see Anglo-American). Caucasian is also considered the race that includes most natives of Europe, West Asia, and North Africa and extends to the Indian subcontinents (Murphy, 1995). This group was proposed first by scientists Johann Riedrich Blumenbach, who coined the term in his treatise, "On the Natural Varieties of Mankind" in 1795. Later anthropologists, such as Carleton Coon, have expanded on the classification of the Caucasian race proposed by Blumenbach (1795/1865) and have subdivided the group into Nordic, Alpine, Mediterranean, and, at times, Dinaric and Baltic. There is extensive debate on the scientific validity of racial classifications, and many people reject systems of racial classification as inherently arbitrary and subject to wide divergences in most populations due to the coexistence of race through conquests, invasions, migrations, and mass deportations, producing a heterogeneous world population ("Caucasian," 2000). *Caucasian* remains a common term in North America to describe Whites of European descent. Caucasian peoples of Asian, African, or, at times, Mediterranean origin, however, are generally excluded from the popular definition of Caucasian. The term retains some accuracy only when applied to forensic anthropology in North America. Its relevance is debatable as an ethnic/cultural or sociopolitical concept. Although the term *Caucasian* is still used to describe the peoples of western Eurasia, the term is generally limited to describe the inhabitants of the Caucasus region of eastern Europe and western Asia.

References

Blumenbach, J. (1865). *On the variety of mankind* (T. Bendysh, Trans.; 3rd ed.). London: Anthropological Society of London. (Original work published 1795)

Caucasian. (2000). In *Columbia encyclopedia.* New York: Columbia University Press.

Murphy, J. (1995, April). Caucasian definition. *Theoretical Anthropology E-Journal, 1*(1), 3.

Chamorro   This is a racial, ethnic, and cultural term that describes the indigenous people of Guam and the Mariana Islands. The terms *Guamanian* and *Chamorro* are used synonymously among residents of Guam (Untalan, 1991). The island of Guam became a U.S. possession in 1898 after 300 years of colonization by Spain. During the years of colonization, the Chamorro race and their values and norms remained intact. Numbering approximately 50,600 in the late 20th century, they are Indonesian with a considerable admixture of Spanish, Filipino, and other strains. Their vernacular, called the Chamorro language, is not a Micronesian dialect but a distinct language with its own vocabulary and grammar. Pure-blooded Chamorros are no longer found in Guam, but the Chamorro language is still used in many native homes, although numerous Spanish words in the vocabulary reflect the three centuries of Spanish rule in Guam. English is the island's official language. The Chamorro culture is known for its dance, sea navigation, unique food, and games. Songs and fashion have been influenced by people from other lands. The Chamorro culture has many complex social protocols centered on respect. Some examples are kissing the hands of elders, passing of legends, and chants. The social status of a Chamorro is determined by his or her family (Munoz, 1990). They are sensitive and concerned about how their behavior will affect family members, and there is a great respect for personal and family privacy. Social activities include the village fiesta, which is a unique cultural activity among Chamorros. As a result of the influence of the Spaniards, the Mariana Islands were Catholic. The center of every village was the church; each had its own patron saint that was celebrated annually with religious and social festivities (Untalan, 1991). In terms of skills, they are masters of canoe making, *belembautyan* making (a musical instrument), sling stone making, weaving, and manufacturing of spears and other tools. The people of Guam (Guahan) are still struggling for an identity. Some refer to themselves as Chamorros, some use the term Chamorus, and some find Chamoris much more to their liking. The last term, Chamoris, is most similar to the term mentioned in the first Spanish document in reference to what their ancestors called themselves. In the earliest Spanish documents, the people of Guahan were called *Chamurre* (Jacobs, 2000). Although the origin of the Chamorro race has never been definitively proven, the original inhabitants of Guam are believed to have been of Indo-Malaya descent originating from Southeast Asia as early as 2000 B.C. and having linguistic and cultural similarities to those of Malaysia, Indonesia, and the Philippines. The first historical Western document relating the physical features of the Chamorro was written by Antonio Pigafetta in 1521 (Athens, 2001).

References

Athens, S. (2001). Asian Chamorro culture and history of the northern Mariana. *Asian Perspectives: The Journal of Archaeology for Asia and the Pacific, 40,* 11–17.

Jacobs, D. (2000, January–March). The struggle for identity. *Pacific Times,* 13–15.

Munoz, U. F. (1990). American policy: Its impact on Pacific Island families. In *Pacific ties, Pacific Islander and Asian news magazine.* Los Angeles: University of California Press.

Untalan, F. F. (1991). Chamorros. In N. Mokuau (Ed.), *Handbook of social services for Asian and Pacific Islanders.* Westport, CT: Greenwood.

Chicano/Chicana This term reflects pride in the indigenous roots of the Mexican people. The term gained wide political and popular favor among Mexican American activists during the 1960s civil rights movement and has emerged as a political term, especially among academics and political activists. *Chicana* is the feminist form of Chicano. Chicano is also the adjective. A Chicano is a Mexican American (i.e., an American of Mexican descent) (*Merriam-Webster Dictionary,* 2003). The word derives from changing the word "Mexicano" by taking out the prefix "Mex" and replacing it with "Chi." The term is used to describe a different culture within a culture (Padilla, Kanellos, & Esteva-Fabregat, 1994). The word can also have different meanings in different situations. For example, one's political and social status can be implied by being called a Chicano. It can be used in a derogatory manner, such as when it was first coined. At one point in time, Chicanos/as were seen as underrated members of society. The word and the stigma attached to it were very negative. Noriega et al. (2001) stated,

> Suffice to say the mainstream social scientist have created a mythical conception of Mexican Americans which sees them as (a) controlled and manipulated by tradition and culture, (b) docile, passive, present-oriented, fatalistic, and lacking in achievement. . . . We have always been thought of as another "minority group" that will, in time, become part of the melting pot. (p. 34)

The proper term is *Chicano*, which is written with a capital "C" as a sign of respect and pride among Chicanos/as (*American Heritage Dictionary*, 2000). The term must be carefully and diplomatically used so as not to offend members of the culture. If the word is pronounced incorrectly, it can be taken as an insult or racial slur. If a person is not a member of the culture, the term *Mexican American* is better suited as a point of reference.

References

American heritage dictionary of the English language (4th ed.). (2000). Boston: Houghton Mifflin.

Merriam-Webster's dictionary. (2003). Springfield, MA: Merriam-Webster.

Noriega, A. C., et al. (Eds.). (2001). *The Chicano studies reader: An anthology of Aztlan, 1970–2000.* Los Angeles: University of California Press.

Padilla, F., Kanellos, N., & Esteva-Fabregat, C. (Eds.). (1994). *Handbook of Hispanic cultures in the United States: Sociology.* Houston, TX: Arte Publico Press/Institution de Instutito de Cooperacion Iberoamericana.

Child rearing   Child rearing is the process of raising, fostering, nourishing, and educating a young boy or girl to the age of puberty or to adulthood (Simpson & Weiner, 1989). Child rearing involves several different aspects, including feeding, toilet training, dependency training, and aggression training (Halfon, Mclean, & Schuster, 2002). The earliest philosophy of child rearing was directed toward self-survival and family survival. According to this "primordial" philosophy, the father of the family hunted, fought off dangerous enemies, and kept a watchful eye on his sons, particularly as they neared the age of puberty. When they became sexually aggressive and a threat to him, the father fought them and drove them off. The newly expelled son usually managed to find a family of his own. The wives bred, bore, suckled, and nurtured the children (McCandless, 1967). McCandless pointed out that Plato's beliefs about child rearing were quite different: Plato taught that in child rearing, the parents should raise the boy to be a man of the most "sophisticated and knowledgeable" type, one who is willing and able to use his education and talents to the benefit of his country. The understanding of childhood and social roles of children has evolved dramatically during the past century. Currently, children are mainly shaped by the very culture in which they grow. The parents are a critical influence in the process of nurturing their child's development, "but so too are political forces, practical economics, and implicit ideological commitments to children and their families" (Halfon et al., 2002, p. 16). From his research on worldwide patterns of parenting, Rohner (1994) concluded that parents in all societies express love, warmth, and affection for their children. He also found that parents everywhere may dislike, disapprove, or resent children, viewing them as an unwanted burden. Child-rearing practices, however, vary with the structure of the family and the cultural context in which the child is raised.

References

Halfon, N., Mclean, K. T., & Schuster, M. A. (2002). *Child rearing in America: Challenges facing parents with young children.* Cambridge, UK: Cambridge University Press.

McCandless, B. R. (1967). *Children: Behavior and development* (2nd ed.). Atlanta, GA: Holt, Rinehart & Winston.

Rohner, R. P. (1994). The warmth dimension in worldwide perspective. In W. Lonner & R. Malpass (Eds.), *Psychology and culture* (pp. 113–120). Needham Heights, MA: Allyn & Bacon.

Simpson, J. S., & Weiner, E. S. C. (1989). *Oxford English dictionary* (2nd ed.). Oxford, UK: Clarendon.

Chinese Americans   The term *Chinese American* is used in some degree to broadly include both citizens and noncitizens. Chinese children that are born and raised in the United States are also considered Chinese Americans. The reason why even noncitizen Chinese are considered Chinese American is that until 1943, the law prevented Chinese immigrants from becoming naturalized citizens. Because such legislation was discriminatory, it was later agreed that Chinese immigrants who had spent most of their lives in the United States would become Chinese Americans. The term began to be used more after World War II. After China became an ally during World War II, the exclusion laws proved to be an embarrassment and were repealed by the Magnuson Act in 1943 (Wong, 1998). This bill made it possible for Chinese to become naturalized citizens and gave them an annual quota of 105 immigrants. Although the bill ended an injustice that had been committed 61 years earlier, the damage to the Chinese community had already been done. Between the 1890s and the 1920s, the Chinese population in the United States declined (Chan, 1988). The worst effect, however, was to undermine the one variable that was most precious to the Chinese—their families. Americanization and, to some degree, Christianity did shape their fortunes and selfhoods; equally important were the countervailing forces of China-centered nationalism and racial exclusion. These conflicting forces sometimes created a sense of ambivalence for the community's self-identity and its relationship to the larger body politic, even as these Chinese immigrants, through a continuous, multifaceted nonlinear process, became Chinese Americans. By 1920, approximately 18,000 (29%) of the 62,000 people of Chinese ancestry were listed in the census as U.S. citizens. Americans by birthright, fluent in English, and familiar with U.S. culture, most, if not all, of the native-born Chinese Americans had nevertheless experienced some form of racial discrimination. Although 90% of Chinese Americans are foreign born, they have shown great accomplishments in language proficiency, acculturation, and political power (Chen, 1995).

References

Chan, S. (1988). *Claiming America: Constructing Chinese American identities during the exclusion era.* Philadelphia: Temple University Press.

Chen, S. A. (1995). Chinese Americans: Their plights and challenges. *Community Psychologist, 21,* 36–37.

Wong, S. (1998, July). Chinese American. *Philadelphia Publication,* iii.

Collectivism   The main focus of collectivistic cultures is on the group as opposed to the individual. The sense of self is tied to group membership. This group may be the family, social or political organizations, or religious affiliations (Hui, Triandis, & Yee, 1991). When asked who he or she is, a collectivistic individual may respond with a family name, unlike an individualist, who usually gives his or her first name. There are variations at the cultural and the individual level. Very few cultures or individuals would claim to be totally collectivistic in all circumstances and at all times. Members of collectivistic cultures value harmony and will defer to the will of the group rather than stand up for individual right. Awards and victories are won for the group, not the individual. Wrongful deeds bring shame not only to the individual but also to the group. Loyalty to the group, cooperation, and contributing to the group with public modesty and without expectation of reciprocity are highly valued (Triandis, 1989). Families in collectivistic cultures tend to be extended, and grandparents usually play a significant role in family decisions. The family structure is hierarchical, with the father being the head of the household. In some collectivistic cultures, such as a traditional Chinese family, the sons have higher status than the mother, who has higher status than the daughters. Sons defer to their fathers even after marriage. Communication is from top (fathers) to bottom (children). Children have little power in decision-making processes. Sex roles tend to be well defined, and the more traditional the culture, the more inflexible the sex role. Children, particularly girls, are likely to live at home until marriage. Individuals in collectivistic cultures tend to be field dependent. Field dependence is the inclination to focus on the whole rather than on parts (Brown, 1994).

References

Brown, H. D. (1994). *Principles of language learning and teaching* (3rd ed.). Englewood Cliffs, NJ: Prentice Hall.

Hui, C. H., Triandis, H. C., & Yee, C. (1991). Cultural differences in reward allocation: Is collectivism the explanation? *British Journal of Social Psychology, 30,* 145–157, 523–524.

Triandis, H. (1989). The self and social behavior in different social contexts. *Psychological Review, 96,* 506–520.

Confucianism   Confucianism is a worldview, a social ethic, a political ideology, a scholarly tradition, and a way of life: The noun is "Confucius," the Latinization of K'ung Fu-tzu or "Master K'ung." The term was coined in Europe in the 18th century. Confucianism is humanism, a philosophy or attitude that is concerned with human beings and their achievements and interests rather than abstract beings and problems of theology. Although Confucian values had their origin with the Chinese philosopher Confucius (551–479 B.C.), these values and beliefs persist today in most East Asian cultures. In this belief system, harmonious social interaction is of the highest value. The individual is never isolated but is part of a unity of mankind (Moore, 1967). In terms of these social interactions, people are bound to one another by *ren* (King & Bond, 1985), and relationships are regulated by *li*, the set of rules and rituals that allow relationships to work without conflicts. In Confucianism, man is the center of the universe, and for human beings the ultimate goal is happiness.

References

King, A. Y. C., & Bond, M. H. (1985). The Confucian paradigm of man: A sociological view. In W. S. Tseng & D. Y. H. Wu (Eds.), *Chinese culture and mental health* (pp. 29–46). Orlando, FL: Academic Press.

Moore, C. A. (1967). Introduction: The humanistic Chinese mind. In C. A. Moore (Ed.), *The Chinese mind.* Honolulu: University of Hawaii Press.

Criollo   This term refers to the children of Spaniards born in the New World (Figueredo, 2002). Moreover, it is also known as *creole*, which refers to an indigenous national who is of Spanish origin (Smith, 1992). In certain instances, the term can also be used to refer to someone who is a coward (Smith, 1992). In Latin America, the noun or adjective version of this term commonly refers to something that is not foreign but indigenous. For instance, when referring to a native dish, one may say that it is *un manjar criollo.* This simply means that one is having a meal that is unique to a particular culture or region. In addition, criollo is used to refer to people who are true to their roots. One may call someone who remains true to their ethnicity a criollo (Gross, 1993). Due to the dissemination of the Spanish culture throughout the New World—for example, in Mexico, Argentina, and the Caribbean—a severe breakdown of their ethnicity began in the late 1700s. This resulted in a separation of individuals based on their generational descent from their parents. Economic and social privileges were given to those with a lesser amount of "mixed" blood (Delgado, 1998). During the 1800s, in the United States, middle-class criollos were considered political exiles. They often published pamphlets and articles in newspapers to be recognized as "true" Spaniards (Figueredo, 2002).

References

Delgado, R. (1998). *The Latin condition: A critical reader.* New York: New York University Press.

Figueredo, D. (2002). *The complete idiot's guide to Latino history and culture.* New York: Alpha.

Gross, R. (1993). *Gran diccionario.* Paris: Larousse.

Smith, C. (1992). *Collins dictionary.* New York: HarperCollins.

Cross-cultural adaptation   This is the long-term process of adjusting and finally feeling comfortable in a new environment. Immigrants who enter a culture more or less voluntarily and who, at some point, decide to or feel the need to adapt to the cultural context experience cultural adaptation in a positive way (Berry, Kim, Minde, & Mok, 1987). Adaptation highlights the relationship between internal equilibrium and environmental challenges. It refers to the process that people who belong to a different culture must go through to adapt to a new environment. A person will attain insight of the similarities and differences between what one is used to and the typical customs and the way of life in the new environment. People will have to understand and adjust to the new traditions and ways of the culture in which they are going to live so that they can feel as if they belong there too (Martin & Nakayama, 2000). Adaptation is similar to any other transition experience that shares some common characteristics and provokes the same kinds of responses (Kim, 1988). Cross-cultural adaptation depends in part on the individual. Each individual has a preferred way of dealing with a new situation. Cross-cultural adaptation may involve one other culture, but it may also involve different ethnicities, races, and cultures (Berry et al., 1987). Briggs and Harwood (1983) believe that training programs in some settings aid the cross-cultural adaptation process. Pusch (1979) views cross-cultural adaptation as a learning continuum with ethnocentrism at one end moving to integration or adaptation at the other end (see Acculturation).

References

Berry, J. W., Kim, U., Minde, T., & Mok, K. (1987). Comparative studies of acculturative stress. *International Migration Review, 21,* 491–511.

Briggs, N. E., & Harwood, G. R. (1983). Furthering adjustment: An application of the inoculation theory to an intercultural context. ERIC Reproduction Service No. ED225.

Kim, Y. (1988). *Communication and cross-cultural adaptation.* Philadelphia: Multilingual Matters.

Martin, J. N., & Nakayama, T. K. (2000). *Intercultural communication in context.* Mountain View, CA: Mayfield.

Pusch, M. D. (1979). *Multicultural education.* New York: Intercultural Press.

Cross-cultural counseling   Cross-cultural counseling and practice took prominence in the United States in the late 1960s and early 1970s, prompted by the civil rights movement and subsequent social movements of the time. This practice arose due to the diverse populations migrating to the United States (Thompson & Carter, 1997). Cross-cultural counseling describes a counseling relationship involving participants who are culturally different from one another (Sue & Sue, 1990). Mental health practitioners mainly consider how culture, race, and other forces related to human diversity and oppression effect a person. Cross-cultural counseling includes the study of factors such as race, ethnicity, social class, gender, intellectual ability, religious preference, physical ability, sexual orientation, and age (Atkinson & Hackett, 1995; Cyrus, 1993). Cross-cultural counseling is based on studies of the life experiences of diverse groups that are inclusive of their sociocultural and sociopolitical perspectives to better understand the different points of view of the patient. It teaches strategies and coping skills for working effectively with a diverse population (Thompson & Carter, 1997).

References

Atkinson, D. R., & Hackett, G. (1995). *Counseling diverse populations.* Madison, WI: Brown & Benchmark.

Cyrus, V. (1993). *Experiencing race, class, and gender in the United States* (3rd ed.). Mountain View, CA: Mayfield.

Sue, D. W., & Sue, D. (1990). *Counseling the culturally different: Theory and practice* (2nd ed.). Oxford, UK: Oxford University Press.

Thompson, C. E., & Carter, R. T. (1997). *Racial identity theory: Applications to individual, group, and organizational interventions.* Mahwah, NJ: Lawrence Erlbaum.

Cross-cultural psychology   Cross-cultural psychology is the scientific study of human behavior and its transmission, taking into account the ways in which behaviors are shaped and influenced by social and cultural factors (Segall, Dasen, Berry, & Poortinga, 1990). This is only one of several definitions of cross-cultural psychology. Another definition (Triandis, Malpass, & Davidson, 1972) states that

> cross-cultural psychology includes studies of subjects from two or more cultures, using equivalent methods of measurement, to determine the limits within which general psychological theories do hold, and the kind of modification of these theories needed to make them universal. (p. 1)

Researchers may be interested in similarities among the cultures being investigated, or they may be searching for differences in the expression of a variable. Furthermore, they may be interested in whether a variable is present in one culture but absent in another. According to Berry, Poortinga, Segall, and Dasen (1992), there is a relationship between cross-cultural psychology both at the population level (sociology and anthropology) and at the individual level (developmental, social behavioral, personality, cognition, and perception).

References

Berry, J. W., Poortinga, Y. H., Segall, M. H., & Dasen, P. R. (1992). *Cross-cultural psychology: Research and applications.* Cambridge, UK: Cambridge University Press.

Segall, M. H., Dasen, P. R., Berry, J. W., & Poortinga, W. H. (1990). *Human behavior in global perspective: An introduction to cross-cultural psychology.* New York: Pergamon.

Triandis, H. C., Malpass, R., & Davidson, A. R. (1972). Cross-cultural psychology. *Biennial Review of Anthropology, 1,* 1–84.

Cross-cultural research   Cross-cultural research is the scientific study of human behavior and its transmission, taking into account the ways in which behaviors are shaped and influenced by social and cultural factors (Segall, Dasen, Berry, & Poortinga, 1990). It is the study of cultural coherence or decoherence within and between human communities that constitute human behavior, beliefs, and institutions (Driver, 1956). It studies human communities and their various practices, beliefs, social roles, norms, expressions, forms of organization, and conflicts that exhibit various sorts of internal coherence as well as cleavages within communities (Levinson, 1980). These coherences and cleavages bear many close connections to the different historical experiences and physical and social environments in which people live (Ogbum, 1982). Cross-cultural research includes configurations of elements and characteristic ways of interrelating that are shared with neighboring and interacting groups and shared among dispersed groups that have common historical experiences and similarities, including common origin, common membership in historical civilizations, and languages that are mutually understood or that derive common families. Lines of cleavage, conflict, and marginality are part of cross-cultural research (Levinson, 1980).

References

Driver, H. E. (1956). *An integration of functional, evolutionary, and historical theory by means of correlations.* Bloomington: Indiana University Press.

Levinson, D. (1980). *Towards explaining human culture.* New Haven, CT: Human Relations Area Press.

Ogbum, W. F. (1982). *Social change.* New York: New York University Press.

Segall, M. H., Dasen, P. R., Berry, J. W., & Poortinga, W. H. (1990). *Human behavior in global perspective: An introduction to cross-cultural psychology.* New York: Pergamon.

Cuban Americans   Cuban Americans are natives of Cuba or descendants of Cubans who began arriving in the United States in large numbers from the island of Cuba.

Cuba is 90 miles south of Florida. It is a Spanish-speaking country, and today many Cuban Americans are either bilingual or Spanish speaking. Although Cubans began arriving as early as the 1800s, the large exodus from Cuba occurred between 1959 and 1980 following the Castro revolution (Gonzalez-Pando, 1998). The 1990 census reported that there are more than 1 million Cuban Americans. Cuban Americans are a heterogeneous group consisting of mixtures of European, Indian, and African descent. The long and continuous history of their immigration to the United States has resulted in various degrees of acculturation into American culture. They arrive as refugees seeking political asylum. The first wave arrived in the 1950s, and the second flotilla of refugees was an exodus from the port of Mariel in 1980. This Mariel boatlift brought approximately 125,000 Cuban refugees to the United States. Refugees are granted permanent residence in the United States. Most of these Cubans settle in the Miami–Fort Lauderdale area in Dade and Broward counties in Florida as well as Los Angeles and New York City (Gonzalez-Pando, 1998).

Reference

Gonzalez-Pando, M. (1998). *The Cuban Americans.* Westport, CT: Greenwood.

Cultural absolutism   According to Berry, Poortinga, Segall, and Dasen (1992), cultural absolutism is the idea that psychological phenomena, such as intelligence and honesty, do not differ from culture to culture: They are the same among cultures. Adamopoulos and Lonner (1994) note that these phenomena or characteristics are found in all cultures, and they can be measured to clarify variations in human behavior. Howard (1995), however, defines cultural absolutism as being related to ethnocentrism—the ethical value of that society's culture is above all others. Howard states, "Cultural absolutists specifically argue that culture is of more value than the internationally accepted (but Western in origin) principle of human rights" (p. 52). Research on cultural absolutism was carried out to find similarities in psychological characteristics and whether the characteristics all had the same psychological meaning in each culture (Berry et al., 1992). The theory behind cultural absolutism is that people of all cultural backgrounds are psychologically the same, with the only variation being the degree (Berry et al., 1992).

References

Adamopoulos, J., & Lonner, W. J. (1994). Absolutism, relativism, and universalism in the study of human behaviour. In W. J. Lonner & R. Malpass (Eds.), *Psychology and culture.* Boston: Allyn & Bacon.

Berry, J. W., Poortinga, Y. H., Segall, M. H., Dasen, P. R. (1992). *Cross-cultural psychology: Research and applications.* Cambridge, UK: Cambridge University Press.

Howard, R. E. (1995). *Human rights and the search for community.* Boulder, CO: Westview.

Cultural bias   This term is used in the cross-cultural literature. It refers to bias that is likely to exist when measuring, analyzing, and interpreting data from different cultures. The more dissimilar the cultures are in values, cognitions, and behaviors, the more likely the evidence of cultural bias. Levine (1991) noted the cultural bias in the psychological concept of field independence and field dependence (see Field Independent and Field Dependent). Researchers assumed that certain levels of independence are achieved at a certain stage of development across all cultures. This was found to be applicable in some cultures but not in others. Because of differences in the cultural value of different cognitive skills and behaviors, intelligence tests that measure Western middle-class intelligence and that are adapted for scientific analysis will discriminate against cultures that have other types of intelligence measured by different tasks (Vernon, 1969). Minorities and middle-class Euro-Americans differ in cognitive skills, but the measurement of IQ has been based on the sampling of Euro-American cognitive skills. Thus, the lower scores may be the result of cultural and cognitive differences that are due to "culture bias" (Greenfield & Cocking, 1994). To reduce or eliminate cultural bias in cross-cultural studies, there must be conceptual equivalence, item or task equivalence, and sample and test situation equivalence (Berry, Poortinga, Segall, & Dasen, 1992).

References

Berry, J. W., Poortinga, Y. H., Segall, M. H., & Dasen, P. R. (1992). *Cross-cultural psychology: Research and applications.* Cambridge, UK: Cambridge University Press.

Greenfield, P. M., & Cocking, R. R. (1994). *Cross-cultural roots of minority child development.* Hillsdale, NJ: Lawrence Erlbaum.

Levine, R. A. (1991). Cultural bias. In P. M. Greenfield (Ed.), *Continuities and discontinuities in the cognitive socialization of minority children.* Washington, DC: Department of Health and Human Services, Public Health Service, Alcohol Drug and Mental Health Administration.

Vernon, P. E. (1969). *Intelligence and cultural environment.* London: Methuen.

Cultural borders   This is "a social construct that is political in origin" and "involves differences in rights and obligations" (Erickson, 1997, p. 42). These cultural borders may be developed around a number of microcultures, which may be based on religion, ethnicity, socioeconomic status, nationality, or region of origin. Affiliations to these cultural groups define the individuals and may be positive when they provide a sense of belonging and contribute to self-esteem. Gollnick and Chinn (2002) maintain that as long as those differences have no "status implication" in which one group is treated differently from another, then the conflict among groups will be minimal. Problems arise when individuals who belong to a microculture denigrate those on the outside and perceive "them" as being inferior to "us" on the inside. Some cultural borders are more easily penetrated than others. A cultural group in which individuals speak a foreign language may be more difficult to penetrate than one that shares the same language as that of the outside group.

References

Erickson, F. (1997). Culture in society and in educational practices. In J. A. Banks & C. A. M. Banks (Eds.), *Multicultural education: Issues and perspectives* (3rd ed., pp. 32–60). Needham Heights, MA: Allyn & Bacon.

Gollnick, D., & Chinn, P. (2002). *Multicultural education in a pluralistic society.* Columbus, OH: Merrill.

Cultural competence Cultural competence is a set of fitting behaviors, attitudes, and policies in a system, agency, or among professionals that facilitate the system, agency, or professionals to work successfully in cross-cultural situations (King, Sims, & Osher, 2000). Ethnoscience is concerned with people's formation and understanding of diverse phenomena. Ethnopsychology is a branch of ethnoscience that is concerned with people's knowledge about human behavior; a specific domain is people's understanding of cognitive competence ("intelligence") in their culture. Studies of this domain have been reviewed by Berry, Poortinga, Segall, and Dasen (2002), who concluded that there are many alternative views about human competence, often distinct with those views that are narrowly cognitive and those that integrate social and moral competencies. Green (1982) defines ethnic competence as "an awareness of prescribed and proscribed behavior within a specific culture" and further suggests that the ethnically competent worker has the ability to carry out professional activities consistent with that awareness (p. 16). Green also emphasizes the trained worker's ability to adapt professional tasks and work styles to the cultural values and preferences of clients (Brown & Brown, 1997). The word culture is used because it implies the incorporated model of human behavior that embraces thoughts, communications, actions, ethnicity, attitudes, principles, and institutes of racial, ethnic, religious, or social groups. The word competence is used because it implies the capability to function in a meticulous way—the ability to function within the context of a culturally incorporated blueprint of human behavior defined by a group (King et al., 2000). Being competent in cross-cultural functioning means discovering diverse patterns of behavior and effectively relating them in the appropriate settings. For example, a teacher of a class of African American children may find that a certain look adequately quiets most of the class. Often, African American adults use eye contact and facial expressions to control their children. Nonetheless, this is not efficient for all African Americans. The unknowing teacher may offend or upset some students by using the wrong words, tone, or body language. Therefore, it is imperative to avoid oversimplification, and by being culturally competent one has the capacity to function productively in other cultural contexts (King et al., 2000). There are five fundamental elements that aid a system's ability to become more culturally competent. The system should value multiplicity, have the capacity for cultural self-assessment, be aware of the "dynamics" inherent when cultures collaborate, institutionalize cultural knowledge, and increase distinctions to service delivery reflecting an understanding of diversity between and within cultures (King et al., 2000). Because of the multiethnic nature of the United States, and the frequent interactions that Americans have with people throughout the world, cultural competence represents a shift in defining ethnic and race relations from conflict to the belief that people should be able to work effectively with other groups. Although the characteristics involved in cultural competency in psychotherapy and counseling have been difficult to specify, it is one of the most discussed concepts among scholars and practitioners interested in ethnic minority issues (Sue, 1998).

References

Berry, J. W., Poortinga, Y. H., Segall, M. H., & Dasen, P. R. (2002). *Cross-cultural psychology: Research and applications* (2nd ed.). Cambridge, UK: Cambridge University Press.

Brown, P., & Brown, D. (1997). *Cross-cultural practice with couples and families.* New York: Haworth.

Green, J. W. (1982). *Cultural awareness in the human services.* Englewood Cliffs, NJ: Prentice Hall.

King, M., Sims, A., & Osher, O. (2000). *Cultural competence.* Paper on the project mandated by the Office of Special Education, Department of Education, Washington, DC.

Sue, S. (1998). In search of cultural competence in psychotherapy and counseling. *The American Psychologist, 53,* 4.

Cultural congruence　According to Au and Kawakami (1994), cultural congruence is the idea of making learning for students of culturally different backgrounds more valuable. It is also the process of incorporating values and practices from the learner's home culture into instruction (Hollins & Oliver, 1999). Cultural congruence studies show that teaching and learning occur in social settings, mostly from teacher-student relations (Au & Kawakami, 1994). The relationship between school practices and the practices that take place in the home greatly affects a student's learning (Hollins, 1996). The theory of cultural congruence is that students from culturally diverse backgrounds frequently do below average work in school because the culture of the school is so different from the culture of the home (Au & Kawakami, 1994). The students are unable to learn because the school's lessons and activities are conducted in a way that is strongly contrasted to the norms of the home (Au & Kawakami, 1994). Hollins asserts that the activities are suited for students of a particular cultural background. It is widely believed that middle-class White students are more comfortable in the classroom than minorities because White parents encourage the exact things that are taught in the classrooms (Bartolomae, 1998). Cultural congruence in no way means to imitate the home culture inside the classroom (Au & Kawakami, 1994). Researchers of cultural congruence understand that school and home are totally different settings, but that some features of the home should be incorporated into class instruction

(Au & Kawakami, 1994). Cultural congruence is also known as culturally compatible instruction and culturally responsive instruction (Au & Kawakami, 1994).

References

Au, K. H., & Kawakami, A. J. (1994). Cultural congruence in instruction. In E. R. Hollins, J. E. King, & W. C. Hayman (Eds.), *Teaching diverse populations: Formulating a knowledge base* (pp. 5–7). New York: State University of New York Press.

Bartolomae, L. I. (1998). *The misleading of academic discourses: The politics of language in the classroom*. Boulder, CO: Westview.

Hollins, E. R. (1996). *Culture in school learning: Revealing the deep meaning*. Mahwah, NJ: Lawrence Erlbaum.

Hollins, E. R., & Oliver, E. I. (Eds.). (1999). *Pathways to success in school: Culturally responsive teaching*. Mahwah, NJ: Lawrence Erlbaum.

Cultural continuity Cultural continuity is the spread of cultural heritage from one generation to another and includes the means by which that transmission is done (Eggan, 1956). Every culture has cultural scripts concerning the favored patterns of thought and action that are considered cultural ideals. When groups move from a homeland to a new country, the scripts move with them. These scripts become a major source of cultural continuity in the transition (Greenfield & Cocking, 1994). As changes occur in values or the environment, aspects of the culture may be lost, leading to changes in cultural continuity (Winer & Boos, 1993). For example, the material circumstances of minority children in the United States or other Western countries are often very different from those of children growing up in the societies of their ancestral origin. Value orientations would therefore more likely be the source of cultural continuity in the developmental processes of minority children (Greenfield & Cocking, 1994). Research on cultural continuity investigates the processes by which cultural models are transmitted from one generation to the next. It focuses on how culturally established mental demonstrations, principle systems, and patterns of performance are developed. Transmission of the human experience establishes the real meaning of cultural continuities (Comunian & Owe, 2000).

References

Comunian, A. L., & Owe, G. P. (Eds.). (2000). *International perspectives on human development* (pp. 177–185). Lengerich, Germany: Science Publishers.

Eggan, D. (1956). Instruction and affect in Hopi cultural continuity. *Southwestern Journal of Anthropology, 12*(4), 347–366.

Greenfield, P. M., & Cocking, R. R. (Eds.). (1994). *Cross-cultural roots of minority child development*. Hillsdale, NJ: Lawrence Erlbaum.

Winer, L., & Boos, H. E. A. (1993). Rights through rings and taws: Marbles terminology in Trinidad and Tobago. *Language in Society, 22*, 41–66.

Cultural difference hypothesis   According to Corsini (1984), cultures differ in many ways, such as in how the people of different cultures work, what they own, and how they think. Corsini further explains that a particular culture's way of thinking and possessions are influenced by the culture's teachings, which he calls cultural symbols. The culture is sustained because the teachings that influenced the way the people of that culture view the world are passed on from generation to generation (Corsini, 1984). Another aspect of cultural difference deals with the individual, such as personality, and not with "designs which compare social system characteristics" (Hofstede, 1999, p. 66). Research on the cultural difference hypothesis indicates that certain behavioral differences are cultural, whereas others are universal (Corsini, 1984). Concerning cultural differences in education, Greenfield and Cocking (1994) identify three types of cultural differences: universal, primary, and secondary. Universal cultural differences are universal because every child from every culture will have to adjust to the new culture of the classroom, which in most cases is very different from that of the home culture (Greenfield & Cocking, 1994). Primary cultural differences occur because different people have their own culture before they are taught by people from a totally different and also dominant culture (Greenfield & Cocking, 1994). Secondary cultural differences focus on the relationship between involuntary and voluntary minorities and the dominant group (Greenfield & Cocking, 1994). The voluntary minorities are willing to overcome the cultural differences, whereas the involuntary minorities are not (Greenfield & Cocking, 1994).

References

Corsini, R. J. (Ed.). (1984). Cultural differences. In *Encyclopedia of psychology* (Vol. 1, pp. 332–333). New York: John Wiley.

Greenfield, P. M., & Cocking, R. R. (Eds.). (1994). *Cross-cultural roots of minority child development.* Hillsdale, NJ: Lawrence Erlbaum.

Hofstede, G. (1999). Empirical models of cultural differences. In J. E. Trimble, P. Arredondo, J. Mio, H. Cheatham, & D. Sue (Eds.), *Key words in multicultural interventions: A dictionary* (p. 66). Westport, CT: Greenwood.

Cultural diversity   Cultural diversity is the variety of human societies found throughout the world, including ethnic, religious, political, age, and economic groups (Pratte, 1979). Cultural diversity has also been defined as differences among people of the same culture (Higgins & Kruglanski, 1996). Kazdin (2000) encompasses both definitions of cultural diversity by stating that it is a "naturally occurring diversity among people within a context and between groups of people who are a part of different contexts" (p. 384). Cultural diversity is reflected in the different dress, languages, and other cultural differences among cultures, even the way various cultures have structured themselves and interact with their surroundings. The fact that when old, one culture would prolong life as long as possible, whereas another would prematurely end life is an outcome of cultural diversity (Macklin, 1999). Cultural diversity is believed to involve many things, although a main factor is undeterminable. Theories are travel, an evolutionary process, or, taken a step further, "different interpretive structures" within an individual causing cultural meanings and practices to be absorbed differently (Higgins & Kruglanski, 1996). The fact that culture is "experimented with, invented, forgotten, and then passed on" offers another explanation for diversity, especially regarding the differences among individuals of the same cultural group (Higgins & Kruglanski, 1996, p. 868). Cultural diversity has been said to be beneficial for humankind, and without it humanity is lost; even so, cultural diversity has occasionally caused problems. The concept of cultural diversity must be understood by researchers; without understanding, validity and generality are not possible (Kazdin, 2000). Cultural diversity is the "central feature of community psychology" based on "a general psychological focus on . . . diversity among a group and between groups" (Kazdin, 2000, p. 384). Recognizing cultural diversity has also been found to improve employer-employee relations, thus reducing miscommunication (Prosser & Sitaram, 1998). Cultural diversity, however, seems to be on the decline as a result of overpopulation, globalization, and imperialism. Studies show that 10% of the languages spoken today are utilized by 100 or fewer people. The diversity in society should be appreciated; as Kazdin (2000) notes, diversity should be taken to appreciate "the plurality of views and experiences in our society" (p. 384). Hence, cultural diversity is a "valued aspect" in society; a jewel in the study of community psychology; and an answer, some believe, to life's problems (Kazdin, 2000, p. 387). See Diversity.

References

Higgins, T. E., & Kruglanski, A. W. (Eds.). (1996). *Social psychology: Handbook of basic principles.* New York: Guilford.

Kazdin, A. E. (Ed.). (2000). *Encyclopedia of psychology.* Oxford, UK: Oxford University Press.

Macklin, R. (1999). *Against relativism.* New York: Oxford University Press.

Pratte, R. (1979). *Pluralism in education: Conflict, clarity and commitment.* Springfield, IL: Charles C Thomas.

Prosser, M., & Sitaram, K. S. (Eds.). (1998). *Civic discourse: Multiculturalism, cultural diversity, and global communication* (Vol. 1). Stamford, CT: Ablex.

Cultural evolution   The term means that all cultures are in the process of advancing up a single evolutionary ladder. Some cultures are at different stages of advancement than others. According to Morgan (1877), human history can be divided into savagery, barbarism, and civilization. Morgan's theories influenced Gordon Childe (1983), who defined three stages of cultural evolution: savagery as pre-Neolithic culture, barbarism as a Neolithic food-producing or herding society, and civilization as urban communities with a written language (Pearson, 1985). The Neolithic culture stemmed from the invention of agriculture. Urban cultures stemmed from population growth, which agriculture made possible (Ember & Levinson, 1996). Eckland (1982) showed the interaction between biological and cultural evolution. He noted that biology and culture mutually influence one another through continuous intergenerational feedback. New patterns invariably emerge through the interaction of heredity and environment. Genes restrict the possible range of human development, and within these limits humans alter their environment or cultural arrangement to change the distribution in the next generation. This change enables them to carry out even more change. Genes prescribe a set of possible biological processes whose exact form is shaped by culture and the physical environment (Shoemaker, 1996). Cultural anthropologists believe in the Spencerian (Spencer, 1883) concept of evolution, which is a change from an indefinite, incoherent, homogeneity to a definite, coherent, heterogeneity through nonstop differentiations and integrations. For Spencer, only changes in the direction of increasing complexity qualified evolution. According to Spencer, evolution consists of development and growth. Development is the emergence of new forms, and growth is an increase in the number of these forms. In addition, there are two forms of cultural evolution: unilinear and multilinear. Unilinear means that all societies follow the same sequence as they evolve, and multilinear means that there are variations in the way societies develop. New cultural elements occur that allow society to cope with environmental conditions. Similar to natural selection, the new cultural forms, if well adapted, may survive and spread. Less adapted traits will disappear. Natural selection works to adapt societies more effectively to their environment. Currently, modern cultural evolutionists look to material factors in accounting for cultural development. Culturological theory explains how culture evolves through the interaction of cultural forms. It states that after requisite conditions are present, inventions follow. Anthropologists, whose concern is cultural evolution, focus on the transformation of culture from its Paleolithic origins to the present (Ember & Levinson, 1996).

References

Childe, V. G. (1983). *Man makes himself.* New York: Meridian.

Eckland, B. (1982). Theories of mate selection. *Social Biology, 29,* 7–21.

Ember, M., & Levinson, D. (1996). Cultural evolution. In *Encyclopedia of cultural anthropology* (pp. 271–276). New York: Henry Holt.

Morgan, L. H. (1877). *Ancient society.* New York: Holt.

Pearson, R. (1985). *Cultural evolution, unilineal: Anthropological glossary.* Malabar, FL: Krieger.

Shoemaker, P. J. (1996). Using biological and cultural evolution to explain the surveillance function. *Journal of Communication, 46*(3), 38–48.

Spencer, H. (1883). *The principles of sociology* (Vol. 11). New York: Appleton.

Cultural loss   Cultural loss is described as a loss of a person's culture, usually due to a change in environment. Such a change may be due to immigration (Sluzki, 1979). When an individual attempts to merge many different cultures into one, the individual ends up with no culture at all. Extensive loss of the unique culture is more likely when the drive for change within the culture is exterior to the group, major changes are made, the changes occur quickly, and the culture has little control over the change progression (Kazdin, 2002). Cultural loss usually occurs when a smaller group encounters or becomes wrapped up in a larger, more dominant culture. Cultural loss has a negative connotation (Brislin, 1981) and has been known to break up families (Sluzki, 1979). In the immigration process, there are five steps in becoming acculturated to the new society: the prep stage, leaving, overcompensation, decompensation, and transgenerational phenomena. It is in the fourth stage, decompensation, when a family or a person begins to shed some aspects of the old culture. This happens simply because some aspects of the old culture are not feasible in the new culture. When one member of a family, usually the male, is working in the community, he becomes more saturated with the new culture than the other family members. This in itself does not cause familial stress, unless prolonged. When roles are reversed so that the woman is the one immersed in the culture, the man may become depressed, an alcoholic, or critical, or there will be a major disorganization of the family. A child caught in the middle of the stress of acculturation may become a delinquent, or viewed as such, because he or she has become more acculturated than the parents (Sluzki, 1979). This shift in power associated with cultural loss may be experienced as a "psychological loss" in which the balance of power is shifted, resulting in a feeling of powerlessness (Pinderhughes, 1989).

References

Brislin, R. W. (1981). *Cross-cultural encounters: Face to face interaction.* New York: Pergamon.

Kazdin, A. E. (2002). *Encyclopedia of psychology.* Oxford, UK: Oxford University Press.

Pinderhughes, E. (1989). *Understanding race, ethnicity and power: The key to efficacy in clinical practice.* New York: Free Press.

Sluzki, C. E. (1979). Migration and family conflict. *Family Process, 18*(4), 379–390.

Cultural oppression According to Kernohan (1998), cultural oppression is "the social transmission of false beliefs, values, and ideals about how to live, and the attitudes, motivations, behavior patterns, and institutions that depend on them" (p. 13). Similarly, cultural oppression is known as "the imposition of a world of meaning on others in such a way that they cannot think about it or question it" (Warren, 1992, p. 6). Kernohan notes that cultural oppression can be both personal and social. A person can easily be culturally oppressed by everything that is expressed in our culture, from what one sees on television, and from society's expectations (Kernohan, 1998). Cultural oppression is a kind of social control that affects every aspect of a minority group, especially African Americans (Semmes, 1996). The educational system widely supports cultural oppression due to the hierarchal structure of society

(Derder, 1991). People from the dominant culture are at the top of the hierarchy, whereas people from minority cultures are at the bottom (Derder, 1991). Kernohan notes that cultural oppression is a type of power. Women can be culturally oppressed by a sexist culture by giving them false beliefs about their worth and their place in a "man's world" (Kernohan, 1998). Another term for cultural oppression is *linguistic standardization* (Williams, 1991).

References

Derder, A. (1991). *Culture and power in the classroom: A critical foundation for bicultural education.* New York: Bergin & Garvey.

Kernohan, A. (1998). *Liberalism, equality, and cultural oppression.* Cambridge, UK: Cambridge University Press.

Semmes, C. E. (1996). *Racism, health, and post-industrialism: A theory of African-American health.* Westport, CT: Praeger.

Warren, M. (1992). *Communications and cultural analysis: A religious view.* Westport, CT: Bergin & Garvey.

Williams, B. F. (1991). *Stains on my name, war in my veins: Guyana and the politics of cultural struggle.* Durham, NC: Duke University Press.

Cultural paranoia   This term was coined by Grier and Cobbs (1968) in their development of a psychological health model for African Americans termed the Black Norm, which covers three defense reactions—cultural paranoia, cultural depression, and cultural antisocialism—that Blacks use to bar against the negative effects of racism (White & Parham, 1991). Racism may affect job performance and interpersonal relationships, impair self-esteem, and even lead to substance abuse (Aponte & Johnson, 2000). Racism may be experienced on an individual basis or institutional (Aponte & Johnson, 2000). Aponte and Johnson refer to attitudinal racism as a dominant group behaving badly toward an ethnic group (p. 31). Included in this are humiliating titles, stereotypes, disassociation from society, and even the denial of "equal rights" (Aponte & Johnson, 2000, p. 31). According to Aponte and Johnson, institutional racism is a "pattern of rules, regulations, and behaviors that are exclusionary and explorative [that] are part of an organization, or social system" (p. 31). For a long time, Blacks have endured both forms of racism, socially conditioning them to be cultural paranoiacs (Ridley, 1984). Cultural paranoia has been described as "a hesitancy about self-disclosure based on one's concern about being misunderstood, hurt, or taken advantage of if personal information is shared" (Arredondo, Cheatham, Mio, Sue, & Trimble, 1999, p. 73). It is considered to be a healthy mechanism against racism (Arredondo et al., 1999). Cultural paranoia is indispensable for the psychiatric and psychological survival of African Americans (and any "person of color") (Cook & Helms, 1999). Thus, every Black man was to have a suspicion and mistrust of the White man and his institutions to "cushion himself against cheating, slander, humiliation, and . . . mistreatment by the official representatives of society, if . . . not . . . [he or she] would live a life of such pain and shock as to find life . . . unbearable" (Grier & Cobbs, 1968, p. 149). Cultural paranoia has been characterized as "playing it cool," as hiding one's true feelings from the White man (Grier & Cobbs, 1968). Grier and Cobbs caution, however, that paranoia of this type should never "impair reality" (p. 161). If it does, the paranoia is no longer healthy but an illness (Ridley, 1984). The healthy paranoiac, according to Ridley (1984), presents a "façade of coolness or smooth compliance unaccompanied by intimate self-disclosure" or hostility or both (p. 1239), whereas a confluent paranoiac (an unhealthy paranoia) maintains a cultural paranoia that has surpassed what is normal—for example, relating all problems to being racially oppressed when in fact this is not the case (Ridley, 1984). The two are not to be confused because one is a healthy response to racism and the other is unhealthy and is in fact an illness. Atkinson (2000) has substituted the term *cultural mistrust* for the term *cultural paranoia*.

References

Aponte, J. F., & Johnson, W. (Eds.). (2000). *Psychological intervention and cultural diversity* (2nd ed.). Boston: Allyn & Bacon.

Arredondo, P., Cheatham, H. E., Mio, J. S., Sue, D., & Trimble, J. E. (Eds.). (1999). *Key words in multicultural interventions: A dictionary.* Westport, CT: Greenwood.

Atkinson, D. R. (2000). *Counseling diverse populations.* Boston: McGraw-Hill.

Cook, D. A., & Helms, J. E. (1999). *Using race and culture in counseling and psychotherapy: Theory and process.* Boston: Allyn & Bacon.

Grier, W. H., & Cobbs, P. M. (1968). *Black rage.* New York: Bantam.

Ridley, C. R. (1984). Clinical treatment of the non-disclosing Black client: A therapeutic paradox. *American Psychologist, 39,* 1234–1244.

White, J. L., & Parham, T. A. (1991). The psychology of Blacks. In R. L. Jones (Ed.), *Black psychology* (3rd ed.). Berkeley, CA: Cobb.

Cultural pluralism   Also known as *multicultural,* this term describes the coexistence of many cultures in a locality without any one culture dominating the region. It is a form of cultural diversity in certain countries in which cultures can maintain their uniqueness and combine to form a great part of a whole. Most societies do not contain a single cultural tradition but are composed of a number of cultural groups interacting in various ways within a larger national framework (Berry, Poortinga, Segall, & Dasen, 1992). It is a state of equal coexistence in a mutually supportive relationship within the boundaries or framework of one nation of people of diverse cultures with significantly different beliefs, behaviors, and colors and, in many cases, with different languages (Stent, Hazard, & Rivlin, 1973). Culturally pluralistic cultures are composed of numerous groups that either by association between minorities or on the basis of their own size are able to resist being lumped together as an unidentifiable mass ("Cultural Pluralism," 2000). Plural cultures have developed as a result of a variety of historical events, including colonization of one culture by another, nation building, by placing borders around a number of distinct cultural groups, and migration of individuals and groups to other countries (Berry et al., 1992). To achieve cultural pluralism, there must be unity with diversity. Each person must be aware of and secure in his or her own identity and be willing to extend the same respect and rights to others ("Cultural Pluralism," 2000).

References

Berry, J. W., Poortinga, Y. H., Segall, M. H., & Dasen, P. R. (1992). *Cross-cultural psychology: Research and applications.* Cambridge, UK: Cambridge University Press.

Cultural pluralism. (2000). In *Encyclopedia of psychology* (Vol. 2). Oxford, UK: Oxford University Press.

Stent, M. D., Hazard, W. R., & Rivlin, H. N. (1973). *Cultural pluralism in education: A mandate for change.* New York: Appleton-Century-Crofts.

Cultural proficiency   Cultural proficiency involves the policies and performance of a group or the value and actions of a person that enable that organization or person to interact successfully in a culturally diverse atmosphere. Cultural proficiency is indicated in the way an organization deals with its employees, customers, and the community (Lindsey, Nuri Robins, & Terrell, 1999). Lindsey et al. refer to cultural proficiency as a set of congruent behaviors, attitudes, and policies that come together in a system, agency, or professional, and they note that this quality enables them to work effectively in cross-cultural situations. The word culture is used because it implies the integrated pattern of human behavior that includes thought, communication, actions, customs, beliefs, values, and institutions of a racial, ethnic, religious, or social group. The term implies having the capacity to function effectively. Thus, Cross (1998) notes,

> A culturally competent system of care acknowledges and incorporates at all levels the importance of culture, the assessment of cross-cultural relations, vigilance toward the dynamics that result from cultural differences, the expansion of cultural knowledge, and the adaptation of services to meet culturally unique needs. (p. 3)

A set of cultural behaviors and approaches included in the practice methods of a system, group, or its licensed professionals enables them to work well in cross-cultural situations. Cultural proficiency is one of the most discussed concepts among scholars and practitioners interested in ethnic minority issues and represents an important philosophical shift in defining ethnic and race relations that was once examined as conflict involving assimilation versus pluralism (Sue, 1998). Cultural proficiency is achieved by converting and combining knowledge about individuals and groups of people into particular practices and policies applied in suitable cultural situations. When professionals are culturally proficient, they set up positive helping interactions, connect with the client, and improve the services they offer (Administration for Aging, 2000). Culturally proficient psychologists value and encourage the natural diversity and individuality of self and others. Professional ethics demand that psychologists be knowledgeable about a range of ideas and practices presented by racial and ethnic groups and how these essentially affect the practice, education, and research of psychology. Culturally proficient psychologists strive to recognize the border between individuals' racial and ethnic psychological theory, tradition, and education (American Psychological Association, 1992). See Cultural Competence.

References

Administration for Aging. (2000). *Achieving cultural competence: A guidebook for providers of services to older Americans and their families.* Washington, DC: Task Force on the Delivery of Services to the Aged.

American Psychological Association. (1992). *Code of ethics.* Washington, DC: Council of National Associations for the Advancement of Ethnic Minority Issues.

Cross, T. (1998, Fall). Cultural competence continuum. In *Focal point: The bulletin of the Research and Training Center of Family Support and Children's Mental Health.* Portland, OR: Portland State University.

Lindsey, R., Nuri Robins, K., & Terrell, R. (1999). *Cultural proficiency: A manual for school leaders* (Multicultural Education Series). Thousand Oaks, CA: Corwin.

Sue, S. (1998). In search of cultural competence in psychotherapy and counseling. *The American Psychologist, 53,* 4.

Cultural psychology   Cultural psychology focuses on the study of behaviors within the context of the culture. This approach rejects the traditional methodology of the experimental method. The experimental method focuses on independent and dependent variables and psychometric analyses. Cultural psychology emphasizes the study of variables within the culture without any interest in cross-cultural comparisons. This is the ethnographic approach. In this approach, behavior patterns are dictated by the values and customs of a culture. The methodology is descriptive rather than quantitative. Information is obtained by open-ended questionnaires or interviews. Cross-cultural studies may be longitudinal. That is, a variable is studied over time to evaluate the process of individual development and change in interaction with the cultural environment (Greenfield, 1997).

Reference

Greenfield, P. M. (1997). Empirical methods for cultural psychology. In J. W. Berry, Y. H. Poortinga, & J. Pandey (Eds.), *Handbook of cross-cultural psychology: Vol. 1. Theory and Method* (2nd ed., pp. 301–346). Boston: Allyn & Bacon.

Cultural relativism   Cultural relativism is the concept that actions in a specific culture should not be judged based on the values of another culture. Cultural relativism is the opposite of ethnocentrism, in which members of one culture believe that their standards are better than those of all other cultures (Goldstein, 2000, p. 25). As stated by Brown (1991), each culture has its "own genius and should be judged in its own terms" (p. 46). This view remains a strong influence, although people still have the tendency to believe that other cultures are less modern and intelligent. This is the case because many people have an ethnocentric judgment toward others, whether they acknowledge it or not (Brown, 1991, p. 55). Another definition of cultural relativism also deals with a person not being able to evaluate and make assumptions about certain occurrences unless they are evaluated using the values and principles of the person's own culture. Therefore, the values of one culture should not be viewed and judged as superior or inferior to those of another culture (Reber, 1995, p. 177). Cultural relativism portrays the view that models of understanding in different cultures are equally good. Also, because this viewpoint holds that the values of each group or culture are equally acceptable, there should not be an attempt to change another group's values and customs. What is pleasing in one culture may be unpleasant in another. These judgments derive from what each individual learns and experiences in his or her particular setting and culture ("Cultural Relativism," 1983, pp. 135–136).

References

Brown, D. E. (1991). *Human universals.* Philadelphia: McGraw-Hill.

Cultural relativism. (1983). *The encyclopedia dictionary of psychology.* Cambridge, MA: Basil Blackwell.

Goldstein, S. (2000). *Cross-cultural explorations: Activities in culture and psychology.* Boston: Allyn & Bacon.

Reber, A. S. (1995).Cultural relativism. In *The Penguin dictionary of psychology* (2nd ed.). London: Penguin.

Cultural transmission   Cultural transmission is defined as "the process of learning through which the values, standards, norms, etc. of a culture are passed on to succeeding generations" (Reber, 1995, p. 177). Cultural transmission is the knowledge that is learned and transmitted to later generations. This ability to transmit knowledge to other people in writing, conversion of abstract information, and explanations is unique to man and can be passed on through time (Cavalli-Sforza & Feldman, 1981, pp. 3–4). This transmission of information between members of a cultural group occurs during the processes of enculturation and socialization. Cultural transmission can be vertical, oblique, or horizontal. Vertical transmission can be either general enculturation from parents or specific socialization, such as child-rearing practices. Oblique transmission can be enculturation from one's own group or acculturation from other groups. Finally, horizontal transmission can be general acculturation or specific socialization from one's peers (Berry, Poortinga, Segall, & Dasen, 1992). In animals, forms of cultural transmission are more limited or sometimes not existent because the range of behavior of animals is small. Examples of cultural activities in animals are tool making and potato washing among monkeys and learning of songs in birds. Because humans are able to use trial-and-error learning and imitation, which are two alternative kinds of learning devices in cultural transmission, they are able to decide whether to pass on what they have learned to later generations (Castro & Toro, 2002).

References

Berry, J. W., Poortinga, Y. H., Segall, M. H., & Dasen, P. R. (1992). *Cross-cultural psychology: Research and applications.* Cambridge, UK: Cambridge University Press.

Castro, L., & Toro, M. A. (2002). Cultural transmission and the capacity to approve or disapprove of offspring's behavior. *Journal of Mathematics—Evolutionary Models of Information Transmission, 6,* 1–3.

Cavalli-Sforza, L., & Feldman, M. (1981). *Cultural transmission and evolution: A quantitative approach.* Princeton, NJ: Princeton University Press.

Reber, A. S. (1995). Cultural transmission. In *The Penguin dictionary of psychology* (2nd ed.). London: Penguin.

Culture The word culture derives from the Latin root *colere*, to inhabit, cultivate, or honor. In general, it refers to human activity; different definitions of culture reflect different theories for understanding, or criteria for valuing, human activity. By the late 19th century, anthropologists argued for a broader definition of symbolic culture that they could apply to a wide variety of societies (Geertz, 1973). They began to argue that culture is human nature and is rooted in the universal human capacity to classify experiences and encode and communicate them symbolically. Consequently, people living apart from one another develop unique cultures, but elements of different cultures can easily spread from one group of people to another (Geertz, 1973). Moreover, from anthropologists' point of view, they understand that symbolic culture refers not only to consumption goods but also to the general processes by which such goods are produced and given meaning and the social relationships and practices in which such objects and processes are embedded (Geertz, 1973). Culture involves at least three components: what people think, what they do, and the material products they produce. Thus, mental processes, beliefs, knowledge, and values are part of culture. Some sociologists define culture entirely as mental rules guiding behavior, although often wide divergence exists between the acknowledged rules for correct behavior and what people actually do. Consequently, symbolic culture is based on arbitrary meanings that are shared by a society (Bodley, 1994). Culture is learned, not biologically inherited, and it involves arbitrarily assigned, symbolic meanings. For example, Americans are not born knowing that the color white means purity, and indeed this is not a universal cultural symbol. The human ability to assign arbitrary meaning to any object, behavior, or condition makes people enormously creative and readily distinguishes culture from animal behavior. People can teach animals to respond to cultural symbols, but animals do not create their own symbols (Bodley, 1994). Finally, Greenfield (1997), a cultural psychologist, explains that symbolic culture, which is shared assumptions, knowledge, and communication, is imbedded in any test of cognitive ability.

References

Bodley, J. H. (1994). *An anthropological perspective.* New York: Cambridge University Press.

Geertz, C. (1973). *Interpretation of culture.* New York: Basic Books.

Greenfield, P. M. (1997). You can't take it with you: Why ability assessments don't cross cultures. *American Psychologist, 52,* 1115–1124.

Culture assimilator   This term has significant variations in meaning. On the one hand, it is used to describe one who undergoes the process of cultural assimilation. On the other hand, it is used to describe the process whereby members of an ethnic group take on the cultural and structural characteristics of another ethnic or national community (Hirsch, Kett, & Tefil, 1988). This results in the group exchanging its previous identity for the new one. Assimilation covers many varieties of culture change and is applicable to individuals who "convert" to the cultures and identities of ethnic groups and civic nations (*Encyclopedia of Nationalism*, 2001). *Webster's Third New International Dictionary* (1993) defines culture assimilator as follows:

A culture assimilator adapts and conforms to another culture; a body of customary beliefs, social forms, and material traits constituting a distinct complex of tradition of a racial, religious, or social group; a complex of typical behavior or standardized social characteristics peculiar to a specific group, occupation or profession, sex, age, grade, or social class. (p. 303)

Not only must the group adapt to the core group but also the core group must come to accept the entering group and treat its members on the basis of their ethnic, religious, or national heritage (Magill, 1994). A more current definition of culture assimilator relates to its similarity in cross-cultural training to the application of critical incidences. The objective of critical incidences is to stimulate thinking about basic and important issues that occur in real-life situations. By analyzing an incident, participants can imagine themselves in the same situation, develop strategies to deal with the situation, and become more realistic in their expectations (Pederson & Allen, 1993). Culture assimilator is a variation on the use of critical incidences to illustrate concepts of cross-cultural counseling (Sue & Sue, 1990). Culture assimilator is also used as a practical application to attribution theory developed by Triandis (1989).

A structured series of incidents and alternative responses is provided in which, for each set, one response is more accurate and appropriate than the others. Explanations are provided for the correctness or wrongness of each choice. To the extent that the culturally accurate and appropriate attributions can be determined for each situation, the cultural assimilator has been extremely successful (Pederson & Allen, 1993). Benefits of the use of culture assimilator include

- Greater understanding of hosts, as judged by the hosts
- A decrease in the use of stereotypes on the part of trainees
- The development of complex thinking about the target culture
- Greater enjoyment among trainees who interact with members of the target culture
- Better adjustment to the everyday stresses of life in other cultures
- Better performance in cases in which performance is influenced by practices addressed in the training material

References

Encyclopedia of nationalism. (2001). New Brunswick, NJ: Transaction Publishers.

Hirsch, E. D., Jr., Kett, J. F., & Tefil, J. (1988). *The dictionary of cultural literacy.* Boston: Houghton Mifflin.

Magill, F. M. (1994). *Survey of social science sociology series* (Vol. 11, p. 442). Pasadena, CA: Salem.

Pederson, P., & Allen, I. (1993). *Culture-centered counseling and interviewing skills: A practical guide.* Westport, CT: Praeger.

Sue, D. W., & Sue, D. (1990). *Counseling the culturally different: Theory and practice.* New York: John Wiley.

Triandis, H. (1989). The self and social behavior in differing cultural contexts. *Psychological Review, 96,* 506–520.

Webster's third new international dictionary, unabridged. (1993). Springfield, MA: Merriam-Webster.

Culture-bond syndrome   This is a psychological problem that affects only people of certain cultures and traditions (Abel, 1996; Alexander, 1984). Culture is defined as a set of accepted ideas, practices, characteristics, and values in a specific society; a bond is a strong relationship with something; and a syndrome is a set of events that work together (Stratton & Hayes, 1999). Other terms that have described culture-bond syndromes during the past 100 years are *atypical psychoses, culture-specific disorder, ethnic psychoses, exotic psychoses,* and *hysterical psychoses* (Abel, 1996; Alexander, 1984; Marsella, 2000). In the late 19th century, the term *culture-bond syndrome* was added to the Western psychiatric literature because Western physicians noticed "exotic" disorders in Asia, Africa, and South America that were different from those of Europe and North America. The earliest reports of these disorders, however, date back to the 16th century (Marsella, 2000). Culture-bond syndrome breaks down into four major disorders: latah, amok, susto, and koro (Abel, 1996; Alexander, 1984). Latah is primarily found in Malaysia and Indonesia. It is present in both males and females but mostly in females (Alexander, 1984). Startle reaction and subsequent imitative behavior are its two main components (Abel, 1996; Alexander, 1984). The term *amok* was used in Southeast Asia by Portuguese travelers in 1552 to describe zealots who vowed to sacrifice their lives in battle (Abel, 1996; Alexander, 1984). Today, amok describes individuals that come out of periods of separation and laziness with a sudden occurrence of mania, agitation, and violent physical attacks (Abel, 1996; Alexander, 1984). Translated, susto means "soul loss"; this disorder causes a strong sense of fear, weight and appetite loss, and fatigue (Abel, 1996). Susto is found in many Hispanic populations; it affects all ages and genders but mainly children and young women (Alexander, 1984). In Southeast Asia, China, and Hong Kong, koro can be found mainly in men. Koro is related to lack of sexual responsibility and can be manifest as strong fearful panic attacks or fear of death (Abel, 1996; Alexander, 1984).

References

Abel, T. M. (1996). Culture-bound disorder. In *Concise encyclopedia of psychology* (2nd ed., pp. 223–224). New York: John Wiley.

Alexander, A. J. (1984). Culture-bound disorders. In *Encyclopedia of psychology* (Vol. 2, pp. 407–410). New York: Oxford University Press.

Marsella, T. (2000). Culture-bound disorders. In *Encyclopedia of psychology* (Vol. 1, pp. 333–334). New York: John Wiley.

Stratton, P., & Hayes, N. (1999). *A student's dictionary of psychology* (3rd ed.). New York: Arnold.

Culture shock   Culture shock occurs as a result of moving to a different location where one's old culture is extremely different from the new culture (Colman, 2001) and one must adjust to new values and behaviors (McMillan, 1996). In 1960, Kalvervo Olberg, an anthropologist, coined the term *culture shock* to describe the reaction of being in a new culture. Olberg mentioned six negative aspects of culture shock: (a) strain resulting from the effort of psychological adaptation; (b) a sense of loss or deprivation produced by the loss of former friends, status roles, or possessions; (c) rejection by or rejection of the new culture; (d) confusion with regard to role definition, role expectations, feelings, and self-identity; (e) unexpected anxiety, disgust, or indignation regarding cultural differences between the old and the new values; and (f) feelings of helplessness as a result of not coping well in the new environment (Bochner, 2000; McMillan, 1996). Peterson (1995) described six indicators that culture shock adjustment is taking place. First, familiar cues about how the person is supposed to behave are missing, or the familiar cues now have a different meaning. Second, values that the person considered good and desirable are not valued by the host culture. Third, the disorientation of culture shock creates an emotional state of anxiety, depression, or hostility ranging from mild uneasiness to rage. Fourth, there is dissatisfaction with the host culture. Fifth, recovery skills that used to work in the past no longer work. Sixth, there is a sense that these experiences are permanent. There are two types of culture shock that deal with contact: within-society and between-society culture shock. By definition, within-society cross-culture contact involves a diverse multicultural society (Bochner, 2000), such as the United States. Between-society cross-culture contact is represented by people who go to areas with different cultures for a specific purpose and then return home (Bochner, 2000). An example is a student from the United States attending college in the Philippines. After he or she graduates, the individual returns to the United States to live and work. Reasons for culture shock include moving to a new location, a feeling of helplessness due to the move, and loss of social skills in the new environment (McMillan, 1996). Just because one moves from one place to another, however, does not mean one will experience culture shock. Culture shock can be reduced by realizing that stress is normal when there is a major transition in one's life, always keeping one's head up high, taking things slow, not rushing oneself, trying to maintain a new set pattern, preparing ahead for the transition (McMillan, 1996), and setting up a support base in the new environment so individuals can provide encouragement during this difficult phase.

References

Bochner, S. (2000). Culture shock. In *Encyclopedia of psychology* (Vol. 2, pp. 410–413). New York: Oxford University Press.

Colman, A. M. (2001). Culture shock. In *Dictionary of psychology* (p. 179). New York: Oxford University Press.

McMillan, J. H. (1996). Culture shock. In *Concise encyclopedia of psychology* (2nd ed., pp. 225–227). New York: John Wiley.

Olberg, K. (1960). Culture shock: Adjustment to new cultural environments. *Practical Anthropology, 7*, 177–182.

Pederson, P. (1995). *The five stages of culture shock: Critical incidents around the world.* Westport, CT: Greenwood.

D

Dhat syndrome   This is also referred to as *prameha* in Sri Lanka or *shenkui* in China. The term *dhat syndrome* was first used by the Indian psychiatrist N. N. Wig in 1960 and J. S. Neki in 1973 (Tseng, 2001). According to Indian psychiatrists Bhatika and Malik (1991), the word dhat derives from the Sanskrit *Dhatu*, which refers to "the elixir that constitutes the body." The syndrome is prevalent in Nepal, Sri Lanka, Bangladesh, and Pakistan. The afflicted person becomes preoccupied with the notion of an excessive loss of semen from "an improper form of leaking," including nocturnal emissions, masturbation, and urination. The belief is that excessive semen loss will result in illness. Tseng reported that patients are predominantly young males who present multiple somatic symptoms, such as fatigue, weakness, anxiety, loss of appetite, and feelings of guilt over having engaged in masturbation or sex with prostitutes. Other complaints include impotence and premature ejaculation. Paris (1992) reported that the main complaint is opaque urine due to the presence of semen. The patient usually asks for tonic to replenish the vitality lost due to the excess leakage of semen.

References

Bhatika, M. S., & Malik, S. C. (1991). Dhat syndrome—A useful diagnostic entity in Indian culture. *British Journal of Psychiatry, 159,* 691–695.

Paris, J. (1992). Dhat: The semen loss anxiety syndrome. *Transcultural Psychiatric Research Review, 29*(2), 109–118.

Tseng, W.-S. (2001). *Handbook of cultural psychiatry.* San Diego, CA: Academic Press.

Discrimination   Discrimination is a negative or positive behavior directed toward a person or a group based on race, nationality, or sex (Colman, 2001; Murrell, 2000; Wolman, 1989). Discrimination originally derived from the Latin words *discriminare*, *discrimen*, and *discernere*, which all generally mean to divide or division (Colman, 2001). The prefix *dis-* means apart, and this explains why the Latin words all deal with division (Colman, 2001). Unlike prejudice, discrimination is a negative behavior toward a group or one of its members. Prejudice is as an attitude that can lead to discrimination. There are three types of discrimination: "classic" discrimination, overt discrimination, and "aversive racism" (Murrell, 2000). Classic discrimination occurs when one can clearly determine who is discriminating against a person and what they are doing (Murrell, 2000). Overt discrimination is when someone wants to keep superiority over a group through power of the group. Groups experience overt discrimination because of race, sex, or nationality (Murrell, 2000). Aversive racism is an unintentional form of discrimination based on one's values and bad attitudes about certain people (Murrell, 2000). There are three levels of discrimination: individual, institutional, and structural (Murrell, 2000; Myers, 2002). Examples of institutional discrimination are racism and sexism. These are institutional practices (even if not motivated by prejudice) that subordinate people of a given race or gender. Racism is the belief that one race is superior to another (Gall, 1996), and sexism is the belief that one gender is better than another (Myers, 2002). Discrimination can be acted out by either avoiding the person or, to the extreme, attacking the person (Cardwell, 1996). Prejudice and discrimination are universal problems (Myers, 2002). One way to decrease discrimination is to positively interact with everyone no matter their nationality, race, or sex (Murrell, 2000). See Prejudice.

References

Cardwell, M. (1996). Discrimination. In *Dictionary of psychology* (p. 74). Chicago: Fitzroy Dearborn.

Colman, A. M. (2001). Discriminability. In *Dictionary of psychology* (p. 208). New York: Oxford University Press.

Gall, S. (1996). Racism. In *The Gale encyclopedia of psychology* (p. 303). Detroit, MI: Gale.

Murrell, A. J. (2000). Discrimination. In *Encyclopedia of psychology* (Vol. 3, pp. 49–54). New York: Oxford University Press.

Myers, D. G. (2002). Discrimination. In *Social psychology* (7th ed., p. 330). Boston: McGraw-Hill.

Wolman, B. B. (1989). Discrimination. In *Dictionary of behavioral science* (2nd ed., p. 95). New York: Academic Press.

Display rules   It is increasingly evident that there are cross-cultural differences in the manifestation of emotion. Emotions are expressed with differing frequency and intensity across cultures. Ekman first introduced the notion of "display rules" following two landmark 1972 cross-cultural studies (Ekman, 2003). In essence, display rules are norms regarding the expected management of facial appearance in certain situations (Berry, Poortinga, Segall, & Dasen, 2002). Within every culture, there are unspoken rules about what "face" a person should put forth to the world on certain occasions; in some cases, the rules dictate whether one should display any emotion at all (Berry, et al., 2002). Matsumoto (1990) presented a theoretical framework to account for differences in display rules according to three cultural dimensions: individualism versus collectivism; power distance, or inequality in social status; and the level of distinction between in-groups and out-groups. Examples of cross-cultural variation in display rules abound. In feudal Japan (until the end of World War I), individuals brought up in the samurai tradition and indoctrinated with the Bushido Code valued strength and absolute dispassion, frowning on open displays of emotion in many social situations as symptomatic of weakness. The emotional display rules from this time period were so strongly woven into the fabric of Japanese culture that they endure to an extent in modern Japan (Ekman, 2003). In collectivist China, openly displaying emotion is sometimes discouraged as selfish. For Eastern Europeans, it is far less appropriate to display negative emotions among family and friends (in-group) than it is for Americans (Matsumoto, 1990). Ultimately, research on display rules suggests that the underlying emotions in a given situation are similar across cultures because they are biologically innate. The manner in which these underlying emotions are expressed, however, varies depending on the culture (Berry et al., 2002).

References

Berry, J. W., Poortinga, Y. H., Segall, M. H., & Dasen, P. R. (2002). *Cross-cultural psychology: Research and applications* (2nd ed.). Cambridge, UK: Cambridge University Press.

Ekman, P. (2003). *Emotions revealed.* New York: Henry Holt.

Matsumoto, D. (1990). Cultural similarities and differences in display rules. *Motivation and Emotion, 14,* 195–214.

Diversity   Diversity refers to the "otherness," or those particular human qualities that are different from one's own and outside the group to which one belongs but are present in other individuals and groups (University of Maryland, 1995). The term also describes a reality created by individuals and groups with a broad spectrum of demographic and philosophical differences (North Carolina State University Administrative Council, 1997). Diversity is defined as differences among groups of people and individuals based on race, ethnicity, socioeconomic status, gender, language, exceptionalities, religion, sexual orientation, and geographic region in which they live (National Council for Accreditation of Teacher Education, 2002). See Cultural Diversity.

References

National Council for Accreditation of Teacher Education. (2002). *Professional standards.* Washington, DC: Author.

North Carolina State University Administrative Council. (1997). *Cultural diversity.* Raleigh: North Carolina State University.

University of Maryland. (1995). *Diversity at UMCP: Moving toward community plan.* College Park: Author.

E

Ebonics The term *Ebonics* was coined in January 1973 by Robert L. Williams, a professor of psychology at Washington University in Missouri, and has produced overwhelming controversy in terms of its origin, usage, and validity as a dialect or language. The term was coined during a small group discussion held with several African American psychologists attending a conference on "Cognitive and Language Development of the Black Child." Ebonics is a compound of two words: "ebony," which means "black," and "phonics," which means "sounds." Thus, the term *Ebonics* literally means "black sounds." The term refers to the "linguistic and paralinguistic features, which on a concentric continuum represent the language and communicative competence of West and Niger-Congo Africa, Caribbean, and United States slave descendants of Niger-Congo African origin" (Williams, 1975, p. 100). Smith and Crozier (1998) contend that Ebonics is not Black English. They point out that when Ebonics is viewed as an African language system that has adopted European words in its usage, it is by "relexification that Ebonics English words such as west, best, and test become; wes, bes, and tes. Left, lift, drift, and swift become; lef, lif, drif, and swif. Wept, crept, slept, except, and inept become; wrep, crep, slep, excep, and enep" (p. 2). According to Leon Todd (1997), "Ebonics is a defective speech and a handicap for Black children" (p. 2). He added that "students and their families who use these unfortunate speech patterns often are in need of a speech therapist to help treat their group reinforced speech pathology if they are to function effectively in the usual mainstream society" (p. 2). In addressing the controversy, Fox (1997) points out that the problem with Ebonics, accurate or not, is that it has become associated with "urban life—poverty, crime, unemployment, substandard housing, and inferior education" (p. 3). He does not believe Ebonics is inferior, but also being adept at Standard American English can contribute to success in the larger American community. See Black English.

References

Fox, S. (1997). The controversy over Ebonics. *Phi Delta Kappa, 73,* 3.

Smith, E., & Crozier, K. (1998). Ebonics is not Black English. *Western Journal of Black Studies, 22,* 2.

Todd, L. W., Jr. (1997). Ebonics is defective speech and a handicap for Black children. *Education, 118,* 2.

Williams, R. L. (1975). *Ebonics: The true language of Black folks.* St. Louis, MO: Institute of Black Studies.

Emic Emic research focuses on how universal behaviors are expressed in other cultures, as opposed to etic research, which examines these universal behaviors (see Etic). These behaviors often emphasize "cultural-specific aspects" (Berry, Poortinga, Segall, & Dasen, 2002):

> In the emic approach an attempt is made to look at phenomena and their interrelationship [structure] through the eyes of the people native to a particular culture, avoiding the imposition of a priori notions and ideas from one's own cultural on the people studied. This point of view finds its origin in cultural anthropology where, via the method of participant observation, the researchers try to look at the norms, values, motives, and customs of the members of a particular community in their own terms. (p. 291)

Reference

Berry, J. W., Poortinga, Y. H., Segall, M. H., & Dasen, P. R. (2002). *Cross-cultural psychology: Research and applications* (2nd ed.). Cambridge, UK: Cambridge University Press.

Enculturation This term was coined by Melville J. Herskovits in 1948 and was first used in the realm of cultural anthropology. Far from being "blank slates" as John Locke suggested (Greenfield & Cocking, 1994), infants are born "hard-wired" to efficiently process information from their surroundings. Much of this information comes from their culture, and one of the main processes by which they acquire it is enculturation. Berry, Poortinga, Segall, and Dasen (2002) define enculturation as "a form of cultural transmission by which society transmits its culture and behavior to its members by surrounding developing members with appropriate models" (p. 19). Berry et al. distinguish between the two principal processes of cultural transmission: enculturation and socialization. Socialization involves deliberate shaping of an individual. Enculturation occurs by osmosis; in other words, it is cultural learning without any sort of deliberate or specific shaping or teaching. Parents (vertical transmission), adults (oblique transmission), and peers (horizontal transmission) comprise a network of influences that help mold a developing individual (Berry et al., 1992). The product of enculturation is an individual who is competent in his or her surrounding culture, including its language, rituals, attitudes, norms, and values (Berry et al., 2002; Greenfield & Cocking, 1994). Ultimately, a distinct cultural identity is formed. Enculturation also occurs when an individual born and raised in one culture must adapt to a new culture as a traveler or as an immigrant (Kim, 1988). Enculturation and socialization create similarities within cultures and differences between cultures. In this sense, enculturation gives rise to some degree of cultural relativism; although some values, attitudes, and norms are universal. The work of Margaret Mead, an anthropologist who studied child rearing and the influence of culture on personality across cultures (most notably in Samoa), is frequently cited when referring to enculturation. Mead suggested that enculturation does not end in adolescence or early adulthood but, rather, continues until death. See Acculturation.

References

Berry, J. W., Poortinga, Y. H., Segall, M. H., & Dasen, P. R. (1992). *Cross-cultural psychology: Research and applications.* Cambridge, UK: Cambridge University Press.

Berry, J. W., Poortinga, Y. H., Segall, M. H., & Dasen, P. R. (2002). *Cross-cultural psychology: Research and applications* (2nd ed.). Cambridge, UK: Cambridge University Press.

Greenfield, P. M., & Cocking, R. R. (1994). *Cross-cultural roots of minority child development.* Hillsdale, NJ: Lawrence Erlbaum.

Kim, Y. Y. (1988). *Communication and cross-cultural adaptation: An integrative theory.* Clevedon, UK: Multilingual Matters.

Ethnic cleansing   In the most general sense, ethnic cleansing is the genocide or the forced migration of an ethnic group out of a region. Genocide targets a specific ethnic group and, like the Jewish Holocaust in Nazi Germany, is usually systematic in nature. Danner (1997) specifically defines ethnic cleansing with regard to the conflict in the 1990s in the former Yugoslavia among the Serbs, Croats, and Muslims as "a process in which the advancing army of one ethnic group expels or eliminates civilians of other ethnic groups from towns and villages it conquers in order to create ethnically pure enclaves for members of its own ethnic group" (p. 9). Danner outlines five steps taken (usually by the Serbs) to ethnically cleanse a region in the Yugoslavian conflict: concentration, or surrounding the region to be cleansed; decapitation, or killing off the political leadership and elite citizenry of the ethnic group to be cleansed; separation, which entails separating women and children from fighting age men; evacuation, which involves the forced migration of women, children, and old men into another region; and liquidation, which involves killing fighting age men and disposing of their bodies. Petrovic (1994) believes the term *ethnic cleansing* came into use as a translation of the word *etnicko ciscenje* in Serbo-Croatian because although the idea of genocide and forced migration is certainly not new, this specific term did not come into colloquial use until the Yugoslavian conflict (and the subsequent conflict in Kosovo) (U.S. Department of Reporting, 1999). As Petrovic notes, however, analysis of ethnic cleansing should not be limited to the former Yugoslavia because 20th-century examples of genocide and forced migration are abundant. The term *ethnic cleansing* is trendy and politically correct, but it should not conceal the fact that the practice of ethnic cleansing still equates to genocide in terms of international law (Petrovic, 1994).

References

Danner, M. (1997). Ethnic cleansing in former Yugoslavia. *New York Review of Books, 40,* 9.

Petrovic, D. (1994). *Ethnic cleansing—An attempt at methodology.* Washington, DC: U.S. Department of Reporting.

U.S. Department of Reporting. (1999). *Ethnic cleansing in Kosovo—An accounting.* Washington, DC: Author.

Ethnic identity   Ethnic identity is the awareness of a person's affiliation with a certain ethnic group (Tajifel, 1981). It can also be defined as recognizing which ethnic group one belongs to by observing the language, customs, and beliefs associated with that group and determining if one's own language, customs, and beliefs correspond with those of that specific group. It can be both symbolic and influential, such as when an individual desires to participate in celebrations such as St. Patrick's Day (La Belle & Ward, 1996). Ethnic identity differentiates one's own ethnicity from any other through identifying the difference in ethnic groups. Some examples of ethnic identities are Jewish Americans, African Americans, and Haitian Americans. They create ethnic distinctiveness, making the ethnic group identifiable (Yang, 2000). Ethnic identity development studies have resulted in a number of models. These various models have focused on the psychological changes the minority individual experiences in reference to the self, the individual's identity group, and the dominant culture (Sue & Sue, 1990).

References

La Belle, T., & Ward, C. R. (1996). *Ethnic studies and multiculturalism.* New York: State University of New York Press.

Sue, D. W., & Sue, D. (1990). *Counseling the culturally different: Theory and practice* (2nd ed.). New York: John Wiley.

Tajifel, H. (1981). *Human groups and social categories.* Cambridge, UK: Cambridge University Press.

Yang, P. Q. (2000). *Ethnic studies, issues and approaches.* New York: State University of New York Press.

Ethnic psychology   This is the study of identity with or membership of a social group in the general population that is distinct and held together by race, language, culture, or nationality (Goetz, 1991). Hirsch, Kett, and Trefil (1988) note that "many minority groups in the United States maintain strong ethnic identity; especially in cities, immigrants are often attracted to ethnic communities established by people from their own country, communities in which many traditional cultural features are maintained" (p. 417). Ethnic psychology is the science of mind or of mental phenomena and activities characteristic of an ethnic group—a group that is united by a common and distinctive cultural heritage, language, and history (Magill, 1994). The focus of ethnic psychologists is the use of culturally appropriate methods in researching these groups. They focus on groups that have been marginalized. It is important to these researchers that instruments normed on mainstream cultures not be used to evaluate members of marginalized groups. Cross (1991) developed a model of nigres-cence or Black racial identity used to explore aspects of mental health among African Americans.

References

Cross, W. (1991). *Shades of diversity in African American identity*. Philadelphia: Temple University Press.

Goetz, P. W. (Ed.). (1991). *The new encyclopedia Britannica* (Vol. 4). Chicago: Encyclopedia Britannica.

Hirsch, E. D., Jr., Kett, J. F., & Trefil, J. (1988). *The dictionary of cultural literacy*. Boston: Houghton Mifflin.

Magill, F. M. (1994). *Survey of social science sociology series* (Vol. 1, pp. 1–442). Pasadena, CA: Salem Press.

Ethnic relations   Genocide, forced removal, imposed assimilation, and involuntary segregation are examples of negative ethnic relations (Hutchinson & Smith, 1996, p. 326). The words ethnic, ethnology, ethnography, ethnocentric, and ethnicity are derived from the Greek word *ethnos*, meaning "group of people sharing [common] characteristics" (Hutchinson & Smith, 1996, p. 21). In common use, these words are taken to describe race (Hutchinson & Smith, 1996). Hutchinson and Smith differenti-ate between ethnic(ity) and race, however. Race is biological, but ethnic as used in eth-nic group implies much more, extending beyond skin color or genetics. Thus, people of different ethnic groups may appear the same on a physical level, but physical traits should not be the only characteristic used to determine an individual's ethnic group-ing (Rose, 1974). Rose defines ethnic groups as "groups whose members share a unique social and cultural heritage passed on from one generation to the next" (p. 12). Ethnic group has also been defined as "a collectivity within a larger society having real or putative common ancestry, memories of a shared historical past, and a cultural focus on one or more symbolic elements defined as the epitome of their peoplehood" (Hutchinson & Smith, 1996, p. 17). Symbolic elements may include kinship patterns, physical congruity, religious affiliation, language, and nationality (Hutchinson & Smith, 1996, p. 17). The most important characteristic a group must have to be con-sidered an ethnic group is to share a "consciousness of kind and an interdependence of fate" (Rose, 1974, p. 13). Therefore, ethnic relations are definable as positive or neg-ative interactions between members of different ethnic groups as previously men-tioned. Ethnic relations are often negative, however. Of seven listed occurrences of ethnic relations, only one was positive (Hutchinson & Smith, 1996). Ethnic groups are able to interact positively with one another when cultural barriers are reduced, according to Hutchinson and Smith. A happy medium must be reached that allows for "codes and values" of different ethnic groups to be similar enough for positive inter-actions at certain levels but dissimilar in other aspects to keep ethnic boundaries intact (Hutchinson & Smith, 1996, p. 80). Interactions such as these have also been labeled as stable by Hutchinson and Smith. Indonesia is an example of a country with stable ethnic relations among its groups, to the point that ethnic minorities are over-represented in the government (Hutchinson & Smith, 1996). The reigning ideology in Indonesian government is "unity in diversity," which helps keep ethnic relations healthy (Hutchinson & Smith, 1996, p. 329). In fact, many countries have approached ethnic conflicts with a particular form of government (Hutchinson & Smith, 1996). The United States does so by placing a liberal emphasis on democracy, meaning "a common domain of values, institutions, and identity" is upheld, nationalism is equated with "citizenship," and all residents of the union are equal irregardless of ethnicity (Hutchinson & Smith, 1996, p. 332). Outright violence, however, seems to be a way of life for some ethnic groups, such as the Palestinians and the Jews. Just as government has been a form of dealing with differences between ethnic groups in some societies, violence has been the course of action in others (Hutchinson & Smith, 1996). Why ethnic differences can be resolved in some societies but not in others goes back to reducing the ethnic barriers. Evidently, ethnic groups with negative ethnic relations are too far divided in their beliefs (Hutchinson & Smith, 1996). See Ethnocultural Groups.

References

Hutchinson, J., & Smith, A. D. (Eds.). (1996). *Ethnicity.* Oxford, UK: Oxford University Press.

Rose, P. I. (1974). *They and we: The United States racial and ethnic relations in the United States* (2nd ed.). New York: Random House.

Ethnicity   According to the *American Heritage Dictionary* (2000), ethnicity is ethnic quality or affiliation resulting from racial or cultural ties. It derives from the ancient Greek word *ethnos,* which refers to situations in which people lived and acted together (Jenkins, 1997). Ethnicity is "fundamentally a political phenomenon based on per-ceived differences between groups" (p. 416). It is the self-awareness a group of people has of their respective ethnic identities (Payne, 1996). When people share a certain way of thinking, eating, dressing, or behaving, they are considered to be of the same ethnic background or share the same ethnicity. It refers to a shared culture or way of life, displayed through language, attire, religion, food, music, literature, and art (Johnson, 2000). Ethnicity should not be confused with race. Race is a social classifi-cation based on physical qualities, whereas ethnicity is classified by cultural factors (Borgatta & Montgomery, 2000).

References

American heritage dictionary of the English language (4th ed.). (2000). Boston: Houghton Mifflin.

Borgatta, E. F., & Montgomery, R. J. V. (2000). *Encyclopedia of sociology* (2nd ed.). New York: Macmillan.

Jenkins, R. (1997). *Rethinking ethnicity.* Thousand Oaks, CA: Sage.

Johnson, A. (2000). *The Blackwell dictionary of sociology* (2nd ed.). Malden, MA: Blackwell.

Payne, M. I. (1996). *A dictionary of cultural and critical theory.* Cambridge, MA: Blackwell.

Ethnocentrism   Ethnocentrism is the belief in the superiority of one's own ethic and culture group and a corresponding disdain for all other groups (Myers, 2002). These individuals have the tendency to view their own ethic or cultural group as the basis for social standards (Reber, 1995). According to Corsini and Auerbach (1996), the concept represents a conflation of two ideas: "(a) the tendency for people to view their own group as the reference against which all other groups are judged, and (b) the tendency to view one's own group as superior to one another" (p. 315). Moreover, ethnocentric individuals have authoritarian tendencies—"intolerance for weakness, a punitive attitude, and a submissive respect for their in-group's authorities" (Myers, 2002, p. 415). Wolman (1988) noted that ethnocentric individuals have a

> personality syndrome characterized by a perception of social reality as composed of in-groups as the frame of reference against which one identifies and out-groups toward which one is hostile; stereotyping people positively or negatively depending on their in-group or out-group membership; authoritarian and power-related social relations. (p. 411)

According to Berry, Poortinga, Segall, and Dasen (1992), there can be several problems related to ethnocentrism in psychology. There may be problems related to the tasks used in cross-cultural studies. The assumption may be that the task in one's culture is superior and sufficient in the study of another culture. Even the choice of a problem to be explored may be based on ethnocentric thinking. Value judgments can lead to incorrect interpretations and incorrect formulation of theories. Unfortunately, ethnocentrism is a universal phenomenon (Levine & Campbell, 1972).

References

Berry, J. W., Poortinga, Y. H., Segall, M. H., & Dasen, P. R. (1992). *Cross-cultural psychology: Research and applications.* Cambridge, UK: Cambridge University Press.

Corsini, R. J., & Auerbach, A. J. (1996). *Concise encyclopedia of psychology* (2nd ed.). New York: John Wiley.

Levine, R. A., & Campbell, D. T. (1972). *Ethnocentrism.* New York: John Wiley.

Myers, D. G. (2002). *Social psychology* (7th ed.). New York: McGraw-Hill.

Reber, A. S. (1995). *The Penguin dictionary of psychology* (2nd ed.). New York: Penguin.

Wolman, B. B. (1998). *Dictionary of behavior science* (2nd ed.). New York: Academic Press.

Ethnocultural groups   This orientation evolved from the multicultural perspective in which there is a mosaic of ethnocultural groups. Such groups preserve a sense of their cultural uniqueness and (on that basis) participate in a social framework that is characterize by some shared customs (legal, economic, and political agreements) about how to live together (Berry, Poortinga, Segall, & Dasen, 2002). The members of these groups contribute to a belief of having a valid heritage, culture, racial background, and ethnicity (Findley, 1998). Every person belongs to an ethnic group, and each identifies with some cultural heritage shared by people of certain national, religious, or language backgrounds or all three. The term *ethnocultural* refers an ethnic identity supported by cultural practice, tradition, and society and to a group of people who believe they are ethnically or culturally distinct from other groups or both. For example, there are a wide variety of ethnocultural groups among people of African, Asian, European, and indigenous North, Central, and South American backgrounds in Canada. Some Canadians experience discrimination because of their ethnocultural attachment (ethnicity, religion, nationality, and language). An ethnocultural minority belongs to an ethnocultural group that is numerically smaller or politically less powerful than the dominant group in a country's population or both. The term *minority*, of course, is a "relative and relational" concept. It is meaningful only in relation to the "majority," and it is not a permanent characterization for any ethnocultural group. Demographic changes, border changes, mass migrations, and radical social changes leading to redefinition of social boundaries can make a minority a majority and vice versa (Yagcioglu, 1996). See Ethnic Relations.

References

Berry, J.W., Poortinga, Y. H., Segall, M. H., & Dasen, P. R. (2002). *Cross-cultural psychology: Research and applications* (2nd ed.). Cambridge, UK: Cambridge University Press.

Findley, T. (1998). *The wars.* Saddle River, NJ: Prentice Hall.

Yagcioglu, O. (1996). Psychological explorations of conflict between ethnocultural minorities and majorities: An overview. In S. A. Allen (Ed.), *Windows to conflict analysis and resolution: Framing our field.* Fairfax, VA: George Mason University, Institute for Conflict Analysis Resolution.

Ethnomethodology   Ethnomethodology is the study of the ways in which people make sense of their social world—understanding the meaning systems and procedures people use in doing what they do. In addition to analyzing the methods people use in social interactions, ethnomethodology also involves the methods that people use to accomplish a reasonable account of what is happening in these social interactions and to provide a structure for the interaction (Garfinkel, 1987). Unlike symbolic interactionists (labeling perspective), ethnomethodologists do not assume that people actually share common symbolic meanings. What they do share is a ceaseless body of interpretive work that enables them to convince themselves and others that they share common meanings (Hawkins & Tiedeman, 1975). In summary, ethnomethodology is the empirical study of methods that individuals use to accomplish their daily actions: communicating, making decisions, and reasoning (Coulon, 1995).

References

Coulon, A. (1995). *Ethnomethodology*. Thousand Oaks, CA: Sage.

Garfinkel, H. (1987). *Studies in ethnomethodology* (Reprint). Englewood Cliffs, NJ: Prentice Hall.

Hawkins, R., & Tiedeman, G. (1975). *The creation of deviance*. Columbus, OH: Chas E. Merril.

Ethnonationalism   This term was coined by U.S. political scientist Walker Connor (2002). It is the phenomenon of political movements launched on the basis of ethnic identity—ethnic groups claiming to be or to possess nations or states in the past or that have the potential of becoming nations or states some time in the future. Ethnic groups demand and assert these claims as historic rights to self-determination for local autonomy or independence (Juergensmeyer, 1993). The term *ethnonationalism* refers to a particular strain of nationalism that is marked by the desire of an ethnic community to have absolute authority over its own political, economic, and social affairs. Therefore, it denotes the pursuit of statehood on the part of an ethnic nation. Ethnonationalist movements signify the perception among members of a particular ethnic group that the group's interests are not being served under the current political arrangements (Rhodes, 1995).

References

Connor, W. (2002). *Ethnonationalism in the contemporary world: Walker Connor and the study of nationalism*. New York: Routledge.

Juergensmeyer, M. (1993). *The new Cold War? Religious nationalism confronts the secular state*. Berkeley: University of California Press.

Rhodes, B. (1995, May). Headlines in the Himalayas. *WorldPress Review, 42*, 42.

Ethos   Ethos is a Greek word meaning the values or characteristics of a specific person, people, movement, or culture (*American Heritage Dictionary*, 1995). Although ethos may imply personality, self, character, and probably most precisely reputation, it usually emphasizes the public character because the private cannot be accessed by a reader or audience unless made public in some way. Thus, in everyday rhetoric, ethos has more to do with public image than with a private self (Austin, 2003). The term is also applied to a person's character or disposition. It is informally defined as the individual character and extended to the social rules that govern and rule our conduct (Iaccarino, 2001). This concept dates back to the early 16th century when Greek philosophers began studying society's morals and ethics. Both the character of a person who aspires to behave ethically and the customs of a people by which one's standards are measured derive from the concept of morality. Morality, a subsidiary of ethics, pertains to distinctions between right and wrong and good and bad. Bateson (1972) highlighted the relationship between ethos and culture.

References

American heritage dictionary (3rd ed.). (1995). Boston: Laureleaf.

Austin, K. (2003). *Rhetoric of religion*. Shepherdstown: West Virginia University.

Bateson, G. (1972). *Steps to ecology of mind*. New York: Ballantine.

Iaccarino, M. (2001). About the precautionary principle. *Embo Reports, 1,* 454–456.

Etic   Etic is the study of a culture and human behavior. The main focus is on human universals, and emic focuses on how these particular human universals are expressed (Berry, 1969) (see Emic). Etic constructs are accounts, descriptions, and analyses conveyed in terms of theoretical schemes and categories viewed as significant and appropriate (Leff, 1990). Etic is analogous to the "outsider" (Harris, 1990). Understanding an etic about another culture may be useful in making predictions about that culture (Harris, 1990). Etic research is concerned with distinguishing resemblances among cultures. The human practice provides an opportunity for creating a cohesive understanding concerning the structure and process of psychological functioning. The etic approach evaluates the extent to which the original factor or structure can be recovered from the imported culture. Child rearing is an example of an etic or a specific human universal and is expressed differently among various ethnic groups. Traditional gender role is another example of a specific etic that may be expressed differently in different cultures. For example, gender roles are more flexible in the United States, whereas in collectivistic cultures they tend to be more traditional (Goldstein, 2000). The study of human universals and how they are expressed is done using the etic and emic approaches.

References

Berry, J. W. (1969). On cross-cultural comparability. *International Journal of Psychology, 4,* 119–128.

Goldstein, S. (2000). *Cross-cultural explorations: Activities in culture and psychology.* Boston: Allyn & Bacon.

Harris, M. (1990). Emic and etic revisited. In T. N. Headland, K. L. Pike, & M. Harris (Eds.), *The insider/outsider debate* (pp. 48–60). Newbury Park, CA: Sage.

Leff, J. (1990). Emic and etics: Notes on the epistomology of anthropology. In T. N. Headland, K. L. Pike, & M. Harris (Eds.), *Emics and etics: The insider/outsider* (pp. 127–142). Newbury Park, CA: Sage.

Euro-American   The term *Euro-American* refers to a U.S. citizen or resident of European descent. This is also used to describe those related to a Euro-American and those who are related to European and to an American (Pickett, 2001). In 1941, it was used for the first time to describe those who were of both European and American descent—that is, Americans who are from Europe, including the English, Irish, Germans, Jews, Italians, Poles, Swedes, and French (Mio, Timble, Arredono, Cheatham, & Sue, 1999). There are, however, some subsets to the term *Euro-American*. The term *Anglo-Saxon* (which sometimes is used interchangeably with Euro-American) is used to describe those of English descent. It excludes many European ethnic groups, such as the French, Poles, and Swedes. Another wider categorization for European Americans is Caucasian because it includes those indigenous to Europe, northern Africa, western Asia, and India (Pickett, 2001). This term was created to avoid the racial implications of the term *White*. Instead, both European American and the less often used Euro-American are a means to compel racial equality in regard to such terms as *Afro-American* and *Polish American* (Herbst, 1997). Because the term to describe a Black American is *African American* (Afro-American), the term *European American* (also used as Euro-American or Euramerican) was created to describe a White American. This is to avoid the presumption that an American is a White person (Herbst, 1997). It brings to mind the origin of the family's background and brings forth its place of heritage (Grant & Ladson-Billings, 1997). See Caucasian.

References

Grant, C. A., & Ladson-Billings, G. (Eds.). (1997). *Dictionary of multicultural education.* Phoenix, AZ: Oryx.

Herbst, P. H. (1997). *The color of words: An encyclopaedic dictionary of ethnic bias in the United States.* Yarmouth, MA: Intercultural Press.

Mio, J. S., Timble, J. E., Arredono, P., Cheatham, H. E., & Sue, D. (Eds.). (1999). *Key words in multicultural interventions: A dictionary.* Westport, CT: Greenwood.

Pickett, J. P. (Ed.). (2001). *The American heritage dictionary.* New York: Dell.

Eurocentrism   Eurocentrism is associated with a philosophy that can become a foundational source of meaning through which individuals, groups, and nations from the continent (Europe) can develop attitudes based on emerging ideologies of racial, religious, cultural, or ethnic supremacy over the various indigenous people they encountered (Amin, 1989). Eurocentrism can be understood as the implicit view that societies and cultures of European origin constitute the "natural" norm for assessing what goes on throughout the rest of the world. It is the real or alleged centrality of Europe in preparing the explosion of economic development, science, and technology, the enlightenment and the expansion of the role of the individual, as well as intensified exploitation and colonial conquest that heralded the modern world (Andre, 1998). Western concepts differ fundamentally from those prevalent in other civilizations. Western ideas of individualism, liberalism, constitutionalism, human rights, equality, liberty, the rule of law, democracy, free markets, and the separation of church and state often have little resonance in Islamic, Confucian, Japanese, Hindu, Buddhist, or Orthodox cultures (Huntington, 1993).

References

Amin, S. (1989). *Eurocentism*. New York: Monthly Review Press.

Andre, G. F. (1998). *Reorient: Global economy in the Asian age*. Berkeley: University of California Press.

Huntington, S. (1993, Summer). The clash of civilizations? *Foreign Affairs*, 22–49.

Evolutionary psychology   Evolutionary psychology is the study of human psychological and physical behavior produced by natural selection (Manstead & Hewstone, 1995). The use of Darwinian ideas to describe human behaviors suggests that all human actions are for survival purposes and have evolved over time (Cardwell, 1996). Research on animals indicates that certain species employ new behaviors with ease, whereas others do so with much difficulty, if at all (Hergenhahn & Olson, 2001). Hergenhahn and Olson state that the aforementioned animals have also been noted within species to establish some relationships easier than others. Cardwell believes that with regard to human nature, stepfathers and their stepchildren have no genetic ties to one another so it is "natural" for stepfathers to kill their stepchildren. According to Cardwell, it is also considered normal and "natural" for men to be sexually promiscuous so that they may increase the chances of reproductive success in a way that women cannot. Because females will always be certain of their maternity to their children, however, males are more likely to be jealous because they cannot be sure of their fatherhood to the alleged children (Daly, Wilson, & Weghorst, 1982).

References

Cardwell, M. (Ed.). (1996). *Dictionary of psychology*. Chicago: Fitzroy Dearborn.

Daly, M., Wilson, M., & Weghorst, S. J. (1982). Male sexual jealousy. *Ethology and Sociobiology, 3*, 11–27.

Hergenhahn, B. R., & Olson, M. H. (2001). *An introduction to theories of learning* (6th ed.). Upper Saddle River, NJ: Prentice Hall.

Manstead, A. S. R., & Hewstone, M. (1995). *The Blackwell encyclopedia of social psychology*. Cambridge, UK: Blackwell.

Exorcism   According to Hardon (1980), this term refers to the religious act in which the devil is either ordered to depart from a possessed person or prohibited to harm someone. This term is commonly referred to as the removal of an evil spirit from a person who is possessed, but it can also be used when trying to remove other evils or even obsessions. In countries that are predominantly Protestant, however, the development of a more scientific view to life has reduced the belief in this act (Brandon, 1970). Notably, the Roman Catholic Church still has an office that deals with the exorcism of evil spirits (Brandon, 1970). For instance, the gospels are filled with lengthy and descriptive stories about exorcisms performed by Christ. In St. Mark's gospel, there are many references to Christ's effortless exorcisms on those who were under evil's control. For somewhat obvious reasons, however, he did not seem to practice any of the now common "steps" that are necessary (Brandon, 1970). Exorcism rituals include a serious statement of belief by the priest or practitioner and also require a realization by the sufferer. In other words, the demon must acknowledge "good" for it to go away (Hardon, 1980). These rituals include intense prayer, incantations, and sometimes physically disturbing rituals (Pye, 1994). For this reason, the practice of exorcism in modern times has been a matter of controversy.

References

Brandon, S. G. F. (1970). *A dictionary of comparative religion*. New York: Scribner.

Hardon, J. A. (1980). *Modern Catholic dictionary*. Garden City, NJ: Doubleday.

Pye, M. (1994). *The Continuum dictionary of religion*. New York: Continuum.

Expressive behavior   This term refers to behavior that communicates emotions or personality. In humans, this occurs especially through facial expression, although it can also occur through other types of affect displays, dress styles, handwriting, and so on (Colman, 2001). It is used interchangeably with emotional expression, which can be traced back to Darwin. He considered the worldwide occurrence of the same expressions as imperative support that emotions are inborn (Berry, Poortinga, Segall, & Dasen, 1992). This claim, however, has been challenged. Culture plays a strong role in how we express emotions. Research shows that human emotional expression is acquired in the process of socialization, at least to a considerable extent. For example, samurai women in Japan will smile when they have lost their husbands (Berry et al., 1992). Expressive behavior is not only what people are doing but also the way they are communicating doing it and the manner in which they are doing it (DePaulo, 1993).

References

Berry, J. W., Poortinga, Y. H., Segall, M. H., & Dasen, P. R. (1992). *Cross-cultural psychology: Research and applications*. Cambridge, UK: Cambridge University Press.

Colman, A. M. (2001). *Dictionary of psychology*. New York: Oxford University Press.

DePaulo, B. M. (1993). *The ability to judge others from their expressive behaviors: In fifty years of personality psychology*. New York: Plenum.

Extended family   The extended family includes the parents, children, grandparents, aunts, uncles, cousins, nephews, nieces, and so on ("India," 2003). Many years ago, it was common for extended families with several generations to live together, but today it is extremely uncommon, mainly because working parents relocate more often than they did in the past to take new, better jobs. Extended families are much more prevalent in collectivistic cultures, such as American Indian culture, than in individualistic cultures, such as European and Anglo-American culture. The life of American Indians is centered on the family, which explains why they live with their extended families. Often, two or more adult generations share a house ("India," 2003). Architecture was greatly influenced by the practice of living with extended families. Instead of building single-family homes, communal structures had to be designed and built. In the majority of these extended families, the grandmother, her daughters, their husbands, and the grandchildren lived together. This practice contradicted the choice of housing of European and American families because they preferred single-family homes. People with whom one becomes friends and establishes a close family-like relationship are also part of the extended family ("India," 2003). Extended families are also defined by the *American Heritage Dictionary* as "a family that includes in one household near relatives, in addition to a nuclear family" ("Extended Family," 2000, p. 367) and "a family group that consists of parents, children, and other close relatives, often living in close proximity" ("Extended Family," 2000, p. 367). In recent times, relatives live close to each other to associate with extended family members but also maintain a separate, private life. An extended family is also defined as a family consisting of the nuclear family and their blood relatives ("Extended Family," 2000).

References

Extended family. (2000). In *American heritage dictionary of the English language* (4th ed.). Boston: Houghton Mifflin.

India. (2003). In *Encarta online encyclopedia*. Redmond, WA: Microsoft Corporation/ Bloomsbury.

Face   Face is defined by Goffman (1956) as the positive social value a person claims for himself or herself during a line of argument to offset feelings of embarrassment. Ting-Toomey's (1988) theory of preservation of face asserts that all cultures seek to save face, but face saving has different referents in collectivistic and individualistic cultures. In collectivistic cultures, the object in an interaction is to preserve harmony. The focus is on saving "us" from embarrassment, not saving "me" from such uncomfortable feelings. For the individualist, especially when others are present and watching the interaction, the individual is more likely to "save face" by rebutting the insult (Ting-Toomey, 1988).

References

Goffman, E. (1956). Embarrassment and social organization. *American Journal of Sociology, 62,* 264–271.

Ting-Toomey, S. (1988). A face negotiation theory. In Y. Kim & W. B. Gudykunst (Eds.), *Theory in intercultural communication.* Newbury Park, CA: Sage.

Falling out   In African American communities, falling out involves seizurelike symptoms resulting from traumatic events, such as robberies (Gaw, 2001).

Reference

Gaw, A. C. (2001). *Concise guide to cross-cultural psychiatry.* Washington, DC: American Psychiatric Publishing.

Fatalismo   Fatalismo is the doctrine that all events are predetermined by fate and are therefore unalterable (*American Heritage Dictionary*, 2000). Fatalismo translated to English is fatalism. It is a belief that all things in the world are under the control of some invisible force, and we are powerless to do anything about it. Knight (2003) notes that "fatalism is in general the view which holds that all events in the history of the world, and, in particular, the actions and incidents which make up the story of each individual life, are determined by fate" (p. 423). Its origins date back to the time of Greek civilization and earlier, when people believed that there was an all-powerful force controlling everything and that all things and people were at its mercy. Common synonyms are *fate* and *destiny*. It has a strong tie with religion because in some religious practices, such as Christianity, God is in charge, and he oversees everything, rather than an all-consuming, all-powerful mysterious force.

References

American heritage dictionary of the English language (4th ed.). (2000). Boston: Houghton Mifflin.

Knight, K. (2003). *The Catholic encyclopedia* (Vol. 5). New York: Robert Appleton.

Field dependent   A field-dependent person is a learner who accomplishes more outside the constraints of a classroom and in tasks involving interpersonal communication skills (Ellis, 1985). Field dependence is, ultimately, the inclination to be dependent on the whole rather than on the parts of the whole. The pieces are not understood as well as the whole. Field dependent and field independent refer to how people perceive and memorize information (Brown, 1994). A field-dependent person has a personal orientation, perceives parts as a whole, is dependent, and is less skilled in interpersonal relationships (Ellis, 1985). The field-dependent learner has the ability to skip minor problems and see the general structure of a major problem or idea (Eliason, 1995). The Group Embedded Figures Test of Oltman, Raskin, and Witkin was administered to 60 high school students (30 with learning disabilities) to measure their cognitive styles of field dependence versus field independence. The analysis showed that the students with learning disabilities scored as more field dependent than those without learning disabilities (Huang, 2000). Field-dependent individuals go through a greater social introduction compared to field-independent people (Messick, 1976). Gruenfeld (1984) noted that in an experiment using Bales' Interpersonal Rating Forms to rate social behaviors of participants, "the field dependents were more task oriented than field independents. The striking negative behavior exhibited by the presumably self-controlled and analytical field independents suggests material for further study" (p. 3). Field-dependent learners tend to focus on the whole rather than the parts, are reality oriented to relationships and social attributes, and demonstrate topic-associating narrative style. They like to work with others to achieve a common goal, they like to assist others, and they care about the feelings and opinions of others. Unlike field independents, if they are approached by a teacher, they openly express their positive feelings for the teacher, ask questions about the teacher's tastes and personal experiences, and seek to become like the teacher. Field-dependent learners also seek guidance and demonstration from the teacher; they seek rewards, which strengthen relationships with the teacher; and they are highly motivated when working individually with the teacher. To facilitate learning, the performance objectives and global aspects of the curriculum should be carefully explained, concepts should be presented in humanized or story format, and concepts should be related to personal interests and experiences (Ramirez & Castaneda, 1974).

References

Brown, H. D. (1994). *Principles of language learning and teaching* (3rd ed.). Englewood Cliffs, NJ: Prentice Hall.

Eliason, P. (1995). *Difficulties with cross-cultural learning styles assessment.* Boston: Heinle & Heinle.

Ellis, R. (1985). *Understanding second language acquisition.* Oxford, UK: Oxford University Press.

Gruenfeld, L. W. (1984). *Human relations: Social behavior of field independents and dependents.* New York: New York Educational Laboratory.

Huang, J. (2000). *Perceptual and motor skills: Field dependence versus field independence with and without learning disabilities.* Missoula: University of Montana.

Messick, S. (1976). *Individuality in learning.* San Francisco: Jossey-Bass.

Ramirez, M., & Castaneda, A. (1974). *Some attributes of field independent and field dependent cognitive styles.* Portland, OR: Northwest Regional Educational Laboratory.

Field independent   A field-independent person excels in classroom learning activities involving analysis and attention to details and succeeds in exercises, drills, and other focused activities (Ellis, 1985). Field independent and field dependent refer to how people perceive and memorize information (Brown, 1994). Field-independent learners have the skill to see the parts of a whole and work on the parts separately rather than on the whole at once. Brown notes,

> A person who can easily recognize the hidden castle or human face in 3-D posters and a child who can spot the monkeys camouflaged within the trees and leaves of an exotic forest in coloring books tend toward a field-independent style. (p. 106)

A field-independent learner has an impersonal orientation and is analytic, independent, and socially sensitive (Ellis, 1985). Cognitive tunnel vision prevents field-independent learners from seeing the whole; instead, they see the parts (Eliason, 1995). Field-independent learners prefer to work by themselves, compete and gain individual recognition, and are task oriented and inattentive to the social environment when working. They do not like teamwork or interaction with teachers. These learners tend to focus on parts rather than on the whole, and they demonstrate a topic-centered narrative style. They also enjoy trying new tasks without the teacher's help and are impatient to begin these tasks. They try to work fast to be the first ones finished, but they seek nonsocial rewards. Field-independent learners' successes increase when the details of concept, mathematics, science, and discovery are emphasized (Ramirez & Castaneda, 1974). Gruenfeld (1984) notes that in an experiment using Bales' Interpersonal Rating Forms to rate social behaviors of participants, "the field independents were less task-oriented than field dependents. Those results caused the striking negative behavior exhibited by the presumably self-controlled and analytical field independents to be further studied and experimented" (p. 5). At an intellectual level, field-independent learners are able to distinguish details as different from their backgrounds compared to field-dependent individuals, who experience all events in the same way. Field-independent learners are likely to learn more effectively under conditions of self-motivation and are affected less by social praises or lack thereof (Messick, 1976).

References

Brown, H. D. (1994). *Principles of language learning and teaching* (3rd ed.). Englewood Cliffs, NJ: Prentice Hall.

Eliason, P. (1995). Difficulties with cross-cultural learning styles assessment. Boston: Heinle & Heinle.

Ellis, R. (1985). *Understanding second language acquisition.* Oxford, UK: Oxford University Press.

Gruenfeld, L. W. (1984). *Human relations: Social behavior of field independents and dependents.* New York: New York Educational Laboratory.

Messick, S. (1976). *Individuality in learning.* San Francisco: Jossey-Bass.

Ramirez, M., & Castaneda, A. (1974). *Some attributes of field independent and field dependent cognitive styles.* Portland, OR: Northwest Regional Educational Laboratory.

Filial piety   Filial piety explains how children should behave toward their mother, father, and other relatives (Zhang, 1998). Filial piety is one of the most important ethics governing social behavior in Chinese society. Ho (1996) states,

> It has been predominantly stressed by Confucian scholars throughout Chinese history as regulating interpersonal, especially intergenerational, relationships among Chinese people. Confucian filial piety surpasses all other cultural ethics in Chinese culture with respect to its historical continuity, the portion of humanity under its governance, and the encompassing and imperative nature of its precepts. (p. 155)

The following behaviors are considered to be related to filial piety: providing for the material and mental well-being of one's aged parents, performing ceremonial duties of ancestral worship, ensuring the continuity of the family line, and conducting oneself so as to bring honor and avoid disgrace to the family name (Zhang, 1998). It has long been thought that the principle of filial piety has meaning surpassing the limits of the family. Filial piety also gives authority to older citizens over younger ones. It justifies not only absolute parental authority over children but also, by extension, the authority of those seniors in generational rank over those junior in rank (Zhang, 1998). Although some component values of filial piety (e.g., obedience) are shared by other cultures (Bond, 1988; Schwartz, 1994), many Chinese scholars believe that filial piety is more indigenous than universal (Ho, 1996; Hsieh, 1967; Yang & Yeh, 1994).

The study of filial piety in Chinese societies is a discipline dominated by historians, philologists, and philosophers (Hsieh, 1967; Tu, 1985). Not much interest was shown from the view of behavioral sciences, or psychology, in studying filial piety. Then, in the 1970s, experimental studies began appearing in psychological journals (Ho, 1996; Hwang, 1977). A hallmark of conservative political culture is filial piety (Szalay, 2002). As research interest in parent care has increased in China, Korea, and Japan, the results have shown that parent-child relationships are based on filial piety (Sung, 1998).

References

Bond, M. H. (1988). Finding universal dimension of individual variation in multicultural studies: The Rokeach and Chinese Value Surveys. *Journal of Personality and Social Psychology, 55,* 1009–1015.

Ho, D. Y. F. (1996). *The handbook of Chinese psychology* (pp. 155–165). Hong Kong: Oxford University Press.

Hsieh, Y. W. (1967). *The Chinese mind: Essentials of Chinese philosophy and culture* (pp. 139–159). Honolulu: University of Hawaii Press.

Hwang, K. K. (1977). Face and favor: The Chinese power game. *Acta Psychologica Taiwanica, 19,* 61–73.

Schwartz, S. H. (1994). Are there universal aspects in the structure and content of human values? *Journal of Social Issues, 50*(4), 19–45.

Sung, K.-T. (1998, Winter). An exploration of actions of filial piety. *Journal of Aging Studies, 12*(4), 331–455.

Szalay, M. (2002, Fall). All the king's men: Or primal crime? *Yale Journal of Criticism, 15*(2), 347–374.

Tu, W. M. (1985). *Culture and self: Asian and Western perspectives* (pp. 231–251). New York: Tavistock.

Yang, K. S., & Yeh, K. H. (1994). *Psychological study of filial piety: Theoretical approaches and discovery, Chinese people and Chinese heart: Traditional perspectives* (pp. 193–260). Taipei: Yuan Lui.

Zhang, J. (1998). Personality and filial piety among college students in two Chinese societies. *Journal of Cross-Cultural Psychology, 29,* 402–417.

G

Ghost sickness   Among American Indians, this involves weakness and dizziness resulting from the action of witches and evil forces. According to Guiley (1992), this term refers to "the belief that the ghosts of the dead can cause illness and death" (p. 140). This term is based on the animistic system of beliefs, which states that everything has a soul and a conscious life. For instance, rocks, trees, rivers, mountains, and the earth are all thought to possess a soul or animae (Brandon, 1970). For many, it is believed that certain places and objects are sacred and have special powers that may be used to help or hurt people. This is characteristic of many tribal societies throughout the world. It is thought that the soul of a dead person remains close to his or her body for a few days until it begins its journey to the land of the dead (Brandon, 1970). According to folklore, it is during this time that the ghost may be particularly dangerous because it is thought that it may be lonely and seeking company from the living. In many African cultures, the spirits of the dead are thought to survive bodily death and have major effects on all types of human affairs (Kohl, 1992). In addition, it is thought that a child's soul is weaker or less attached to his or her body, thus making him or her more susceptible to ghost sickness. For this reason, children of the Kwakiutl Indians of British Columbia are sometimes referred to as adults or even disguised to confuse ghosts into thinking that they are older than their true age (Guiley, 1992). Interestingly, fear of the dead has resulted in many strange practices, such as the removal of corpses from homes via a man-made hole in the wall rather than through a door or window, to confuse or make the ghosts' trip back home more difficult. Although ghosts may cause greater fear soon after death, many societies believe that any sighting or sounds of a ghost may carry with them disease or death, even if some time has passed (Guiley, 1992).

References

Brandon, S. G. F. (1970). *A dictionary of comparative religion*. New York: Scribner.

Guiley, R. E. (1992). *Ghosts and spirits*. New York: Facts on File.

Kohl, H. (1992). *From archetype to zeitgeist*. Boston: Bay Back Books.

H

Haitians This group of people is characterized by their tendency to be passive and nonassertive (Brown & Shalett, 1997). They are generally very warm and hospitable (Culture Grams, 2002). Personal greetings are a must when entering a room, and superiors are generally addressed by title and last name (Culture Grams, 2002). They have a very acute awareness and knowledge of their culture and history (Brown & Shalett, 1997; Culture Grams, 2002). By nature, Haitians also possess exceptionally strong survival skills (Brown & Shalett, 1997). Most Haitians are descendants of Black African slaves who came to the country in approximately the 16th century. Only a small percentage of them are of mixed heritage. Their social roots, however, derive as much from Europe as from Africa (Leyburn, 1966). One of the languages used more frequently among Haitians is Creole. This language is a combination of several African dialects and French (Brown & Shalett, 1997; Leyburn, 1966). The predominant religion is Roman Catholicism, although many Haitians practice voodoo, which is more a belief than a religion (see Voodoo). Also practiced, but less popularized, are the Pentecostal and Baptist religions, among others (Culture Grams, 2002; Leyburn, 1966). Haitians typically do not like to be referred to as, or associated with, African Americans. It is almost seen as an insult to them because they take great pride in their culture (Brown & Shalett, 1997). Families are generally very close and include extended family. Marriages can be legal, or a man and woman may simply choose to live together as husband and wife (Culture Grams, 2002). In the typical Haitian family, the man makes all the decisions and acts as head of the household. If the woman serves as sole breadwinner, however, the roles are sometimes reversed and may even cause problems in the relationship (Brown & Shalett, 1997). Disciplinary action taken against children tends to be violent, a form of punishment readily accepted within the Haitian culture. Because the educational system in Haiti is very poor and not available to everyone, education is held in very high esteem among Haitians (Brown & Shalett, 1997; Foster & Valdman, 1984; Leyburn, 1966). In large part due to the poor living conditions and limited opportunities, many Haitians have migrated to the United States illegally by way of boat (Foster & Valdman, 1984; Leyburn, 1996).

References

Brown, P. M., & Shalett, J. S. (1997). *Cross-cultural practice with couples and families.* New York: Haworth.

Culture Grams. (2002). *World edition: The Americas* (Vol. 1). Lindon, UT: Axiom.

Foster, C. R., & Valdman, A. (1984). *Haiti—Today and tomorrow: An interdisciplinary study.* Lanham, MD: University Press of America.

Leyburn, J. G. (1966). *The Haitian people.* New Haven, CT: Yale University Press.

High-contact cultures   High-contact cultures are described as cultures that customarily maintain small distances among themselves (Hall, 1959; Vargas, 1986). Madonik (2001) states that communities that give great significance to physical contact as a form of communication are deemed high-contact cultures. She notes that the communicator's message will make a greater impact if the recipient of the message also experiences an often delayed touch. In terms of contact, distance can be defined as a relational concept, usually measured in terms of how far one individual is from the other (Leather, 1978). Jimenez Arias (1996) maintains that "people have certain patterns for delimiting the distance when they interact, and this distance varies according to the nature of the social interaction" (p. 32). To make sense of why certain cultures keep certain distances among each other, Hall (1959) categorized contacts into four types of distances: intimate, personal, social, and public. Hall further pointed out that these distances can vary according to personality and environmental factors. An abnormal situation could bring people closer than they usually are. Researchers conclude that civilizations such as those of Arabs, Latin Americans, Greeks, Turks, the French, and Italians are considered high-contact cultures (Hall, 1959; Vargas, 1986).

References

Hall, E. T. (1959). *The silent language.* Garden City, NY: Doubleday.

Jimenez Arias, I. (1996). Proxemics in the ESL classroom. *Forum, 34*(1), 32.

Leather, D. (1978). *Nonverbal communications systems.* Boston: Allyn & Bacon.

Madonik, B. G. (2001). *I hear what you say, but what are you telling me? The strategic use of nonverbal communication in mediation.* San Francisco: Jossey-Bass.

Vargas, M. (1986). *Louder than words.* Ames: Iowa State University Press.

Hinduism   Hinduism represents a wide range of beliefs and practices that involve worship of trees and stones and the like in India. Hindu originated from those who lived beyond the river Sindu. Hinduism does not have a religious founder. Hinduism is not just a single belief system, such as monotheistic, pantheistic, panentheistic, theistic, and monistic systems: It is a combination of all (Fowler, 1997). Hindu society includes many races and cultures. In popular Hinduism, God is worshiped in different forms; Hindus worship God in a certain figure in Hindu mythology. The nameless and formless have different names, and different forms are recognized to God, but it is remembered that God is one (Sen, 1978). The Hindu social structure is known as the caste system, which consists of four *vanas* or social groups that have traditional types of occupations: the Brahmins, who are priests and scholars; the Kshatriyas, who are warriors and rulers; the Vaishyas, who engage in imports and trades; and the Shudras, who are serfs who serve the three higher groups. Some law books recognize a fifth group, the vana, who are the untouchables. They are lower than the Shudras. Each group is considered separate, and intermarriage is forbidden between the groups (Kinsley, 1982). Customs and festivals are an important part of life for Hindus. Daily customs include *pratahkritya* and *sandy*, which are meditations, prayers, and rituals that high-caste Hindus must perform every day. Some worship in temples called *mandiras*, and some worship at home, where images of gods or symbols on shrines are used. Some Hindus have weekly religious customs, such as fasting on a particular day of the week. Prayers are also performed during the full moon and new moon. Women perform *vratas* (vows), which are wishes for the welfare of the family or the community. *Savitri Vrata* is for the welfare of the husband, *Shashthi Vrata* for the well-being of the children, *Maghamandala Vrata* for sunshine in the winter, and *Pausha Vrata* for good crops. Annual religious festivals are associated with the worship of particular gods and goddesses of the Hindu. An annual festival that is associated with the seasons is the *Holi*, the spring festival, where people throw colored powder and water on each other. Religious ceremonies are performed at every stage of life. *Namakarana* is the ceremony for naming a child, *annaprasana* is the ceremony for weaning it, *upanayana* is the ceremony performed when a high-caste boy is introduced to the rights and duties of his caste and is given a sacred thread for the symbol of new birth, *vivaha* is the marriage ceremony, and *sraddha* (meaning respect) is the ceremony for a funeral (Sen, 1978). People associate Hinduism with a god, Brahman, and everything in life, whether living or not. All creatures, plants, individuals, stones, trees—everything in existence—come from Brahman. Brahman is considered an It, which is why It is not called God. All things are part of Brahman and are considered sacred; this is called pantheism. Hindus believe in *Samsara*, which is the cycle of reincarnation—the idea that when someone dies, the individual is born again in another form to carry on the evolutionary path. Another belief is *Karma*, meaning action or activity. This is the belief that all things happen for a reason, and that all actions produce results. *Dharma* is doing what is right, and *Moksa* is when the individual realizes purity (Fowler, 1997).

References

Fowler, J. (1997). *Hinduism: Beliefs and practices*. Portland, OR: Sussex Academic Press.

Kinsley, D. R. (1982). *Hinduism*. Englewood Cliffs, NJ: Prentice Hall.

Sen, K. M. (1978). *Hinduism*. London: Cox & Wyman.

Hispanic American   A Hispanic is a person who descends from one of the world's Spanish-speaking peoples (Ochoa, 2001). People from these Spanish-speaking countries migrated to the United States. The term *Hispanic America* is most often used to refer to the 18 Western Hemisphere countries that were once colonies of Spain and in which Spanish is still the predominant language: Mexico, Guatemala, El Salvador,

Honduras, Nicaragua, Costa Rica, Panama, Cuba, the Dominican Republic, Colombia, Venezuela, Ecuador, Peru, Bolivia, Paraguay, Argentina, Uruguay, and Chile (Ochoa, 2001). It was difficult for Hispanics to blend into the two groups, Black and White. Some Hispanics do not associate themselves with either group. Hispanics have many different complexions (Benson, 1996). Various terms are used to identify individuals of Hispanic origin. For example, among U.S.-born educated individuals, the term *Chicano(a)* is preferred to *Mexican American* or *Hispanic American*. Some Hispanic Americans prefer the term *Latino*, and individuals of Cuban origin may prefer to be called *Cuban American* rather than *Latino* (Padilla, 1995). Brazilians, although they are from South American, are not considered Hispanics because their language is Portuguese, whereas Hispanics speak Spanish.

References

Benson, S. G. (1996). *The Hispanic American almanac* (3rd ed.). New York: Thomson & Gale.

Ochoa, G. (2001). *Atlas of Hispanic-American history.* New York: Checkmark.

Padilla, M. A. (1995). *Hispanic psychology: Critical issues in theory and research.* Thousand Oaks, CA: Sage.

Holocultural method   Terminologies associated with the term *holocultural method* are the hologeistic approach and the cross-cultural approach. These methods use a global sample of societies to test a hypothesis (Rohner, 2002). These terminologies originated from the ancestral analogies formed by Sir Edward Tylor, William Sumner, Gottfried Keller, and George Murdock, who were anthropological and ethnological psychologists (Rohner, 2002). Levinson (1977), an anthropological psychologist, stated that a holocultural method is "designated to test or develop a proposition through the statistical analysis of data on a sample of 10 or more nonliteral societies, from three or more geographical regions of the world" (p. 6). In this approach, "cultural traits are taken out of the context of the whole culture and are compared with cultural traits in widely diverse cultures to determine patterns of regularities and differences within the broad base of a test or study" (Levinson, 1977, p. 28). Subsequently, to enhance cross-cultural research, researchers developed the Human Relations Area Files (HRAF) in 1949 to collect and organize ethnographic information on all known cultures (Ember & Ember, 2001). Ember and Ember note,

> If one wanted to locate a set of cultures for a comparative project that met certain criteria, it would be a long and difficult task to wade through hundreds of ethnographic reports searching for specific groups that would serve this purpose. (p. 15)

Fortunately, the HRAF eliminates these obscurities: "One may be able to direct one's activity more effectively toward fruitful questions when one eventually goes to the field" (Ember & Ember, 2001, p. 26). The HRAF is based on two classifications, namely of societies and of topics, that are believed to be applicable worldwide (Moore, 1971): the outline of the world cultures (Murdock, 1983) and the outline of cultural materials (Murdock et al., 1987). The first is "a comprehensive listing of many of the world's cultural (including ethnic and political) units, which constitutes the population from which researchers may identity and sample cultures" (Murdock et al., 1987, p. 109). A more specific population of cultures is the Ethnographic Atlas, which includes 863 societies arranged into six "culture areas": sub-Saharan Africa, circum-Mediterranean, east Eurasia, Oceania, North America, and South America (Murdock, 1967). Another listing of societies is contained in the HRAF Standard Cross Cultural Sample, which includes 186 representative cultures (Murdock & White, 1969). The outline of cultural materials contains 79 topics that are considered to be a universal set of categories found in all cultural groups (Barry & Schlegel, 1980). These topics are organized into eight broad categories, including general characteristics (language and communication), food and clothing (food quest and food consumption), housing and technology (processing of basic information and structures), and economy and transport (property and transportation). With this native archive, virtually any feature of a society can be sought and found by the researcher (Barry & Schlegel, 1980).

References

Barry, H., & Schlegel, A. (1980). *Cross-cultural samples and codes.* Pittsburgh, PA: University of Pittsburgh Press.

Ember, C. R., & Ember, M. (2001). *Cross-cultural research methods.* Landham, MD: Alta Mira.

Levinson, D. (1977). *A guide to social theory: Worldwide cross-cultural tests* (Vol. 1). New Haven, CT: Human Relations Area Files Press.

Moore, F. W. (1971). *Readings in cross-cultural methodology.* New Haven, CT: Human Relations Area Files Press.

Murdock, G. P. (1967). Ethnographic atlas. *Ethnology, 6,* 109–236.

Murdock, G. P. (1983). *Outlines of world cultures* (6th ed.). New Haven, CT: Human Relations Area Files Press.

Murdock, G. P., Ford, G. S., Hudson, A. E., Kennedy, R., Simmons, L. W., & Whiting, J. W. M. (1987). *Outlines of cultural materials* (5th ed.). New Haven, CT: Human Relations Area Files Press.

Murdock, G. P., & White, D. R. (1969). Standard cross-cultural sample. *Ethology, 8,* 329–369.

Rohner, R. P. (2002). Toward a conception of culture. *Journal of Cross-cultural Psychology, 15,* 111–138.

Hwa byung   This is a Korean term that means illness (byung) of fire (hwa). The term corresponds to the meaning of fire, which is anger in Asian metaphysical thinking; hwa byung is "an illness of anger." The illness affects women more than men, and Koreans believe it is related to suppression of anger and indignation (Gaw, 2001). The affected individual complains of pain in the chest, a hot sensation in the body, indigestion, fatigue, sighing, and headache. Emotional symptoms include fearfulness, panic, dysphoria, sad mood, loss of interest in daily activities, suicidal ideas, and guilt (Kim, 1993).

References

Gaw, A. C. (2001). *Concise guide to cross-cultural psychiatry.* Washington, DC: American Psychiatric Publishing.

Kim, L. I. C. (1993). Psychiatric care of Korean Americans. In A. C. Gaw (Ed.), *Culture, ethnicity and mental illness.* Washington, DC: American Psychiatric Press.

I

Identity development theories   Identity development or development of self is defined as a series of stages that everyone must go through to determine who they are as an individual ("Identity," 2001). The *Gale Encyclopedia* ("Identity," 2001) defines identity formation as follows:

> Identity formation . . . described by Erik Erickson in his theory of developmental stages, which extends from birth through adulthood. According to Erickson, identity formation, while beginning in childhood, gains prominence during adolescence. Faced with physical growth, sexual maturation, and impending career choices, adolescents must accomplish the task of integrating their prior experiences and characteristics into stable identity. Erickson coined the phrase identity crisis to describe the temporary instability and confusion adolescents experience as they struggle with alternatives and choice. (p. 419)

Racial identity and racial identity development theory are defined by Janet Helms (1990) as

> a sense of group or collective identity based on one's perception that he or she shares a common racial heritage with a particular racial group. . . . Racial identity development theory concerns the psychological implications of racial-group membership, that is belief systems that evolve in reaction to perceived differential racial-group membership. (p. 3)

It is assumed that in a society in which racial-group membership is emphasized, the development of racial identity will occur in some form in everyone. According to Cross's (1971, 1978; Cross, Parham, & Helms, 1991) model of Black identity development, there are five stages in the process: preencounter, encounter, immersion/emersion, internalization, and internalization-commitment. See Black Identity Development.

References

Cross, W., Jr. (1971). The Negro to Black conversion experience: Toward a psychology of black liberation. *Black World, 20*(9), 13–27.

Cross, W., Jr. (1978). The Cross and Thomas models of psychological nigrescence. *Journal of Black Psychology, 5*(1), 13–19.

Cross, W. E., Jr., Parham, T. A., & Helms, J. E. (1991). The stages of Black identity development: Nigrescence models. In R. Jones (Ed.), *Black psychology* (3rd ed., pp. 319–338). San Francisco: Cobb & Henry.

Helms, J. E. (Ed.). (1990). *Black and White racial identity: Theory, research and practice.* Westport, CT: Greenwood.

Identity/identity formation. (2001). In *Gale encyclopedia of psychology* (2nd ed.). Farmington Hills, MI: Gale.

Ideocentrism   Other terminologies for ideocentrism are *individualistic-individualism* (Triandis, 1989) and *independent self-idiocentrism* (Markus & Kitayama, 1991; Triandis, Leung, Villareal, & Clark, 1985). It is defined as the inability to view the world from a different ideological perspective. In cross-cultural research, one of the variables that has been thoroughly studied is individualistic dimensions (Triandis, 1989). Individualistic cultures focus on independence and group harmony (Hofstede, 1984; Triandis, 1995). Bravery, creativity, self-reliance, solitude, and frugality are valued in individualistic cultures (Triandis, 1989). According to Triandis et al., idiocentrism is the expression of individualist values and norms on an individual level. In addition, it concerns values such as a comfortable life, pleasure, competition, and social recognition. Moreover, idiocentrism is related to the need for achievement, alienation, and anomie. According to Markus and Kitayama (1991), independent self is similar to idiocentrism. Their notion of self is that it is a cognitive construct that others cannot know directly and that is beyond "a physical or ecological sense of self . . . and of the continuous flow of thoughts and feelings" (p. 225). According to Schwartz (1992, pp. 878–891), the subdimensions of individualism are power (social status and prestige, and control and dominance over people or resources), achievement (personal success through demonstrating competence according to social standards), hedonism (pleasure and sensuous gratification for oneself), stimulation (excitement, novelty, and challenge in life), and self-direction (independent thought, action choosing, creating, and exploring).

References

Hofstede, G. (1984). *Culture's consequences: International differences in work-related values.* Beverly Hills, CA: Sage.

Markus, H. R., & Kitayama, S. (1991). Culture and the self: Implications for cognition, emotion, and motivation. *Psychological Review, 98,* 224–253.

Schwartz, S. H. (1992). Universals in the content and structure values: Theoretical advances and empirical tests in 20 countries. *Journal of Personality and Social Psychology, 58,* 878–891.

Triandis, H. C. (1989). Cross-cultural studies of individualism and collectivism. In J. Berman (Ed.), *Nebraska symposium of motivation* (pp. 41–133). Lincoln: University of Nebraska Press.

Triandis, H. C. (1995). *Individualism & collectivism*. Boulder, CO: Westview.

Triandis, H. C., Leung, K., Villareal, M. J., & Clark, F. L. (1985). Allocentric versus idiocentric tendencies: Convergent and discriminant validation. *Journal of Research in Personality, 19,* 395–415.

Immigrant   An immigrant is a person who leaves one country to settle permanently in another (*American Heritage Dictionary*, 2000). The number of first-generation, documented and undocumented immigrant individuals in the United States in 1996 was 19.8 million, an increase of 106% from 1970 (Booth, 1997). In 2000 this number increased to 56 million with an estimated 8 million illegal aliens (U.S. Census Bureau, 2000). What has been called the "new immigration" has had a profound impact on all three countries that are traditional recipients of immigration—the United States, Canada, and Australia—but the impact has been very different in each case. The new immigration essentially is immigration from non-European countries (Reitz, 1998). Recent immigrants earn less and have higher jobless rates than do earlier postwar immigrants and U.S. natives; educational attainment and English fluency are important factors in labor market success. Some of the differences are due to external circumstances that affect immigrant flows, such as the U.S. border with Mexico and proximity to Latin America, the Canadian and Australian connections to the British Commonwealth, and Australia's Pacific location near emerging Asian economies (Reitz, 1998).

References

American heritage dictionary of the English language (4th ed.). (2000). Boston: Houghton Mifflin.

Booth, A. (1997). *Immigration and the family: Research and policy on U.S. immigrants.* Mahwah, NJ: Lawrence Erlbaum.

Reitz, J. (1998). *Warmth of the welcome: The social causes of economic success for immigrants in different nations and cities.* Boulder, CO: Westview.

U.S. Census Bureau. (2000). Profile of foreign born population. Washington, DC: Department of Commerce.

Immigration   Immigration is defined as the entrance of a person, an alien, into a new country for the purpose of establishing permanent residence (*Columbia Encyclopedia*, 2000). America is a country of immigrants. Historically, immigrants throughout the world used this "land of opportunity" and created the nation (Yang, 1995). Motives for immigration, like those for migration generally, are often economic, although religious or political factors may be very important (*Columbia Encyclopedia*, 2000). Family unity has been and continues to be the cornerstone of immigration policy for the United States (Booth, 1997). Of all nations, the United States has received the largest number of permanent immigrants since World War II (Fawcett,

Carino, Park, & Gardner, 1983). Family-based immigration is alleged to be an inefficient means of selecting workers that contributes to a decline in the skill levels of the workforce. Much of this argument misjudges the character of family-based immigration (Booth, 1997). High rates of immigration are frequently accompanied by militant, and sometimes violent, calls for immigration restriction or deportation by nationalist groups (*Columbia Encyclopedia*, 2000). Immigrants were largely responsible for the rapid development of the United States, and their high birthrates did much to swell the U.S. population (*Columbia Encyclopedia*, 2000). Immigrants are typically admitted under family reunification provisions but may also qualify for admission in virtually all professional and technical occupations specified in immigration laws (Booth, 1997). In the history of contemporary immigration to the United States, 1965 marked a milestone. From 1966 to 1988, the United States admitted more than 11 million immigrants, with an average annual influx of 481,513 (U.S. Naturalization and Immigration Services, 1989). In recent decades, immigration to Europe from Asia and Africa has also substantially increased, as has emigration from Eastern Europe to the newly reunified Germany (*Columbia Encyclopedia*, 2000).

References

Booth, A. (1997). *Immigration and the family: Research and policy on U.S. immigrants.* Mahwah, NJ: Lawrence Erlbaum.

Columbia encyclopedia (6th ed.). (2000). New York: Columbia University Press.

Fawcett, J. T., Carino, B., Park, I. H., & Gardner, R. W. (1983). Selectivity and diversity: The effect of U.S. immigration policy on immigrant characteristics. *International Migration Review, 17*(3), 470–484.

U.S. Naturalization and Immigration Services. (1989). *Immigration statistics.* Washington, DC: U.S. Government Printing Office.

Yang, P. Q. (1995). *Post-1965 immigration to the United States: Determinants.* Westport, CT: Greenwood.

Implicit theories of intelligence   Implicit theories of intelligence are the ideas that everyday people have about what constitutes intelligence. For example, one may associate an intelligent person with being verbally fluent, sociable, modest, and organized; working efficiently; speaking clearly and articulately; seeing all aspects of a problem; making clear decisions; and being knowledgeable about a particular field of study (Goldstein, 2000). Data gathered to study implicit theories may consist of characteristics of an intelligent person or definitions of intelligence provided by research participants (Goldstein, 2000). Studying implicit theories of intelligence is important for understanding the cultural differences in conceptions of intelligence (Goldstein, 2000; Ruzgis & Grigorenko, 1994). Ruzgis and Grigorenko observed that positive social competence corresponds to the social component in implicit theories of intelligence studied in individualistic cultures, such as those of Australia, Canada, and the United

States. These authors noted that receptive social competence tends to correspond to the social component in implicit theories of intelligence in collectivistic cultures, such as Asian and African societies. Sternberg, Conway, Ketron, and Bernstein (1981) explored the implicit theories of intelligence held by American laypersons and experts (researchers of human intelligence). They found that the laypersons' conceptions could be classified into three categories: practical problem solving, verbal ability, and social competence (more similar to positive social competence than to receptive social competence) (Goldstein, 2000; Sternberg et al., 1981). Dweck, Chiu, and Hong (1995) published a questionnaire on a survey of implicit theories about the malleability of intelligence, morality, and global principles of the world theories. Spinath and Stensmeier-Pelster (2001) noted that

> this questionnaire is postulated to be antecedents of motivational orientation, and differences in achievement motivation. The authors presented extended proof for the reliability and validity of this questionnaire. The paper presented summarized several studies in which a German version of the questionnaire was applied and tested for its psychometric properties. The relationships between implicit theories of intelligence and specific abilities and other variables of Dweck's theory, goal orientation, and self-concept of ability were assessed. (p. 53)

Dweck et al. evaluated relationships between implicit theories and age, gender, and type of school attended. It was proven that theories of intelligence, morality, and the world's global principles are empirically independent in the studies reported by Dweck et al. Implicit theories showed no significant correlations to age or gender, social political attitudes, or self-presentational concerns. The lack of relationship with cognitive abilities, self-confidence in personal capability, and optimism was interpreted as proof of the construct's discriminate validity as opposed to incremental validity (Spinath & Stensmeier-Pelster, 2001).

References

Dweck, C. S., Chiu, C., & Hong, Y. (1995). Implicit theories and their role in judgments and reactions: A world from two perspectives. *Psychological Inquiry, 6,* 267–285.

Goldstein, S. (2000). *Cross-cultural explorations: Activities in culture & psychology.* Boston: Allyn & Bacon.

Ruzgis, P., & Grigorenko, E. L. (1994). Cultural meaning system, intelligence, and personality. In R. J. Sternberg & P. Ruzgis (Eds.), *Personality & intelligence* (pp. 248–270). New York: Cambridge University Press.

Spinath, B., & Stensmeier-Pelster, J. (2001). Implicit theories about the malleability of intelligence and ability. *Psychologische Beiträge, 43,* 53–76.

Sternberg, R. J., Conway, B. E., Ketron, J. L., & Bernstein, M. (1981). People's conceptions of intelligence. *Journal of Personality and Social Psychology, 41,* 37–55.

Independent self Independent self is the normative imperative to become independent from others and to discover and express one's unique attributes (Johnson, 1980). Achieving the cultural goal of independence requires construing oneself as an individual whose behavior is organized and made meaningful primarily by reference to one's own internal repertoire of thoughts, feelings, and action rather than by reference to the thoughts, feelings, and actions of others. This view of the self derives from a belief in the wholeness and uniqueness of each person's configuration of internal attributes (Sampson, 1976). The essential aspect of this view involves a conception of the self as an autonomous, independent person; it is thus referred to as the independent construal of the self (Shweder, 1991). The independent self must, of course, be responsive to the social environment.

References

Johnson, H. C. (1980). *Human behavior and social environment: New perspectives: Vol. 1. Behavior psychopathology & the brain.* Portland, OR: Curriculum Concepts.

Sampson, E. E. (1976). *Social society and contemporary society.* New York: John Wiley.

Shweder, R. A. (1991). *Thinking through cultures.* Cambridge, MA: Harvard University Press.

Indigenous psychology Indigenous psychology is psychological knowledge that is native, that is not transported from another region, and that is designed for its people (Kim, 1990). In other words, indigenous psychology is an understanding rooted in a particular associated cultural context. "Psychology" has traditionally meant Western psychology, using the assumption that human universals hold true for humankind because they hold true in Western society. As practiced in other areas of the world, however, psychology raises an alternative view of human behavior. Indeed, human universals are problematic and need to be revealed through an examination of multiple indigenous psychologies to establish comparisons between cultures (Kim & Berry, 1993). There are cultures in which firmly drawn boundaries marking sharp self-nonself separations define the culture's indigenous psychology. According to the indigenous psychology currently dominant in the United States, for example, there exists a region intrinsic to the person and a region of "other" (Heelas & Lock, 1981).

References

Heelas, P., & Lock, A. (Eds.). (1981). *Indigenous psychologies: The anthropology of the self.* London: Academic Press.

Kim, U. (1990). Indigenous psychology: Science and applications. In R. W. Brislin (Ed.), *Applied cross-cultural psychology.* Newbury Park, CA: Sage.

Kim, U., & Berry, J. W. (Eds.). (1993). *Indigenous psychologies: Research and experience in cultural context.* Newbury Park, CA: Sage.

Individual racism   The major classifications of racism are individual and personal. Individual racism is evident when personal actions or reactions are overt and exercised with every intention to hurt; destroy; inflict death or wounds; cause violence, hate, or displeasure toward a person, group, or organization based solely on the physical appearance of the subject; or all these (Ponterotto & Petersen, 1993). Racism in the United States has existed since the country's inception. It is an institution that has dramatically shaped U.S. society. European settlers began with overt acts of racial discrimination, such as the enslavement and genocide of African and Native American people. The use of direct force and political subjugation helped White people maintain unconditional authority over non-White inhabitants and elevated White power and privilege. Exploitation of non-Whites also helped constitute much of the rapid economic growth and prosperity seen throughout U.S. history (Jones, 1997). Throughout the years, however, many non-White and White citizens fought against the institutionalization of power based on the color of one's skin. As historic legislation against racial discrimination increased, the semblance of overt racism was replaced by more covert racism so that the generations of institutional and individual racial prejudice continue to affect how members of different races think, act, and feel toward one another. Individual racism may be overt or covert (Sue et al., 1998). Most people are familiar with overt racism because it is easily detectable and takes the form of direct behavioral or verbal racially discriminatory acts. An example is when an Arabic male student is brutally murdered out of hate. Covert racism is more subtle but occurs more often than overt racism and is more easily hidden, denied, or discounted. An example of covert racism is when an employer decides not to hire an Asian American employee because she believes that the employee might drive away business but tells the person that there are no more openings available. A child is not born a racist. Racism is a learned social phenomenon via family, education, religion, the law, and the media. It is difficult to grow up in society without adopting the biases of that society. It takes a strong-willed person to overcome the tendency toward individual racism.

References

Jones, J. M. (1997). *Prejudice and racism* (2nd ed.). New York: McGraw-Hill.

Ponterotto, J. G., & Pedersen, P. B. (1993). *Preventing prejudice: A guide for counselors and educators.* Newbury Park, CA: Sage.

Sue, D. W., Carter, R. T., Casas, J. M., Fouad, N. A., Ivey, A. E., Jensen, M., LaFramboise, T., Manese, J. E., Ponterotto, J. G., & Vazquez-Nutall, E. (1998). *Multicultural counseling competencies: Individual and organizational development.* Thousand Oaks, CA: Sage.

Individualism   Individualism is a belief in the primary importance of the individual and in the virtues of self-reliance and personal independence. It stresses individual initiative, action, and interests (*American Heritage Dictionary*, 2000). The term *individualism* appears to have its roots outside of the North American continent, namely in the French Revolution. It appears that the term *individualism* was first used to describe the negative influence of individual rights on the well-being of the commonwealth. The rising tide of the individual rights movement was feared; it was thought that individualism would make community "crumble away, be disconnected into the dust and powder of individuality" (*American Heritage Dictionary*, 2000, p. 512). In this usage, individualism describes a worldview antagonistic to community and collective social structure (Llewelyn & Kelly, 1980). Individualism was synonymous with liberalism and included the ideas of maximum freedom of the individual, the existence of voluntary groups that individuals could join or leave as they pleased, and equal participation of individuals in group activities. Individualism usually pertains to ethics. One can also speak of metaphysical individualism (that only particular, individual things exist), epistemological individualism (that only individual minds can come to have knowledge), and political individualism (respect for individual rights) (Bellah, 1987). The preferred definition is ethical individualism. It is the expression of the ethics of rational self-interest. It holds that a human being should think and judge independently, respecting nothing more than the sovereignty of his or her mind; thus, it is intimately connected with the concept of autonomy. This seems to be the most popular definition because we live in an affluent society in which people's basic material needs for food, clothing, and shelter are met. The individualism and competitiveness fostered by capitalism cause us to continually evaluate whether our choices are self-serving or ethically correct.

References

American heritage dictionary of the English language (4th ed.). (2000). Boston: Houghton Mifflin.

Bellah, R. N. (1987). The quest for the self: Individualism, morality, politics. In P. Rabinow & W. M. Sullivan (Eds.), *Interpretative social science: A second look.* Berkeley: University of California Press.

Llewelyn, S. P., & Kelly, J. (1980). Individualism in psychology: A case for a new paradigm? *Bulletin of the British Psychological Society, 33,* 407–411.

Industrialized culture   Industrialized culture is found in any nation that is industrial. Industrial countries or nations are characterized by highly developed industries or by being economically dependent mainly on industry. Industrialized culture has survived, adapted, and adopted a higher standard of lifestyle since the industrial revolution. This type of culture exists in several countries: In some, it exists in certain areas, whereas in others it exists throughout the entire country. The industrial revolution that began quietly in Europe in the 18th century triggered a wave of economic, political, social, and cultural changes. This resulted in increased migration between Europe and the Americas. People left farming communities and moved to industrialized cities. People who migrated in the 19th and early 20th centuries went to what were then called Euro-American nations: the United States, Brazil, Uruguay, Chile,

Argentina, Canada, and other areas in the Americas. These Euro-American nations started to become industrialized; as a result, when immigrants from other areas of the world entered, they were compelled to adapt to the ways of the country to which they migrated. This process was called the "melting pot" in the United States (Gall, 1998). Therefore, the industrialized culture is not restricted to certain nations but every nation that depends on an industry for population and economic survival. The industrialized culture can be found in North and South America and other areas of the world.

Reference

Gall, T. (1998). *Worldmark encyclopedia of cultures and daily life* (Vol. 2). Detroit, MI: Gale.

Informant   An informant is a person who gives information. It is also one who supplies cultural or linguistic data in response to interrogation by an investigator ("Sociology," 2003). In the context of field research in the social sciences, informants may be a major source of useful information (Orenstein & Phillips, 1978). They were first used in the 19th century when sociology developed into an independent study. Subjects are called research informants. Social psychologists use informants as a source for their data and are responsible for securing their anonymity and privacy in both quantitative and qualitative research. The informant transmits information from the natural setting to the researcher. The informant must also be well informed. The tasks of the informant include collecting, retaining, and transmitting information. In addition, the informant must be motivated to perform the assigned tasks (Beck, 1960). Distinctions are sometimes made among informants according to the degree of complexity of the data required from them. When they are used for describing data, such as topographical details and buildings (e.g., for the military), and when they are used in credit investigations and in journalism, they are referred to as "sources" (Beck, 1960). An alternate definition of an informant is a linguist who studies a modern language, analyzing the speech of one or more native speakers of that language. The more popular definition of informant is an individual who provides useful and credible information either to a law enforcer regarding felonious criminal activities or to a scientist as a research informant. Payment of informants is discouraged, and their consent should be obtained in advance.

References

Beck, K. (1960). The well-informed informant. In R. N. Adams & J. J. Preiss (Eds.), *The human organization research: Field relationship and techniques.* Homewood, IL: Dorsey.

Orenstein, A., & Phillips, W. R. F. (1978). *Understanding social research: An introduction.* Boston: Allyn & Bacon.

Sociology. (2003). In *Encyclopedia Britannica.* Retrieved from Encyclopedia Britannica Premium Service, http://www.britannica.com/premium.

In-group/out-group   In-group is defined as the social definition of who you are (race, religion, sex, academic major, social class, etc.). This also implies a definition of who you are not. The circle that includes "us" (the in-group) excludes "them" (the out-group). The in-group bias is the tendency to favor one's own group at the expense of the out-group (Brewer, 1979). This "favoring" can manifest in varying degrees. The extreme is a complete exclusion of a group from the moral boundaries of another group. The Nazi treatment of Jews during World War II provides a stark instance of in-group bias. In this situation, there is clearly no question that the Jewish people had been excluded from the moral rules of the Nazis' more "pure" community. It is certain that they did not regard or treat their family and friends the same as they did the concentration camp inhabitants. In this instance, there was an in-group, the German Aryans, and an out-group, the non-Aryans (Wilder & Shapiro, 1984). Obviously, the simple act of categorizing people into members of one's in-group versus one's out-group is enough to trigger discrimination (Hinkle & Schopler, 1986). It is also enough to trigger stereotyping and prejudice. Members of the out-group tend to be stereotyped and evaluated on relatively few dimensions, and they are liked less than in-group members.

References

Brewer, M. B. (1979). In-group bias in the minimal inter-group situation: A cognitive-motivational analysis. *Psychological Bulletin, 86,* 307–324.

Hinkle, S., & Schopler, J. (1986). Bias in the evaluation of in-group and out-group performance. In S. Worchel & W. G. Austin (Eds.), *Psychology of inter-group relations* (pp. 196–212). Chicago: Nelson Hall.

Wilder, D. A., & Shapiro, P. (1984). Facilitation of out-group stereotypes by enhanced in-group identity. *Journal of Experimental Social Psychology, 27,* 431–452.

Institutional racism   Blum (2002) defines institutional racism as "racial inferiorizing or antipathy perpetuated by specific social institutions such as schools, corporations, hospitals, or the criminal justice system as a totality" (p. 9). It is also referred to as "the practices and the nonpractices that help to maintain Black people in a disadvantaged position" (Ghaill, 1999, p. 63). Newman and Newman (1995) note that "social institutions such as family, church, school, business, and government create patterns of injustice and inequality based on the color of a person's skin" (p. 12). Institutional racism may not be intentional, but institutions may still be guilty of such practices. An institution that inadvertently denies access to an already disadvantaged group through exorbitant financial or educational requirements is discriminating without intending to do so. Rex (1986) reported that systematic disadvantage is the result of discrimination; hence, it is difficult to identify and blame any individual for the practice of institutional racism.

References

Blum, L. (2002). *I'm not a racist, but . . .* Ithaca, NY: Cornell University Press.

Ghaill, M. M. (1999). *Contemporary racisms and ethnicities.* Buckingham, UK: Open University Press.

Newman, G., & Newman, L. E. (1995). *Racism: Divided by color.* Springfield, NJ: Enslow.

Rex, J. (1986). *Race and ethnicity.* Milton Keynes, UK: Open University Press.

Intercouple   This is any romantic relationship in which the partners are of different races, religions, cultures, or all three (Reiter, Krause, & Stirlen, in press). Breger and Hill (1998, p. 7) defined these types of relationships at the marital stages as "mixed" or "cross-cultural" marriages—that is, marriages between two people from different linguistic, religious, or ethnic groups or nations. Intercouple relationships, however, do not necessarily have to consist of marital partners. Other terms for this dyad are *interethnic relationships*, in which partners differ in their racial, cultural, and/or religious memberships (Baptiste, 1984), and *intermarriage*, which indicates that individuals in the couple are from different social groups (Merton, 2000) or "denotes marriage across religious, racial, ethnic, or other social divisions" (Smith, 1996, p. 4).

References

Baptiste, D. A., Jr. (1984). Marital and family therapy with racially/culturally intermarried stepfamilies: Issues and guidelines. *Family Relations, 33,* 373–380.

Breger, R., & Hill, R. (Eds.). (1998). *Cross-cultural marriage: Identity and choice.* Oxford, UK/New York: Berg.

Merton, R. K. (2000). Intermarriage and the social structure: Fact and theory. In W. Sollors (Ed.), *Interracialism: Black-White intermarriage in American history literature and law* (pp. 473–491). Oxford, UK: Oxford University Press.

Reiter, M. D., Krause, J., & Stirlen, A. (in press). Inter-couple dating on college campuses. *College Student Journal.*

Smith, R. C. (1996). *Two cultures: One marriage.* Berrien Springs, MI: Andrews University Press.

Intercultural communication   Communication is one of the most important aspects of life. It is through communication that we discover who we are and what the world or our surroundings are like. It allows us to convey our beliefs and views to others as well as fulfill our own needs (Nolan, 1999, p. 33). Intercultural communication has been a topic of study since the 1960s. Samover and Porter, communication scholars, define it as taking place when the two people interacting are from different cultures. Collier and Thomas describe it as interaction between people who think of themselves as different from the other in terms of culture (Guirdham, 1999, p. 193). Intercultural communication is defined as the communication involving individuals of different cultures. It concentrates on face-to-face contact between people. All cultures are different in one way or another, whether it is their language, behavior patterns, or values. Because cultures vary greatly in their views and manners, intercultural communication promotes the realization and the understanding that cultures are different. It is important that one understands the objective culture and the subjective culture. The objective culture includes social, economic, political, and linguistic systems. The subjective culture deals with the everyday thinking and behavior that make up a group of people. If one understood only the objective culture, one would be knowledgeable about that culture but probably would not understand the thinking behind the culture's actions. This is why both are so crucial in accomplishing intercultural communication. To succeed in intercultural communication, all stereotypes must be eliminated. They are usually not correct and cause a misleading sense of understanding or cause people to view an individual in biased ways that in turn support people's stereotypes. The common mistake individuals make when engaging in intercultural communication is not realizing that they are using their own rules in a culture whose rules are not the same. Sometimes, the person does not comply with the "new" rules intentionally and instead tries to push his or her own rules on the system. When engaging in this form of communication, one must be open-minded, patient, and understanding. One should be knowledgeable about the culture so that mistakes can be limited. Young Y. Kim states that the most important goal for attaining intercultural communication competence is to be able to cope with cultural "differences and unfamiliarity, intergroup posture, and the additional stress that is experienced" (as quoted in Bennett, 1998, p. 3). Knowing and understanding the rules and customs of everyday interactions is the most important kind of cultural knowledge for truly understanding and appreciating intercultural communication (Guirdham, 1999, p. 192).

References

Bennett, M. (Ed.). (1998). *Basic concepts of intercultural communication* (pp. 2–6, 154). Yarmouth, ME: Intercultural Press.

Guirdham, M. (1999). *Communicating across cultures* (pp. 192–193). West Lafayette, IN: Purdue University Press.

Nolan, R. (1999). *Communicating & adapting across cultures: Living & working in the global village.* Westport, CT: Greenwood.

Intercultural conflict   Intercultural conflict is a struggle between at least two parties who perceive incompatibility due to a difference in what meaning is produced or interpreted (Hall, 2002). Ting-Toomey and Oetzel (2001) note that "intercultural conflict often starts with different expectations concerning appropriate or inappropriate conflict behavior in a conflict scene" (p. 2). Intercultural conflict is based on cultural ignorance or misunderstanding but is not always caused by miscommunication. Racism and stereotyping may also play a role (Ting-Toomey & Oetzel, 2001). Cahn (1994) suggests three reasons for intercultural conflict in the United States: changing demographic trends of the U.S. population, an increase in intercultural and interracial marriages, and probing to understand other cultures.

References

Cahn, D. D. (1994). *Conflict in personal relationships*. Hillsdale, NJ: Lawrence Erlbaum.

Hall, B. J. (2002). *Among cultures: The challenges of communication*. Belmont, CA: Wadsworth.

Ting-Toomey, S., & Oetzel, J. G. (2001). *Managing intercultural conflict effectively*. Thousand Oaks, CA: Sage.

Interdependent self   Interdependent self is "the sense of being both one and many, of being different from everyone else and like them at the same time" (Elkind, 1994, p. 220). According to Markus and Kitayama (1991), being part of interdependence is recognizing that one is part of a relationship and noticing that the self's behavior is determined by what one thinks are the thoughts, ideas, and actions of others. Hofstede (1997) explains it in terms of business organizations. He found that in low power distance countries, subordinates prefer managers who use a consultative "give-and-take" style, whereas high power distance subordinates prefer the more autocratic approach.

References

Elkind, D. (1994). *Ties that stress: The new family imbalance*. Cambridge, MA: Harvard University Press.

Hofstede, G. (1997). *Cultures and organizations* (2nd ed.). London: McGraw-Hill.

Markus, H., & Kitayama, S. (1991). Culture and the self. *Psychological Review, 98*, 224–253.

Intergenerational conflict   Intergenerational conflict is defined as stresses and disagreements between generations in the family and in society (Bengtson & Achenbaum, 1993). Intergenerational conflict can be defined as the struggle between family members and families to meet the needs of all the members (Cowan, Field, Hanson, Skolnick, & Swanson, 1992). According to Cahn (1994), intergenerational conflict occurs because generational differences are a source of conflict; adult daughters are more likely than adult sons to be caught between work demands and caregiving and to be stressed; and the chances for conflict increase the closer people are and the more time they spend together. Intergenerational conflicts are exaggerated when generations are differentially acculturated in a host culture. When families migrate to a new culture, conflicts often arise between grandparents and their children and also grandchildren born and raised in the host culture.

References

Bengtson, V. L., & Achenbaum, W. A. (1993). *The changing contract across generations*. Hawthorne, NY: de Gruyter.

Cahn, D. D. (1994). *Conflict in personal relationships*. Hillsdale, NJ: Lawrence Erlbaum.

Cowan, P. A., Field, D., Hanson, D., Skolnick, A., & Swanson, G. E. (Eds.). (1992). *Family, self, and society: Toward a new agenda for family research.* Hillsdale, NJ: Lawrence Erlbaum.

Intracouple   This is any romantic relationship in which the partners are from the same race, religion, and culture (Reiter, Krause, & Stirlen, in press). Khatib-Chahidi, Hill, and Paton (1998) discuss this type of couple in terms of homogamy, "where like tends to marry like" (p. 49). Smith (1996) defines homogamy as two persons coming together in a relationship with similar backgrounds. This is based on the predisposition of people to find others who are socially, psychologically, and physically similar to them. The intracouple or homogamous couple is the normative pairing based on societal expectations (Killian, 2002).

References

Khatib-Chahidi, J., Hill, R., & Paton, R. (1998). Chance, choice and circumstance: A study of women in cross-cultural marriages. In R. Breger & R. Hill (Eds.), *Cross-cultural marriage: Identity and choice* (pp. 49–66). Oxford, UK/New York: Berg.

Killian, K. D. (2002). Dominant and marginalized discourses in interracial couples' narratives: Implications for family therapists. *Family Process, 41,* 603–618.

Reiter, M. D., Krause, J., & Stirlen, A. (in press). *College Student Journal.*

Smith, R. C. (1996). *Two cultures: One marriage.* Berrien Springs, MI: Andrews University Press.

Issei   In Japanese, this term literally means "first generation." The word *issei* is derived from the Japanese character for the generation number, in this case, one. The first group of Issei came to the United States between 1885 and 1924 (Niiya, 2001). An Issei is a refugee of Japan, mainly to the United States. Unfortunate economic circumstances in various areas of Japan were a cause for the mass departure of men and women in the late 1890s and early 1900s. Distinct from the Europeans, who were drawn to the United States by advertisers, the majority of Japanese emigrants left to recover their economic situation. Because of the Oriental Exclusion Proclamation of 1907, Issei were not entitled to U.S. citizenship until 1952. Issei who were Japanese born but to some extent raised in the United States became known as *Yobiyosi.* They were tightly bound to their homeland traditions and tended to live in segregated communities, and they upheld their Japanese identity and resisted acculturation (Padilla, Wagatsuma, & Lindholm, 1985). Following Japanese custom, marriages among the Issei were arranged by a *baishakunin* (go-between). Many Issei men saved or borrowed money to return to Japan to meet their prospective brides and take part in the wedding ceremony. Others, for financial or other reasons, had matches arranged by a go-between through exchange of photographs, popularizing the term "picture marriage." Although no stigma is attached to picture marriages, the women still prefer to meet their prospective spouses, if only briefly (Glen, 1986). Today, a small number of pre-1924 Issei are still alive, the majority of whom are women (Niiya, 1993).

References

Glen, E. N. (1986). *Issei, nisei, war brides: Three generations of American women in domestic service.* Philadelphia: Temple University Press.

Niiya, B. (1993). *Japanese American history: An A-to-Z reference from 1868 to the present.* New York: Facts on File.

Niiya, B. (2001). *Encyclopedia of Japanese American history, updated edition: An A-to-Z reference from 1868 to the present.* New York: Facts on File.

Padilla, A. M., Wagatsuma, Y., & Lindholm, K. J. (1985). Acculturation and personality as predictors of stress in Japanese and Japanese Americans. *Journal of Social Psychology, 125,* 295–305.

Item equivalence   Item equivalence means that each item used in cross-cultural studies should have the same meaning in the cultures being studied. Any cross-cultural comparison presupposes cross-culturally identical scale. Data obtained in different cultures are considered incomparable or biased when there are differences in the scales (Berry, Poortinga, Segall, & Dasen, 1992). A lack of equivalence implies that an observed difference on a measurement scale (e.g., a test or questionnaire) is not matched by a corresponding difference on the comparison scale (Berry et al., 1992). Hui and Triandis (1985) noted three different types of equivalence (conceptual, item, and scalar) and the different strategies for assessing equivalence, which include item response theory approaches and factor analytic approaches. Cross-cultural researchers are sensitive to item equivalence when examining, comparing, and contrasting values and variables in different cultures. A number of researchers have demonstrated the use of various techniques for assessing cross-culture equivalence through the highly criticized etic approach (see Etic), in which a measurement structure derived in one culture is assumed to be universal and is applied to all cultures (Ryan, Chan, Ployhart, & Slade, 1999). The emic approach is not without its problems (see Emic). This approach is often impractical because of the need to keep methods and measures standard worldwide (Ryan et al., 1999). Research has focused on diagnosing measurement equivalence in cross-cultural studies (Adler, Schwartz, & Graham, 1989; Mullen, 2002).

References

Adler, N. J., Schwartz, T., & Graham, H. L. (1989). Business negotiations in Canada (French and English speakers), Mexico and the United States. *Journal of Business Research, 15,* 411–429.

Berry, J. W., Poortinga, Y. H., Segall, M. H., & Dasen, P. R. (1992). *Cross-cultural psychology: Research and applications.* Cambridge, UK: Cambridge University Press.

Hui, C. H., & Triandis, H. C. (1985). Measurement in cross-cultural psychology: A review and comparison of strategies. *Journal of Cross-Cultural Psychology, 16,* 131–152.

Mullen, M. R. (2002). Diagnosing measurement equivalence in cross-national research. *Journal of International Business Studies, 26*(4), 573–600.

Ryan, A. M., Chan, D., Ployhart, R. E., & Slade, L. A. (1999). Employee attitude surveys in a multinational organization: Considering language and culture in assessing measurement equivalence. *Personnel Psychology, 52*(1), 37–55.

J

Jewish culture Jewish culture is centered on holidays and fasts following the traditional value placed on the rituals and social laws in relation to God and society (Bloch, 1978). Also known as Judaism, the Jewish culture's foundation—rich history, life values, and understanding of the world—is a direct representation of the sacred meaning placed on its holidays (Greenberg, 1988). In addition, the culture's expression is cultivated within what is held very highly among the Jewish—their holy days. These days provide an alternative means of becoming educated on the teachings and practices of Judaism (Greenberg, 1988). Another important part of the culture is the Torah, which symbolizes a particular way of life. The Torah is a scroll composed of the first five books of the Old Testament and is used in a synagogue. The Jewish covenant states that in accepting the Torah, Jews have agreed to persist in their quest of universal redemption by living meaningful lives, full of great accomplishment and purpose (Greenberg, 1988). One of the most sacred days to the Jewish people is Rosh Hashanah, known as the Jewish New Year and commonly celebrated in September or October. Although not originally spoken of in the Hebrew Bible in terms of its celebration, it was referred to as "the day of the blowing of the horn," and now it is understood to be a day of rest (Feliner, 1995). Yom Kippur is another important day, once concentrating specifically on sacrificial rituals of atonement. It was to be taken as a day of spiritual cleansing and forgiveness of sins. A person would not only ask forgiveness from God but also ask forgiveness from the person to whom he or she wronged, whose pardon would in turn guarantee his or her own sins absolved (Bloch, 1978; Feliner, 1995). In addition to holidays, Jews used terms that denoted special meaning to them, such as the *Sukkah*, which symbolizes protection and peace, similar to a safe place. It was meant to provide security to those who prayed for it during times of distress (Bloch, 1978). Included in the holiday festivities is mealtime. During Passover, symbolic foods are arranged on the dinner table on a Seder (i.e., order) plate. On it is *haroset* (chopped-up fruit and spices, wine, or all three), which symbolizes the mortar used for building by enslaved Hebrews, and *karpas* (green vegetables), a symbol of spring. Also on the plate is *z'roa*, a paschal sacrifice usually represented by a roasted lamb shank bone; *beitzah*, a roasted egg used as a festival sacrifice; and *maror*, bitter herbs emblematic of the bitterness of slavery. Passover serves as a time for family, friends, tradition, and happiness. It also serves as a reminder of the need to continue to work hard and a reminder of a time of enslavement. Jews are also to open their hearts and help those less fortunate during this time (Feliner, 1995).

References

Bloch, A. P. (1978). *The biblical and historical background of the Jewish holy days.* New York: Ktav.

Feliner, J. B. (1995). *In the Jewish tradition: A year of food and festivities.* New York: Friedman.

Greenberg, R. I. (1988). *The Jewish way: Living the holidays.* New York: Summit.

Johrei Fellowship   Johrei Fellowship was founded in 1931 by a Japanese philosopher, Mokichi Okada, also known as *Meishu-sama.* This is a contemporary religion that appeals to both Christians and Buddhists and represents a blend of multicultural influences (Dresser, 1996). Johrei means purification of the spirit, and the three main tenets of this Japanese-based religion are to give service to others, to appreciate beauty and art, and to care for one's physical health. Congregations are located in Vancouver, Canada, and many U.S. cities, including Miami; Los Angeles; San Diego; Fresno, California; Denver; and Boston. Offerings include monetary donations as well as vegetables, cake, cookies, kelp, and seaweed.

Reference

Dresser, N. (1996). *Rules of etiquette for a changing society.* New York: John Wiley.

K

Karoshi *Karoshi* is defined by Evans (1997) as death from overwork. Karoshi is primarily used for those in pursuit of workers compensation, especially in cases dealing with cardiovascular diseases caused by a tremendous work schedule and the profession. Uehata (1980) coined the term *karoshi*. He defined it as

> a permanent disability or death brought on by worsening high blood pressure or arteriosclerosis resulting in diseases of the blood vessels in the brains, such as cerebral hemorrhage, subarachnoidal hemorrhage, and cerebral infarction, and acute heart failure and myocardial infarction induced by conditions such as ischemic heart disease. (p. 1)

Karoshi became known in Japan in the early 1970s, but the public did not know of its existence until almost 20 years later ("Worked to Death," 1991). Annually, 30 deaths are attributed to karoshi, for which the government pays punitive damages to the families. Most karoshi cases occur among blue-collar workers; seldom are white-collar workers victims ("Japan Says," 1992).

References

Evans, T. M. (1997). *A dictionary of Japanese loanwords.* Westport, CT: Greenwood.

Japan says an executive worked himself to death. (1992, July 16). *New York Times,* p. D4.

Uehata, T. (1980). A medical study of Karoshi. In *National Defense Council for victims of Karoshi.* Tokyo: Mado-sha.

Worked to death in Japan. (1991, March). *World Press Review,* p. 51.

Kibei The *American Heritage Dictionary* (2000) defines *kibei* as "a person born in the United States of Japanese immigrant parents and educated chiefly in Japan" (p. 516). Prior to World War II, these individuals were sent to Japan for purposes of education, socialization, or both, with the full expectation that they would later return to the United States. Glenn (1986) noted that this move by Japanese parents was motivated by economic reasons and by the desire to have their children imbibe the Japanese way of life and not to become Americanized. They wanted their children to have traditional Japanese values, such as respect for the elderly, discipline, and appreciation of the arts. Those who returned were perceived as fundamentally Japanese in their outlook, speech, and behavior. Their "Japaneseness" became a handicap in the dominant culture. They also did not fit in with the other first-generation Japanese *(nisei)*, and they tended to marry other kibei. Many never became fluent in English, and this resulted in limited occupational choices. The kibei comprised only a small portion of the population of Japanese Americans who were incarcerated during World War II. Glenn postulated that 9.2% of the population in one evacuation camp was kibei. Galen Fisher's opposition to mass evacuation of enemy aliens in 1942, as reported by Dudley (1997), evaluated first-generation Japanese as loyal, with possibly the exception of the kibei. Niiya (1993) reported that the kibei remain a subgroup of the nisei, distinct in their degree of Japanese and English language ability, their socialization as Japanese or Americans, and their identity.

References

American heritage dictionary of the English language (4th ed.). (2000). Boston: Houghton Mifflin.

Dudley, W. (1997). *Asian Americans: Opposing viewpoints.* San Diego, CA: Green Haven.

Glenn, E. K. (1986). *Issei, neissei war bride: Three generations of Japanese women in domestic service.* Philadelphia: Temple University Press.

Niiya, B. (1993). *Japanese American history. An A-to-Z reference from 1868 to the present.* New York: Facts on File.

Kirpan   The *kirpan* is a knife worn by members of the Khalsa Sikh religious community that originated in the Punjab area of northwest India. The kirpan is one of the five holy symbols these followers must wear after they are formally initiated. This is a tradition that dates back 300 years. The five K's must be worn at all times, even when bathing or sleeping: long hair *(kesh)*, a comb in the hair *(kangha)*, a steele bracelet on the right wrist *(kara)*, special cotton undershorts *(kachha)*, and a sword *(kirpan)* held close to the body by means of a shoulder harness. The kirpan has blunted sides, an approximately 3-inch blade, and is not intended to cause harm (Dresser, 1996).

Reference

Dresser, N. (1996). *Rules of etiquette for a changing society.* New York: John Wiley.

Koro   This is a term from a Malaysian word meaning "tortoise" (Yap, 1965). It involves the sensation that one's penis is retracting into the abdomen and the belief that when fully retracted death will result. There are frantic attempts to keep the penis from retracting. This effort may result in physical damage. Many cases have been described in Southeast Asia, but there have also been cases in non-Asian individuals (Gaw, 2001). Koro is predominantly a male affliction, but Burnstein and Gaw (1990) reported females with anxiety over breast and labial involution.

References

Burnstein, R. L., & Gaw, A. C. (1990). Proposed classification for *DSM IV*. *American Journal of Psychiatry, 147,* 1670–1674.

Gaw, A. C. (2001). *Concise guide to cross-cultural psychiatry.* Washington, DC: American Psychiatric Publishing.

Yap, P. M. (1965). *Comparative psychiatry. A theoretical framework.* Toronto: University of Toronto Press.

Kwanzaa   This is a 7-day event that starts on December 26 and ends on January 1. It was established to honor the African tradition of African Americans. Kwanzaa is derived from the Kiswahili phrase "*mutunda ya kwanza*" ("first fruits of the harvest"), which is a depiction of the celebration of harvesting the first crops in traditional Africa. This cultural celebration was started in 1966 by Dr. Maulana Karenga, a Black studies professor at California State University (Karenga, 1972). Kwanzaa was formally established as a nonreligious celebration of family and social values. There are some variations in practice, however, including the degree to which Christian theology is incorporated into the ceremony (Hutchinson, 1997). Kwanzaa celebrates each day with one of its seven established principles: *Umoja,* which means unity; *Kujichagulia,* which means self-determination; *Ujima,* which stands for collective responsibility; *Ujamaa,* which means cooperative economics; *Nia,* which means purpose; *Kuumba,* which means creativity; and *Imani,* which means faith. These principles are referred to as *Nguzo Saba* and should be used for guidance while meditating and during daily activities. Each day of Kwanzaa should begin with the greeting "*Habari Gani,*" and the response should be the same, accompanied by that day's principle. During the evening, the family lights a candle in the *kinara,* which is a seven-branched candelabrum that represents parents and ancestors, and the *mshumaa* (seven candles), which represent the seven principles of Kwanzaa. Family members converse about the principle of the day (Riley, 1995). Kwanzaa includes not only the celebration of social values but also gift giving and an African feast, which is referred to as *karamu.* Kwanzaa celebration is a cultural nationalist movement that seeks to preserve unity and an appreciation of an African diaspora history and culture (Hutchinson, 1997).

References

Hutchinson, J. F. (1997). *Cultural portrayals of African Americans.* Westport, CT: Bergin & Garvey.

Karenga, R. M. (1972). *Kwanzaa.* Chicago: Institute of Positive Education.

Riley, D. W. (1995). *The complete Kwanzaa: Celebrating our cultural harvest.* New York: HarperCollins.

L

La Fiesta La Fiesta is a September weekend event that takes place in Santa Fe, New Mexico. At this event, there is the burning of *Zozobra*, a 40-foot-tall puppet stuffed with shredded paper. Zozobra means Old Man Gloom, and it represents everyone's bad luck. This yearly ritual has been taking place since 1924. The burning symbolizes the destruction of one's problems. The ritual begins at dusk, marked by the beating of 12 slow gongs. The effigy will moan and groan as green, yellow, and red fireworks light up the sky. Zozobra's enemy, the red-clad fire dancer, eventually ignites it. This event is supposed to provide a cathartic effect on the thousands of spectators, who afterward participate in street dance, concerts, arts and craft shows, and children's and pet parades (Dresser, 1996). The religious roots of La Fiesta date back to the 17th century, when Don Diego de Vargas vowed to the Holy Mother Mary to bring Spanish back to Santa Fe. To celebrate Vargas's success, a special parade features individuals carrying a statue of *La Conquistadora*, America's oldest Madonna (Dresser, 1996).

Reference

Dresser, N. (1996). *Rules of etiquette for a changing society*. New York: John Wiley.

Laotian The Laotian are people from the lowland country of Laos who speak the Lao language. Approximately 85% of the inhabitants practice Theravada Buddhism (Hockings, 1995). Laos is a landlocked Southeast Asian country bordered by Myanmer (Burma), Thailand, Vietnam, Cambodia, and China (Ember & Ember, 2001). "*Pathet Lao*," which means "the country of Lao," is the customary name for the Laos country and was applied to the insurgent Communists during the Second Indochina War. Today, the country is named the Laos Peoples Democratic Republic (Levinson, 1995). During the eighth century, Tai-speaking peoples from the north arrived, but they were later displaced by the larger number of Laos migrants who had already settled there. The area emerged as a separate political entity by the 14th century (Levinson, 1998). During the 18th century, the province remained separated variously under Thai, Burma, and Vietnamese influence and control, and the French entered in 1893. By the 19th century, France controlled it as part of French Indochina. In 1954, the Laos slowly moved toward independence because Japan had taken the region from France in World War II. Due to the instability of the government and the lag in economic development, Laos remains one of the poorest nations in the world. Several urban Chinese and Vietnamese have assimilated into the Lao culture; an ethnic hierarchy exists, however, placing ethnic Lao at the apex (Ember & Ember, 2001). The term *ethnic minorities* refers to the hill tribes (Levinson, 1998). The ethnic composition accounts indicate that there are 48 ethnic groups in Laos; findings suggest, however, that there are 68 or more different groups. Ethnic Lao and minorities can be divided into a threefold categorization based on language: The Lao Loum or Lao Lum (lowland) includes those who speak Lao-Tai languages; the Lao-Theung (midland), which is the second major linguistic-based group; and the Lao Soung (highland).

References

Ember, M., & Ember, C. (Eds.). (2001). *Countries and their cultures* (Vol. 3, pp. 1247–1251). New York: Macmillan/Gale.

Hockings, P. (1995). *Principles of visual anthropology.* New York: Mouton.

Levinson, D. (Ed.). (1995). *East and Southeast Asia* (Vol. 5). Boston: Hall.

Levinson, D. (1998). *Ethnic groups worldwide: A ready reference handbook.* Phoenix, AZ: Oryx.

Latah   This is a Malaysian term that means "ticklish" and involves imitative behavior that seems beyond the individual's control. It is often characterized by hypersensitivity to sudden fright or startle, often with echolalia, command obedience, and dissociative or trancelike behavior. Afflicted individuals typically respond to a sudden stimulus with exaggerated startle, sometimes dropping or throwing objects held in the hand and often uttering obscene words. Most of those with latah are middle-age women of low socioeconomic status (Gaw, 2001).

Reference

Gaw, A. G. (2001). *A concise guide to cross-cultural psychiatry.* Washington, DC: American Psychiatric Publishing.

Law of Contagion   This is also called the Law of Contact. The law states that things that have been in contact with each other continue to interact after separation (Frazer, 1959). Emphasis is on objects or people that have been in physical contact. This is the latter of the principles of thought on which magic is based. Law of Contagion follows from the Law of Similarity (Frazer, 1951), which states that like things produce like things, or that an effect resembles its cause (Frazer, 1994). From these principles, the magician makes inferences. From the Law of Similarity, the magician infers that he or she can produce any effect that he or she desires just by imitating it. Also, from the Law of Contact, the magician infers that whatever he or she does to a material object will equally affect the person who once had contact with or possessed the object. This is the reason why, when performing a spell, the practitioner may have in his or her possession something personal of the person, such as a lock of hair, nail clippings, a piece of clothing, or a photograph, for whom the spell is being cast (Frazer, 1951). A branch of magic such as contagious may be understood under the common name of sympathetic magic. In sympathetic magic, there must exist a cause-and-effect relationship; if not, the magician's inferences would never function. Charms based on the Law of Contagion or contagious magic are founded on the connection of contiguity (Frazer, 1951), which is two events occurring at the same time or the same place (Frazer, 1994). Anything that has come into contact with any form of power or person acquires some of that power (Jones & Zusne, 1989). An example of a charm based on contagious magic is when a magician uses hair and nails of a victim, or some object close to the person, in a ceremony designed to cause pain (Frazer, 1951). This illustrates the principle of contiguity that operates to establish relations between ideas of objects or events in close proximity (Jones & Zusne, 1989). Practice based on the Law of Contact or Contagion is derived from a false consensus of natural law in its final analysis (Frazer, 1959). When there is a cause-and-effect relationship that is not firm, magical modes of thinking may result (Frazer, 1994).

References

Frazer, J. (1951). *The golden bough: A study in magic and religion.* New York: Macmillan.

Frazer, J. (1959). The new golden bough. In P. H. Gaster (Ed.), *A new abridgment of the classic works* (Vol. 1). Hillsdale, NJ: Phillips.

Frazer, J. (1994). The golden bough. In J. Frazer (Ed.), *A study in magic and religion* (Vols. 2–3). New York: Oxford University Press.

Jones, W., & Zusne, L. (1989). *Anomalistic psychology: A study of magical thinking.* Mahwah, NJ: Lawrence Erlbaum.

Law of Similarity   This law states that like things produce like things or that an effect resembles its cause (Frazer, 1981). This is the first of two sublaws contained within the Law of Association; the second is the Law of Contact or Contagion. Objects similar to one another tend to be seen as a unit (Goldstein, 2000). Two principles of thought on which magic is based are that like produces like, or effect resembles its cause, and that things that have been in contact with each other continue to act on each other after physical contact has been severed. The second principle is contained in the Law of Contagion (Frazer, 1959). Practices of the Law of Similarity are based on homeopathy magic or imitative magic. It is the belief that resemblance or contact with a target and imitating a desired outcome through a specific procedure will cause it to occur (Beals & Hoijer, 1971). A well-known application of homeopathy magic is an attempt to destroy or injure an image of a target (Frazer, 1994). Another principle that corresponds to the "two roots" of sympathetic magic is contagious magic, which is an effort to manipulate an object to influence a person or object directly associated with it. Both principles of sympathetic magic are a misapplication of the association of ideas (Frazer, 1994). Homeopathy assumes that things that resemble each other are alike and mistakenly assumes that when things have been in contact with one another they are always in contact. The principles act on one another at a distance through secret sympathy (Frazer, 1994). The most familiar example of the Law of Similarity is that in many cultures it is believed that by stepping on footprints it is possible to injure the feet that made them (Frazer, 1959, 1981). Numerous traditional cultures are known for using different forms of magic that resist logic and reason. Magical thinking exists in everyday life and is not limited to traditional cultures (Frazer, 1959, 1981).

References

Beals, R. L., & Hoijer, H. (1971). *An introduction to anthropology.* Aurora, CO: Scuzzydog.

Frazer, J. (1959). The new golden bough. In P. H. Gaster (Ed.), *A new abridgment of the classic works* (Vol. 1). Hillsdale, NJ: Phillips.

Frazer, J. (1981). *The golden bough: The roots of religion and folklore* (Vols. 1–2). New York: Avenal.

Frazer, J. (1994). The golden bough. In J. Frazer (Ed.), *A study in magic and religion* (Vols. 2–3). New York: Oxford University Press.

Goldstein, S. (2000). *Cross-cultural explorations: Activities in culture & psychology.* Boston: Allyn & Bacon.

Low-contact culture   Cultures differ in the degree to which physical contact is permissible and for whom (see Personal Space). In low-contact cultures, touch occurs in limited circumstances. Low-contact cultures include the British, other northern European cultures, and those of North America and Japan. Too much contact in these cultures is viewed as intruding on a person's privacy. When low-contact cultures associate with high-contact cultures, the person from a low-contact culture may be viewed as unapproachable, distant, and hostile, whereas the person from a high-contact culture may be viewed as pushy and possibly intrusive. Very little touching can be expected from low-contact cultures such as that of Japan. Low-contact cultures differ from high-contact cultures in the amount of personal space that people require to feel comfortable (Gudykunst, 1998). People from low-contact cultures may feel uneasy when their personal space is invaded. People in low-contact cultures touch each other less frequently, preserve more interpersonal space, and verbalize in a softer tone of voice. Low-contact cultures are known as low-immediacy cultures. There is a greater reliance on verbal communication with less emphasis given to feeling, and almost all information is conveyed in the message (Shiraev & Levy, 2000). Schedules are rigid, and time is tangible. Knowledge is obtained through analytical reasoning and written procedures; laws and policies are more important than oral agreements (Henderson, 1994).

References

Gudykunst, W. (1998). *Bridging differences: Effective intergroup communication* (3rd ed.). Thousand Oaks, CA: Sage.

Henderson, G. (1994). *Social work interventions: Helping people of color.* Westport, CT: Bergin & Garven.

Shiraev, E., & Levy, D. (2000). *Introduction to cross-cultural psychology: Critical thinking and contemporary applications.* Boston: Allyn & Bacon.

M

Machismo   This is a Latino American cultural value associated with the Latin male. It is a gender role behavior that alludes to the assumed cultural expectation for men to be dominant in social relationships (Yep, 1995). It includes both positive and negative evaluations. From the positive perspective, machismo imbibes courage and responsibility, and the male is the family protector (Sorenson & Siegel, 1992). The negative connotations include being irresponsible, domineering, jealous, violent, insensitive to women, unfaithful, promiscuous, and abusive; abusing alcohol; and having antisocial and narcissistic characteristics (Castro, Proescholdbell, Albeita, & Rodriquez, 1999). Boys may be socialized into a machismo lifestyle by older youths and men (Arcaya, 1999).

References

Arcaya, J. (1999). Hispanic American boys and adolescent males. In A. M. Horne & M. S. Kiselica (Eds.), *Handbook of counseling boys and adolescent males: A practitioner's guide* (pp. 101–116). Thousand Oaks, CA: Sage.

Castro, F. G., Proescholdbell, R. J., Albeita, L., & Rodriquez, D. (1999). Ethnic and cultural minority groups. In B. S. McCrady & E. E. Epstein (Eds.), *Additions: A comprehensive guide* (pp. 499–526). New York: Oxford University Press.

Sorenson, S. B., & Siegel, J. M. (1992). Gender, ethnicity and sexual assault: Findings from a Los Angeles study. *Journal of Social Issues, 48,* 93–104.

Yep, G. A. (1995). Communicating the HIV/AIDS risk to Hispanic populations: A review and integration. In A. M. Padilla (Ed.), *Hispanic psychology: Critical issues in theory and research.* Thousand Oaks, CA: Sage.

Macroculture   This term refers to the national or shared culture of a nation or state. It is a shared core culture. It consists of a set of values, formation of ideas, and symbols. The values, ideologies, and symbols of such a culture may also be shared by microcultures within the larger state (Banks, 1994). Although the microcultures all share, to some degree, the features of the macroculture, they each express them differently. The United States is an example of a macroculture that consists of a number of microcultures, but representatives of any one of these microcultures can claim distinctiveness, autonomy, and educational rights (Webster, 1997). The term *macroculture* is frequently favored over *majority* or *dominant culture*. The macroculture in the United States may be described as Anglo-Western European. As a sociological term, it deals with the language, religion, and customs of the larger culture (Mitchell & Salsbury, 1999).

References

Banks, J. R. (1994). *Multiethnic education: Theory and practice.* Needham Heights, MA: Allyn & Bacon.

Mitchell, B. M., & Salsbury, R. E. (1999). *Encyclopedia of multicultural education.* Westport, CT: Greenwood.

Webster, Y. O. (1997). *Against the multicultural agenda: A critical thinking alternative.* Westport, CT: Praeger.

Mainstream The most popular usage for the term *mainstream* is to describe a demographic majority. Over time, this term has come to pertain to a cultural meaning rather than a demographic one. Some components of mainstream culture are style of clothing, demeanor, speech, and food. Other terms for mainstream culture are *majority culture* and *dominant culture*. Factors considered as fitting the norm or standard are suggestive of a mainstream culture. The term *mainstream* dates back to the 1800s, regarding literary trends and music. Other aspects of mainstream phenomena include Ramirez's (1991) examples of mythical ideas based on qualitative comparisons of human characteristics ranging from skin color to gender intelligence and competence in arts and sciences. Scholars have defined mainstream as the act of placing children with disabilities in regular education classrooms (Bilken, 1992; Knoblock, 1982). Mainstreaming was formally used by psychologists to define the release of patients from a mental institution to the real world. The fervor of this movement occurred in the 1960s following John F. Kennedy's address to Congress in 1963. Sue (1990) emphasized the mainstream culture's approach to counseling and its negative impact on working with minority clients. He referred to the mainstream culture approach to counseling as generic and proposed new approaches to counseling Third World clients. Katz (1985) described mainstream culture as White American culture and reported that their values and beliefs have influenced the practice of counseling and psychotherapy.

References

Bilken, D. (1992). *Schooling without labels.* Philadelphia: Temple University Press.

Katz, J. (1985). The sociopolitical nature of counseling. *The Counseling Psychologist, 13,* 615–624.

Knoblock, P. (1982). *Teaching and mainstreaming autistic children.* Denver, CO: Love.

Ramirez, J. D. (1991). *Final report: The longitudinal study of immersion strategy, early-exit and late-exit transitional bilingual education programs for language minority children.* San Mateo: CA: Aquirre International.

Sue, D. (1990). *Counseling the culturally different: Theory and practice* (2nd ed.). New York: John Wiley.

Marginal man   Robert Park (1928) studied human migration and coined the term *marginal man*. A marginal man, not specifically limited to any culture or person, has a feeling of suspension between his own original culture and another culture in which he inhabits. This person fits into neither culture nor society but, rather, denies both, desiring at times one while rejecting the other but never fully living in either one. The marginal individual resides on the margin of two distinct societies and cultures, which never combine into one culture or reach integration (Leung, 1994). One explanation of this phenomenon indicates that people of the same culture join together and view other societies with more scrutiny, which results in finding faults and ensuing feelings of fear and hatred. The concept of marginal man also developed through the theories of ethnocentrism and in-group/out-group behaviors. For example, group solidarity correlates to a great extent with animosity toward an out-group. Psychologically living in two or more different and often antagonistic cultures results in the development of a marginal behavior. The marginal personality type occurs at a time and place in which there is a significant merging of cultures and people. Such people find themselves always on the margins rather than comfortably integrated. The positive aspect is that marginal persons are by definition more civilized human beings. They can observe their own group and other groups with considerable objectivity. Because of personal detachment, they can learn to accept differences, develop wide appreciations, and make mature adjustments (Davis, 1997). The intercultural adaptation of an individual and his or her psychological adjustment concludes that cultural shock and cultural adaptation may lead to personal development over time or result in marginality. Factors such as personality characteristics, technical skills, and communication behavior may determine an individual's adaptation to cultural change (Kim, 1989). The intensity of urban change may lead to a "cultural fatigue" toward schizophrenia, usually if an individual does not learn to accept either integration or objective nonconformity (Leung, 1994). Stonequist (1937) described the marginal man as one who experiences psychological uncertainty between two or more social worlds. In this uncomfortable situation, the marginal man experiences all kinds of discords and harmonies, repulsions and attractions of these different worlds.

References

Davis, B. (1997). Marginality in pluralistic society. *Psi Chi, 2*(1), 28–31.

Kim, Y. Y. (1989). Intercultural adaptation. In M. K. Asante & W. B. Gudykunst (Eds.), *Handbook of international and intercultural communication.* Newbury Park, CA: Sage.

Leung, W. (1994). Survival of the marginal person from a city in transition: Resolution of the Hong Kong mentality in films set in America. *Regent Journal of Film and Video, 1,* 2.

Park, R. (1928). Human migration and the marginal man. *American Journal of Sociology, 6,* 881–893.

Stonequist, E. V. (1937). *The Marginal Man—A study in personality and culture conflict.* New York: Scribner.

Marianismo   Marianismo is a stereotyped gender role of females in Mexican society and culture. Marianismo, the female counterpart of machismo, is character-ized by hyperfeminine behavior. It is the belief that women are morally and spiritually superior to men, allowing a woman to place her needs after those of her family and spouse. The "Mariana" is also pure; submissive to her father, brothers, and spouse; and lacks sexual desires. Unfortunately, this misconception has been accepted as an unjus-tified generalization of a woman's behavior, most notably in Mexican culture. The his-torical meanings of marianismo are both cultural specific and encountered in many regions of the Hispanic culture. The word marianismo was believed to signify a move-ment within the Roman Catholic Church and its theology, emphasizing dedication to the Virgin Mary, who was both a virgin and a Madonna. Marianismo, however, is not a religious practice (Stevens, 1994). Being a figure of worship, the Virgin Mary sym-bolizes the ideal Mariana, thus contributing to the notion of marianismo. As such, she was, in the religious sense, spiritually better than men (Comas-Diaz, 1988). Since the 1970s, marianismo has taken on a new meaning. In conjunction with the women's movement, marianismo has evolved into an idea of feminine spiritual superiority, which teaches that women are semidivine, morally superior to and spiritually stronger than men, and have a much greater capacity for sacrifice (Stevens, 1994). In Hispanic folk culture, marianismo is a characterization of the ideal personality of women. Throughout the literature, this ideal woman is emotional, kind, instinctive, whimsical, docile, compliant, vulnerable, and unassertive. Symbolically, the Mariana is also a representation of a woman's power to produce a living human being from within her own body (Stevens, 1994). Consequently, she has a higher status in the community if she has children. Therefore, marianismo alludes to the expectation that the ideal wife or mother is required to be immaculate and spiritually superior to men. This translates into a kind of sex-based role behavior in which the ideal woman is expected to suffer without complaining and to place the needs of her husband and children before her own wishes and desires (Enos, 1996).

References

Comas-Diaz, L. (1988). *Women of color: Integrating ethnic and gender identities in psychotherapy.* New York: Guilford.

Enos, R. (1996). *Correctional case management.* Cincinnati, OH: Anderson.

Stevens, E. P. (1994). Marianismo: The other face of machismo in Latin America. In G. M. Yeager (Ed.), *Confronting change, challenging tradition: Women in Latin American history* (No. 7). Wilmington, DE: Jaguar Books on Latin America.

Matriarchal   This is a hypothetical social system in which women empower familial and political authority. It is used to describe a society in which power and property are held by women and handed down through matrilineal descent also controlled by women or dominated by women with the traditional qualities. A matriarchal figure shows strength and assurance as the most respected in the group: "My grandmother was a powerful, matriarchal figure." Under the influence of Darwin's theories of evolution and particularly the work of the Swiss anthropologist J. J. Bachofen (1815–1887), some 19th-century scholars believed that matriarchy followed a stage of general promiscuity and preceded male superiority (patriarchy) in human society's evolutionary sequence. Like other elements of the evolutionist view of culture, the concept of matriarchy as a universal stage of development is now generally discredited, and the modern consensus is that a strictly matriarchal society has never existed. In societies in which matrilineal descent occurs, however, access to socially powerful positions is arbitrated through the maternal line of relations. The Minangkabau social system in Sumatra is a matriarchal example for several reasons. There is an archetypal maternal symbol, a dominant symbol in anthropological terms, who condenses in her being primitive principles of conduct. According to these principles, the mother-child bond is sacred, part of natural law. Being grounded in natural law, customs associated with matrilineal descent are treated as an absolute part of the foundation of Minangkabau identity. The defining principles of conduct in family, clan, and village life revolve around men and women being connected through females by a common ancestress. Not all matrilineal societies should be labeled matriarchal, however, nor does this imply female dominance or male subordination. Although Minangkabau men have important roles as leaders in some realms of social or public life, their titles are inherited through females, and their political activities are established not only in the matrilineal principle but also in women's ceremonies. Women are leaders in the public realm by virtue of the life-cycle ceremonies revolving around tradition and face-to-face political action. Women's life-cycle ceremonies soil the traditional political atmosphere by bringing members of the different clans together. Women nurture and uphold tradition (called *adat*) in today's world by giving male and female leaders and opinion makers an opportunity to perform and uphold their duties to their clan. Because women follow the old ways in their ceremonies, men have a moral obligation to also follow these ways (Sanday, 2002). Examples of matrilineal societies with high female status include the Khasi (India), Innu/Naskapi (Canada), Musuo (China), Tuareg (Sahara), Keres (New Mexico), Minangkabau (Sumatra), Haudenosaunee (New York/ Ontario), Amahuaca (Peru), Seri (Mexico), and Vanatinai (Pacifica) (Dashu, 2000).

References

Dashu, M. (2000). *Review: The myth of matriarchal prehistory: Why an invented past won't give women a future by Cynthia Eller.* Boston: Beacon.

Sanday, P. R. (2002). *Women at the center: Life in a modern matriarchy.* Ithaca, NY: Cornell University Press.

Melting pot   The term *melting pot* refers to the idea that societies formed by immigrant cultures, religions, and ethnic groups will produce new social and cultural forms. The notion derives from the pot in which metals are melted at great heat, melding together into a new compound with great strength and other advantages. In comparison with assimilation, it implies the ability of new or minor groups to affect the values of the dominant group. Sometimes, it is referred to as amalgamation, opposing the views of both assimilation and pluralism (Laubeová, 2000). In social science, the term is defined as a society composed of many different cultures—a place where people of different ethnic groups are brought together and can assimilate or integrate, such as in a culturally diverse region or country, and a place where immigrants of different cultures or races form an integrated society. The United States is a prime example of a country accepting immigrants from throughout the world, historically combining the different component metals—represented by immigrants from various countries—into the new metal, Americans. Traditionally, the United States has been described as a melting pot—a place where the previous identities of each immigrant group are melted down to create an integrated, uniform society. Although the term *melting pot* may be applied to many countries, such as Brazil, Bangladesh, or even France, mostly referring to increased levels of mixed race and culture, it is predominantly used with reference to the United States and the creation of the American nation as a distinct "new breed of people" amalgamated from many various groups of immigrants. This is roughly referred to as the process of Americanization. The theory of the melting pot has been criticized as both unrealistic and racist because it has focused on the Western heritage and excluded non-European immigrants. Also, despite its proclaimed "melting" character, results have been assimilationist (Laubeová, 2000). The history of the melting pot theory can be traced to 1782 when J. Hector de Crevecoeur, a French settler in New York, envisioned the United States not only as a land of opportunity but also as a society in which individuals of all nations are melted into a new race of men, whose efforts and posterity would one day cause changes in the world (Parrillo, 1997). The new nation welcomed virtually all immigrants from Europe in the belief that the United States would become, at least for Whites, the melting pot of the world. This idea was adopted by the historian Frederick Jackson Turner in 1893, who updated it with the frontier thesis. Turner believed that the challenge of frontier life was the country's most crucial force, allowing Europeans to be "Americanized" by the wilderness (Takaki, 1993). Since the 1960s, many Americans have rejected the melting pot metaphor in favor of the image of the mosaic, a picture created by assembling many small stones or tiles. In a mosaic, each piece retains its own distinctive identity while contributing to a larger design or commonality. Advocates of the mosaic metaphor assert that it better represents the diverse multicultural society of the United States. Today, many Americans value their immigrant heritage as an important part of their identity. Different countries have different combinations of minorities within their borders. In the United States, nationality is quite widely assumed to be hyphenated. Even the aboriginal population is identified as "Native American" to distinguish it from Anglo-American, African American, and so on. Accordingly, the United States is perceived throughout the world as a successful experiment in ethnic mixing; to many, it is considered the greatest melting pot.

References

Laubeová, L. (2000). *Encyclopedia of the world's minorities*. Chicago: Fitzroy Dearborn.

Parrillo, V. (1997). *Strangers to these shores. Race and ethnic relations in the United States.* Boston: Allyn & Bacon.

Takaki, R. (1993). *A different mirror. A history of multicultural America.* Boston: Little, Brown.

Mestizo   This is a term of Spanish origin describing people of mixed racial background or combined ancestry. In Hispanic America, the term originally referred to the children of one European and one American Indian parent. Originally the term meant the offspring of a European (Spaniard) and Indian ancestry (Amerindians). The children of these unions became known as Mestizos, which originates from the Spanish word meaning mixed. The modern connotation of this term means any non-White individual who is fluent in Spanish and observes Hispanic cultural norms. The term also became common for all people of mixed European and indigenous ancestry in the Spanish American colonies. Mestizos officially make up the majority of the population in Mexico, El Salvador, Honduras, Nicaragua, Colombia, Venezuela, and Chile and are significant in most other Hispanic countries, with the exception of Cuba and the Dominican Republic. Many Americans of Hispanic and Latino origin identify themselves as Mestizos as well, particularly those who also identify themselves as Chicano (Mexican American). Since the time of the European conquest in South America, intermarriage and sexual relations have occurred between Native Americans and Europeans (Library of Congress, 2000). Mestizos form the largest population group in many Latin American countries and constitute a large proportion of the population in Guatemala, Ecuador, Peru, and Bolivia. In some countries, such as Ecuador, it has acquired social and cultural implications: A pure-blooded Indian who has adopted European dress and customs is called a *Mestizo* (or *Cholo*). In Mexico, the term's meaning has varied so greatly that it has been abandoned in census reports. In the Philippines, it denotes a person of mixed foreign (e.g., Chinese) and native ancestry. It also refers to people of mixed Malay and Chinese or Spanish descent. It is often very difficult to distinguish people who are of pure indigenous ancestry from those who are Mestizo. In reality, the classification of people as indigenous is usually more of a cultural distinction than a biological one, counting only those people who have not yet abandoned their indigenous ways of life. Today, the majority of indigenous people in Central and South America live in villages away from urban areas. The views of Mestizo psychology are as follows: (a) The person is an open system; (b) the spiritual world holds the key to destiny, personal identity, and life mission; (c) community identity and responsibility to the group are of central importance in development; (d) emphasis is on liberation, justice, freedom, and empowerment; (e) total development of abilities and skills is achieved through self-challenge; (f) the search for self-knowledge, individual identity, and life meaning is a primary goal; and (g) duality of origin and life in the universe and education within the family plays a central role in personality development (Ramirez, 1999).

References

Library of Congress. (2000). *Mestizos.* Washington, DC: Author.

Ramirez, M. (1999). *New developments in Mestizo psychology: Theory, research, and application.* East Lansing: Michigan State University, Julian Samora Research Institute.

Middle Easterners   These people are from an array of countries consisting of Algeria, Bahrain, Egypt, Iran, Iraq, Israel, Jordan, Kuwait, Lebanon, Libya, Morocco, Oman, Qatar, Saudi Arabia, Syria, Tunisia, United Arab Emirates, Western Sahara, and Yemen (International Coalition, 2001). According to Islamic law, there is no distinction between believers. Classic Islam, however, does hold that there is a difference between man and woman, freeman and slave, and believer and infidel (Lewis, 1995). Included in Middle Eastern origins are Palestinians, Arabs, Kurds, Assyrians, and Sunni Muslims (International Coalition, 2001). The predominant religion practiced among most is Islam, although some of the countries do tolerate practice of other religions (International Coalition, 2001). The Islamic religion requires that at least once during their lifetime, every Muslim must make a trip to Mecca in Saudi Arabia. They call this the *Hajj*. It is a tradition held every year in which Muslims from all over gather to perform certain rites and rituals (Lewis, 1995). Middle Easterners use many symbols that have significant meaning to their culture. One is called the *Ankh*, which stands for the Egyptian cross of life and is viewed as a universal charm. Another that is familiar to many Americans is the Eye of Hours. This symbol appears on the dollar bill and represents the god inside a tomb waiting to be reborn. The open eye indicated that his soul was alive, and he was ever watchful (Shira). Traditionally, Middle Easterners manufactured goods in their home with the help of their families. Most industrial organizations did not engage in international trade. Products that Middle Easterners are known for include pepper, carpets, and sugar (Lewis, 1995). At one time, Islamic education consisted of two forms of literature and learning. The *adab* consisted of poetry, history, belles lettres, and a large number of works that identified what a man of culture should know. The *ilm*, meaning knowledge, was basically religious education (Lewis, 1995).

References

International Coalition for Religious Freedom. (2001). *Religious freedom world report.* Silver Springs, MD: Author.

Lewis, B. (1995). *The Middle East: A brief history of the last 2,000 years.* New York: Scribner.

Shira. Symbols from the Middle East. Available from http://www.shira.net/symbols.htm

Mojado   Mojado (*mo-ha-doh*) is a translation of the word "wetback," sometimes spelled moja'o, which literally means wet. This is an expression that is sometimes used by Mexican people to describe themselves and their experiences of illegally crossing the Rio Grande to enter the United States (Castro, 2000). Unfortunately, this term has come to be used against all Mexican immigrants with some of the same prejudicial meanings as "cracker," which is commonly used when referring to Anglos. Mexican immigrants, however, currently use the term to differentiate themselves from recent or undocumented immigrants. The word mojado has also been translated to English by Mexican immigrant teens to the term *wets*. Mojado is also interchangeable with the term *alambrista*, meaning "wires," which is also used to describe a person who has crossed from one country to another and has cut wires along a fence dividing the United States and Mexico (Herrera-Sobek, 1998). Interestingly, alambrista takes into consideration the fact that the immigrant must have gotten wet at some point in the journey. The reverse does not necessarily have to be true, however. In recent years, many stories have been written depicting the journey that these individuals have endured. In Mexico, the term sometimes used is *espaldas mojadas*, which literally means wetbacks. The term has received notoriety in films and novels about the Chicano experience (Castro, 2000). The term has also been applied to immigrants from other nationalities that share a similar plight (Herrera-Sobek, 1998).

References

Castro, R. (2000). *Dictionary of Chicano folklore*. Santa Barbara, CA: ABC-CLIO.

Herrera-Sobek, M. (1998). *In culture across borders*. Tucson: University of Arizona Press.

Monochronic   Monochronic is defined as relating to one period of time (Boisvert, 1998). In monochronic cultures, "one thing at a time" and "time is money" are important concepts (Hall, 1983). Monochronic people tend to do one thing at a time, concentrate on the job, and take time commitments very seriously, whereas polychronic people do many things at once, are easily distracted, and perceive time commitments as objectives (Kenton & Valentine, 1997). Monochronic is also referred to as "M-time" or "M-people" (Boisvert, 1998). Americans and most people in English-speaking countries are monochronic; they concentrate on one task at a time (Hall, 1983). People from Asian, Arabic, and Spanish-speaking countries are polychronic (Hall, 1983). Monochronic people view time as a straight line moving forward and never returning (Hall, 1983). Tasks are scheduled to happen at specific times, and being "on time" is a virtue (Hall, 1983). Viewing time in this way can ensure that tasks are completed in a scheduled time period. M-people, however, can become obsessed with things having to happen on time (Kenton & Valentine, 1997).

References

Boisvert, R. D. (1998). *John Dewey: Rethinking our time*. Albany: State University of New York Press.

Hall, E. T. (1983). *The dance of life.* New York: Anchor.

Kenton, S., & Valentine, D. (1997). *Communicating in a multicultural workplace.* Englewood Cliffs, NJ: Prentice Hall.

Monocultural   This term is used to characterize a homogeneous society or culture. Van Rheenen (1996, 1997) states that it is the assumption that all other people are like us, resulting in the tendency to judge other peoples' actions and attitudes on the basis of our own. It also refers to the practice of growing a single crop plant in a large field (e.g., a cereal crop such as wheat or corn). Used within context, a monocultural society is one that has the tendency to acknowledge only one culture. This can lead to ethnocentrism, in which one's own culture is used as a measuring rod to compare other cultures. This monocultural society tends to lack respect for other peoples' ways, customs, and norms. During the 19th and 20th centuries, the Anglo-conformity theory gave the United States the characteristic of being a monocultural country. Being "American" has been implied as being able to adopt the customs, language, and morality of the majority—the White, middle-class, Anglo-American. The United States, therefore, has one dominant culture, and it is expected that immigrants will assimilate these norms. *E pluribus unum* (the making of many into one) translates well the emphasis given to this assimilation. The Anglo-conformity theory has been challenged by the melting pot theory, in which it is believed that all the diverse cultures that migrate to the United States are contributing to the "melting" of all into one so as to form a new breed. Finally, the theory of cultural pluralism rejects both of the previous approaches and explains that although immigrants are being Americanized, they still retain their own culture, norms, and values.

References

Van Rheenen, G. (1996). *Missions: Biblical foundations and contemporary strategies.* Grand Rapids, MI: Zondervan.

Van Rheenen, G. (1997). Modern and postmodern syncretism in theology and missions. In C. Douglas McDonnell (Ed.), *The Holy Spirit and mission dynamics* (pp. 164–207). Pasadena, CA: William Carey Library.

Monogamy   Monogamy is defined as marriage to only one spouse at a time. Monogamy contrasts with bigamy, polygamy, or infidelity (Phillips, 1999). It is thought that monogamy evolved based on the idea that offspring will have a much better chance at survival when both parents cooperate in child rearing (Ehrlich, Dobkin, & Wheye, 1988). Monogamous behavior varies depending on gender, age, and ethnicity. According to population-based sampling surveys done in the United States (Kelly & Kalichman, 1995), a significant number of people engage in nonmonogamous behavior and have sex with multiple partners or during brief serial relationships. Monogamy is practiced in the West and is considered the only just and civilized form of marriage, whereas polygamy continues to be practiced by some Muslims throughout the Muslim world. The concept of monogamy was introduced into the Christian philosophy to conform to Greek and Roman marriage. Although it prevailed as the only legitimate form of marriage in Greece and Rome, it cannot be said that Christianity introduced obligatory monogamy to the Western world, and certain groups, including the Mormons, regard polygyny as a divine institution (Westermarck, 1930) (see Polygamy). The assertion that monogamy is the natural form of marriage because there is an equal number of men and women is refuted. There is monogamy in cases in which the numbers are not equal and polygyny in cases in which the sexes are equal in number or the males form the majority, such as among Australian tribes (Westermarck, 1930).

References

Ehrlich, P., Dobkin, S., & Wheye, D. (1988). *The birder's handbook: A field guide to the natural history of North American birds*. New York: Simon & Schuster.

Kelly, J. A., & Kalichman, S. C. (1995). Increased attention to human sexuality can improve HIV-AIDS prevention efforts: Key research issues and directions. *Journal of Consulting and Clinical Psychology, 63*(6), 907–918.

Phillips, A. (1999). *Monogamy*. New York: Random House Value.

Westermarck, E. (1930). *A short history of marriage*. New York: Macmillan.

Monolingual   Monolingual means of one language (*Merriam-Webster's Collegiate Dictionary*, 1993). Monolinguals do not function the same way as their bilingual counterparts on tasks of sentence processing (Hernandez, Bates, & Avila, 1994). For instance, studies show that Spanish monolingual adults use noun-verb agreement to determine the agent of a sentence, and English monolingual adults rely on word order cues to determine the agent (Hernandez et al., 1994). Spanish-English bilinguals combine these two strategies (Hernandez et al., 1994). They favor noun-verb agreement in Spanish and word order cues in English but not to the same extent as their monolingual counterparts, thus demonstrating an "in between" profile (Hernandez et al., 1994).

References

Hernandez, A., Bates, E., & Avila, L. (1994). Sentence interpretation in Spanish-English bilinguals: What does it mean to be "in between"? *Applied Psycholinguistics, 15*, 417–446.

Merriam-Webster's collegiate dictionary. (1993). Springfield, MA: Merriam-Webster.

Multiculturalism   Multiculturalism came into public use during the early 1980s mostly in the context of school reform (Erickson, 1992). Being multicultural means being tolerant toward racial minorities with regard to language, food, religion, and other cultural manifestations (Francis, 1998). Multiculturalism advocates a greater sensitivity along with a better inclusion of racial minorities and women in society (Francis, 1998). Multiculturalism in the United States includes the main agenda of having White Americans become more sensitive to minorities by adopting a "politically correct" language (Francis, 1998). A second agenda of multiculturalism is to have all groups included in institutions such as schools. No group should be left out (Berman, 1992). Multiculturalism also allows for a broad definition of cultural groups, such as the homeless and single mothers (Francis, 1998). Multiculturalism is an individual psychological and theoretical view that all cultures and national groups are equal. Multiculturalism acknowledges that cultures and national groups vary in norms, values, worldviews, and traditions, but there is no superior versus inferior culture. Multiculturalism in psychology is an expression of the sociopolitical climate. As cultural issues, concepts, and values are explored, there is the underlying assumption of equality irrespective of any implicit or explicit differences.

References

Berman, P. (1992). *Debating P.C.: The controversy over political correctness on college campuses*. New York: Dell.

Erickson, P. (1992). What multiculturalism means. *Transition, 55*, 105–114.

Francis, S. (1998). The other face of multiculturalism. *Chronicles, 1*, 33.

Multiracial   This term pertains to people of two or more races (Goldberg, 1997). Multiracial people do not fit specifically into a well-defined category, such as Caucasian or African American (Fanon, 1952). Many multiracial individuals prefer to associate with the minority heritage (Fanon, 1952). In 2000, approximately 7 million people indicated that they belonged to more than one race in their responses to the U.S. census (Schmitt, 2001). Through 1996, more than 100,000 infants were born annually to parents of interracial marriages (Schwartz, 1998). People of mixed race must deal with problematic racial identity issues (Jacobs, 1992). Many studies have been performed on multiracial children, adolescents, and young adults to understand their identity development (Jacobs, 1992). For these age groups, issues of racial identity are mixed with general identity development and therefore are difficult to deal with (Jacobs, 1992). There has been race mixing for centuries, but only during the past few decades have multiracial people demanded to have all their ancestries acknowledged (Sollors, 1997).

References

Fanon, F. (1952). *Black skin, White masks*. New York: Grove.

Goldberg, D. T. (1997). *Racial subjects: Writing on race in America*. New York: Routledge.

Jacobs, J. H. (1992). Identity development in biracial children. In M. P. P. Root (Ed.), *Racially mixed in America* (pp. 190–207). Newbury Park, CA: Sage.

Schmitt, E. (2001, March 13). For 7 million people in census, one race category isn't enough. *New York Times*, pp. A1, A14.

Schwartz, W. (1998). *The identity development of multiracial youth.* Washington, DC: Office of Educational Research and Improvement.

Sollors, W. (1997). *Neither Black nor White, yet both.* New York: Oxford University Press.

Muslims   Muslims are defined as followers of Islam, a world religion founded by the Prophet Mohammed. Islam is the principal religion of much of Asia, including the Middle East and Indonesia, which has the largest Muslim population. The word Islam means "submission" and derives from a word meaning "peace." In Europe, Albania is predominantly Muslim. Elsewhere in Europe, there are immigrant communities of Muslims in North Africa and Turkey. In the United States, the Islamic population has increased in recent years from both conversions and due to immigration of Muslims from throughout the world. The number is estimated to be 5 to 6 million, and there are more than 1 billion Muslims worldwide ("Islam," 2000). Muslims believe that the Quran is the word of God. The Quran is a record of the words of God revealed through the angel Gabriel to the prophet Muhammad. Muslims believe in one god, who is unique and incomparable. They also believe in the existence of angels, who are honored creatures, and in prophets and messengers of God. In addition, they believe in the Day of Judgment, when all people will be resurrected for God's judgment according to their beliefs and deeds. They believe in *Al Qadar*, which encompasses the following principles: (a) God knows everything; (b) God has recorded all that has happened and all that will happen; (c) whatever God wills to happen happens, and whatever he wills not to happen does not happen; and (d) God is the creator of all things. A Muslim's life consists of five pillars: faith, prayer, the *Zakat* (meaning purification and growth), the fast, and the pilgrimage. The family is the foundation of the Islamic society. Children are greatly treasured and do not usually leave home until they marry. Typically, women keep their family name when they marry. The religion of Islam allows for polygamy, providing the husband is fair (Embassy of Saudi Arabia, 2001).

References

Embassy of Saudi Arabia. (2001). *Understanding Islam and the Muslims.* Washington, DC: Department of Islamic Affairs.

Islam. (2000). In *Columbia encyclopedia* (6th ed.). New York: Columbia University Press.

N

Native Americans This is the name given to the first people descended originally from cavemen in Asia (White, 1965). They have lived in America for thousands of years, and today there are numerous Indian communities (White, 1965) (see American Indian). Five main cultures are studied among Native Americans: the Northwest culture, the Californian culture, the Southwest culture, the plains culture, and the eastern woodland culture. In each of these cultures, Native Americans have somewhat different lifestyles. For example, in the Northwest culture, they live in wooden lodges, their predominant food is salmon, and their clothing is made of tree bark. In the Californian culture, they live in *wickiups* (circular homes with arched poles covered with brush and mat); their predominant food is acorns, fish, and shellfish; and their clothing is made of animal skins (Payne, 1965). In the Southwest culture, they live in pueblos; their predominant food is corn, beans, and squash; and their clothing is made of cotton fibers (Payne, 1965). In the plains, they lived in tepees (tentlike structure), their food of choice is the buffalo, and their clothing is made of buffalo skin (Luling, 1978). In the eastern woodland culture, Native Americans live in long houses; their food of choice is deer, squirrels, rabbits, and berries; and their clothes are made of the skin of small animals (Sheppard, 1975).

References

Luling, V. (1978). *Indians of the North American plains.* London: MacDonald Educational Press.

Payne, E. (1965). *Meet the North American Indians.* London: Random House.

Sheppard, S. (1975). *Indians of the eastern woodlands.* New York: Franklin Watts.

White, A. (1965). *The American Indian.* London: Random House.

Navajo Indians This is the name given to the second largest tribes of North American Indians, the largest being the Cherokee. The Navajo Indians are a tribe from the Southwest. They are also called *Dine*, "the people" (Haslam & Parsons, 1995). They originated as a group of people known as the Athapascans, who migrated from Canada and Alaska to settle in the Southwest (Josephy, 1994). The Navajo Indians lived in homes made of wooden poles, tree bark, and mud that were called hogans. In the 1600s, the Spanish started to intrude on the Pueblo Indians of Arizona (Josephy, 1994). In 1680, the Pueblos revolted against these European invaders, and many Pueblos moved northward to join Navajo settlements. The Navajo began to adopt the Pueblo agricultural, sheep-raising, and weaving ways (Josephy, 1994). Their clothes were made of sheep wool, and the sheep was the predominant food (Roessel, 1995). The Navajo Indians were known as the healthiest tribe in the country. Most Navajo Indians currently live in Arizona, Utah, and New Mexico, and the Navajo reservation is the largest in the United States (Josephy, 1994). They engage in pottery carving, and they use turquoise to make jewelry because it represents the stone of happiness and good fortune for them (Roessel, 1995).

References

Haslam, A., & Parsons, A. (1995). *Make it work: North American Indians, the hands-on approach to history.* London/Belmont, CA: Two-Can/Thomson.

Josephy, A. M. (1994). *500 Nations: An illustrated history of North American Indians.* New York: Knopf.

Roessel, M. (1995). *Songs from the loom: A Navajo girl learns to weave.* Minneapolis, MN: Lerner.

Neurasthenia   Neurasthenia was one of the most diagnosed disorders of the late 19th and early 20th century and mostly prevalent in women (Showalter, 1985). Neurasthenia, like hysteria, presented symptoms such as blushing, vertigo, headaches, insomnia, and depression (Showalter, 1985). Neurasthenia also included sensations of pain or numbness in parts of the body, chronic fatigue, fainting, anxiety, and uterine irritability (Beard, 1880). Originally, neurasthenia was considered an American disorder and was also described as "American nervousness" (Sicherman, 1977). The majority of U.S. neurasthenic patients were female, but men also presented some characteristics of the condition (Showalter, 1985). The diagnosis was developed in the United States by physicians George Beard and Silas Weir Mitchell (Sicherman, 1977). There is no physical treatment, but antidepressants such as fluoxetine, amineptine, and desipramine are sometimes helpful (Showalter, 1985). Today, neurasthenia is referred to as chronic fatigue syndrome (Sharpe & Campling, 1999). This may be related to the multiple roles that women play in a complex industrialized culture such as that of the United States. In association with the introduction of modern psychiatry into China in the late 19th century, the medical term *neurasthenia* was introduced and translated literally as *shenjing-suairu* ("nerve weakened disorder") (see Shenjing-Suaruo). It became widely known as a mild body disorder related to nerve exhaustion, a concept compatible with traditional Chinese concepts and easily understood by the layman (Tseng, 2001).

References

Beard, G. (1880). *A practical treatise on nervous exhaustion (neurasthenia).* New York: Treat EB.

Sharpe, M., & Campling, F. (1999). *Chronic fatigue syndrome: The facts*. London: Oxford University Press.

Showalter, E. (1985). *The female malady: Women, madness, and English culture, 1830–1980*. New York: Pantheon.

Sicherman, B. (1977). The uses of a diagnosis: Doctors, patients, and neurasthenia. *Journal of the History of Medicine, 6,* 33–54.

Tseng, W. (2001). *Handbook of cultural psychiatry*. San Diego, CA: Academic Press.

Non-Standard English   Non-Standard English is defined as English that has not undergone standardization (Trudgill, 1992). Such standardization consists of processes such as language determination, which is a selection of a particular language for particular purposes in the society or nation in question, and codification, which is a publicly recognized and fixed form found in dictionaries and grammar books (Trudgill, 1992). There are numerous differences between Standard English and non-Standard English. In non-Standard English, there is a distinction between "did" and "done," as in "You done it, did you?" (Cheshire, 1982). Non-Standard English also allows multiple negation, such as "I don't want none." Non-Standard English uses possessive forms such as "hisself" and "theirselves" (Cheshire, 1982). Where Standard English fails to distinguish between second-person singular and second-person plural pronouns using "you" in both cases, non-Standard English maintains the older English distinction between "thou" and "you" and uses newer pronouns, such as "you" and "youse" (Cheshire, 1982). Non-Standard English has the same form for all persons, such as "I be," "you be," "he be," "we be," "they be," "I were," "you were," "he were," "we were," and "they were" when conjugating the verb "to be" (Cheshire, 1982). It is sometimes difficult to determine which grammatical forms are and are not Standard English (Labov, 1966). In general, there is a tendency for these grammatical forms to change from nonstandard to standard (Labov, 1966). There are some difficulties in distinguishing features of non-Standard English, which makes it possible for nonstandard features to become standard and vice versa (Labov, 1966). See Black English.

References

Cheshire, J. (1982). *Variation in an English dialect*. London: Cambridge University Press.

Labov, W. (1966). *The social stratification of English in New York City*. Washington, DC: Center for Applied Linguistics.

Trudgill, P. (1992). *Introducing language and society*. London: Penguin.

Nonverbal communication   Nonverbal communication is defined as behavior other than written or spoken language that creates meaning for someone (Beebe, Beebe, & Redmond, 2002). It consists of the tone of voice, eye contact, facial expression, posture, movement, and appearance, and it is believed to be the primary way in which feelings, emotions, and attitudes are communicated (Beebe et al., 2002).

Nonverbal communication is also called body language (Young, 2001). It has been estimated that at least 80% of communication occurs on the nonverbal level, 38% of emotions are conveyed by the voice, and 55% are conveyed by the face (Mehrabian, 1972). Nonverbal communication plays a major role in interpersonal relationships and often is more credible than verbal communication (Beebe et al., 2002). Although people rarely notice their presence, nonverbals have a tremendous effect and often make a difference in the way messages are interpreted (Young, 2001). For instance, it has been found that an eyebrow can be raised in only one sixth of a second but can be detected at a distance of more than 150 feet (Blum, 1998). It is very important to acknowledge the power of nonverbal communication. This is why most important decisions are handled face to face or "in person" (Young, 2001). Nonverbals play a vital role in getting the message across and can be powerful tools of persuasion (Young, 2001). Prominent people, such as Martin Luther King, have used their voice tone and gestures in moving orations in front of thousands, and these nonverbal skills help in persuasive communication (Young, 2001).

References

Beebe, S., Beebe, S. A., & Redmond, M. (2002). *Interpersonal communication: Relating to others*. Boston: Allyn & Bacon.

Blum, D. (1998). Face it! *Psychology Today, 31*(5), 32–70.

Mehrabian, A. (1972). *Nonverbal communication*. Chicago: Aldine.

Young, M. (2001). *Learning the art of helping: Building blocks and techniques*. Englewood Cliffs, NJ: Prentice Hall.

Norms   Norms are defined as the rules of daily living that members of the group adhere to and are generally called group norms ("Group Norms," 1998). Norms are also defined as rules that tell us what is "right" or " wrong" to do and when, where, and with whom (Alloy, Jacobson, & Acocella, 1999). Norms are passed from one generation to the next as early as infancy ("Group Norms," 1998). Members of a homogeneous culture share a language and a lifestyle and therefore have a clear set of norms that the group follows, whereas members of a heterogeneous culture do not necessarily have one language and one lifestyle in common ("Group Norms," 1998). Norms also vary from culture to culture. For instance, personal space is a concept that differs from one culture to the next. In North America, two people that do not know each other stand approximately 3 feet apart, but in South America they stand closer, and in Asia they stand much farther apart (Alloy et al., 1999). One study revealed that when Japanese, American, and Venezuelan students were asked to have a 5-minute conversation with a stranger of the same nationality, the Japanese sat approximately 40 inches apart, the Americans sat 35 inches apart, and the Venezuelans sat 32 inches apart (Sussman & Rosenfeld, 1982). Norms are also used in a culture to judge others, depending on how well others conform to the culture's norms (Alloy et al., 1999). It has even become a standard in some cases to define abnormal behavior. In other words, norm violation can be viewed as abnormal (Alloy et al., 1999).

References

Alloy, L., Jacobson, N., & Acocella, J. (1999). *Abnormal psychology: Current perspectives.* New York: McGraw-Hill.

Group norms. (1998). In *Gale encyclopedia of childhood & adolescence.* Detroit, MI: Gale Research.

Sussman, N., & Rosenfeld, H. (1982). Influence of culture, language, and sex on conversational distance. *Journal of Personality and Social Psychology, 42,* 66–74.

Nuclear family   Also called a natural family, a nuclear family is composed of a mother, a father, and their biological children or children they adopt (Beebe, Beebe, & Redmond, 2002). The nuclear family is considered the traditional family. It is also called an idealized natural family because today this family type is no longer typical. Changes in culture, values, and economics have given rise to more predominant types of family, such as the single-parent family, composed of one parent and at least one child, and the blended family consisting of two adults and their children, possibly from other marriages or adoption. Another type of family that has become common is the extended family, in which relatives are a central part of the family unit. Instead of being taken care of by traditional parents, children are raised by grandparents, uncles, aunts, or other relatives. In the extended family, the caretakers are sometimes not even relatives but people who are treated like family. They are called surrogate family members. The newest type of nuclear family, once considered inconceivable, is the gay and lesbian parent trend. According to the Gay and Lesbian Parents Coalition International, approximately 4 million gay men and lesbians are raising 8 to 10 million children in the United States. Most of them were former heterosexual parents who left their previous marriages and took their children with them (Carroll, 2000).

References

Beebe, S., Beebe, S. A., & Redmond, M. (2002). *Interpersonal communication: Relating to others.* Boston: Allyn & Bacon.

Carroll, J. D. (2000, August 28). The new nuclear family. *Austin Chronicle,* 1–3.

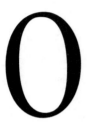

Obeah/obeahism   This is the name given to the practice of witchcraft on the island of Jamaica. The word is a corruption of the Twi (the language of the Akan people of Ghana) *obayi* or sorcery. The man or the woman who practices obayi is known as *obayifo.* In Jamaica, all aspects of the craft are included under this heading. It is used to designate the person who practices this craft and uses it to harm others through a variety of means—powders, curses, lotions, lizard's tail, and alligator's teeth. An Obeah Law of Jamaica was passed in 1760 prohibiting its practice (Barrett, 1977). Today, obeah is still practiced on the island and remains a secret endeavor. It is difficult to identify both the client and the practitioner; either could be a person who lives next door. Obeah has never been part of mainstream healing practice, and very few individuals openly acknowledge their belief in its tenet. When there is excessive hardship or illness that seems mysterious or incurable, however, individuals may turn to the obayi as a last resort (Hall, 2001).

References

Barrett, L. (1977). *The sun and the drum: African roots in Jamaican folk traditions.* Kingston, Jamaica: Sangster's Educational Books.

Hall, L. E. (2001). *Working with the Jamaican client.* Unpublished manuscript.

Ojibwa Indians   The Ojibwas are spread over 1,000 miles of territory from southeastern Ontario, Canada, westward across the upper Great Lakes of the United States and Canada as far as Saskatchewan and Montana (Johnson, 1976). Although classed as one people in the Algonquian linguistic family, they have several alternate regional names and are divided into approximately 100 separate bands or reservation communities. The Ojibwas probably number approximately 200,000, two thirds of whom reside in Canada, with an estimated 20,000 fluent in one of the three or four dialects of Ojibwa (Tanner, 1992). On 17th-century French maps, a form of the word Ojibwa identified a village on the north shore of Lake Superior, but use of the term expanded to include allied communities along the eastern side of Lake Superior. Depending on its division into syllables, the Ojibwa name has been interpreted as a reference either to the puckered toe of the Ojibwas' distinctive moccasins or to their use of glyphs to inscribe historical and religious information as well as simple messages on birch bark or rock surfaces. The name has no standard spelling in English and has been corrupted into *Chippewa*, the form still used by tribal organizations recognized by the U.S. government (Warren, 1984).

References

Johnson, B. (1976). *The Ojibwa heritage.* Toronto/New York: McClelland & Stewart/ Columbia University Press.

Tanner, H. H. (1992). *The Ojibwa.* New York: Chelsea House.

Warren, W. W. (1984). *History of the Ojibway people.* St. Paul, MN: Historical Society Press.

Ontogenetic theory of culture   The word *ontogenetic* derives from the word *ontogeny,* which means "growth, growing, and development," or from the word *ontogenesis,* "the process of an individual organism organically; a purely biological unfolding of events involved in an organism changing gradually from a simple to a more complex level" (Robinson, 1969, p. 33). The word *ontogenetic* means of, relating to, or appearing in the course of development, especially of an individual organism (*Merriam-Webster's Collegiate Dictionary,* 2003, p. 867). The analogy of biological recapitulation was later applied to the theories of psychoanalysis by Sigmund Freud and to the stages of child development by G. K. Hall in 1904. The ontogenetic theory of culture was developed by Geza Roheim (Robinson, 1969). He is credited as one of the first to apply psycho-analysis to the study of world cultures and is one of the first anthropologists to suc-cessfully apply Freudian theories to the analysis of cultures. This theory is considered a great contribution to his field of study. Ontogenetic theory of culture contended that cultural differences were largely the result of an individual's childhood traumas. The childhood experiences of the individual were ultimately reflected in adult personality and in the collective institutions of a given culture (Robinson, 1969). In *Civilization and Its Discontents,* Freud (1930) stated that the evolution of culture is a special process comparable to the normal growth of an individual to maturity. Differences in behavior that are found across cultures do not just exist at a particular moment in time but have a history and a reason for occurring (Vygotsky, 1978).

References

Freud, S. (1930). *Civilization and its discontents, standard edition* (Reviewed by J. Strachney; Vol. 21, pp. 59–145). New York: Norton.

Merriam-Webster's collegiate dictionary. (2003). Springfield, MA: Merriam-Webster.

Robinson, P. (1969). *The Freudian Left: Wilhelm Reich, Geza Roheim, Herbert Marcuse.* New York: Harper & Row.

Vygotsky, L. S. (1978). *Mind in society: The development of higher psychological processes.* Cambridge, MA: Harvard University Press.

P

Pacific Islanders Pacific Islanders come from approximately 50 countries and ethnic groups, each with distinct cultures, traditions, and histories. According to the Asian American Health Forum (1990), Asian Americans have geographic origins in more than 20 countries, with more than 60 different ethnicities represented. Pacific Islanders speak more than 100 Asian and Pacific Islander languages. Pacific Islanders have origins from areas of Polynesia, Micronesia, and Melanasia as well as Hawaii and Guam Samoa. Until the 18th century, they had very little contact with Europeans; by the beginning of the 20th century, however, all Pacific Islanders had come (at least nominally) under the rule of Western powers (Campbell, 1992). Currently, there are approximately 12 million Pacific Islanders living in the United States, or approximately 5% of the total population of Asian American and Pacific Islanders. By 2020, the Pacific Islander population is projected to be 20 million (Asian Americans & Pacific Islanders, 2003). Hawaiians are the largest Pacific Islander group; they comprise 58% of the Pacific Islander population in the United States (U.S. Department of Commerce, 1993). Approximately 75% of Pacific Islanders live in Hawaii and California (U.S. Department of Commerce, 1993). These two states have more than 100,000 Pacific Islanders. Their migration to the United States has been through complex avenues involving a multistage, multipath phenomenon. Whereas some have emigrated directly from their country of origin to the United States, others have used a more circuitous route by either going to another country before entry or entering as a nonimmigrant and subsequently changing their status (Barkan & Doob, 1992).

References

Asian American Health Forum. (1990). *Dispelling the myth of a health minority.* San Francisco: Author.

Asian Americans & Pacific Islanders. (2003, April). *Pacific Islanders.* Social Security data accessed at http://www.ssa.gov/aapi/who.htm.

Barkan, E. R., & Doob, L. W. (1992). *The Asian and Pacific Islander migration to the United States: A model of new global patterns.* Westport, CT: Greenwood.

Campbell, I. C. (1992). *A history of the Pacific.* Christchurch, NZ: University of Canterbury Press.

U.S. Department of Commerce, Bureau of the Census. (1993, September). *We the American Asians*. Washington, DC: U.S. Government Printing Office.

Padrino   The word *padrino* translates into "godparents." In the Andes culture, padrinos play an important role in the child's spiritual, social, and physical development. They aid the child's spiritual growth by ensuring that he or she attends catechism and maintains the Christian faith (Bourque, 1995). Godparents are present in most cultures; they are considered to be the "second-parents" to the child. Everything parents provide for their children (i.e., protection, education, and financial security) godparents also provide. In the Andes culture, the role of the padrino is more significant: "The significance of padrinos in the physical development of their godchildren is evident during the baptismal feast. They must eat and drink to excess, else the child will not learn to walk or talk" (Bourque, 1995, p. 75). In Colombia, the baptism plays a very important role with regard to the godparents' responsibility and luck. They believe that with material objects, a child's welfare is enhanced. Bourque notes,

> The power of baptism to promote growth is illustrated by the beliefs surrounding *el bautizo del billete* (the baptism of the bill). The padrino secretly holds a peso bill during a baptism ceremony; it will be baptized instead of the child. The bill will receive a name and when it enters into circulation it will "grow" by continually returning to its owner and bringing more money with it. (p. 75)

Cultural understandings of a padrino's role in a child's life differ. Some believe padrinos provide moral and emotional support. Wells (2000) notes that "even in a 'private' baptism, the godparents represent the community of faith. And the role of the community of faith is vital" (p. 3). The idea of godparents entered into the Mexican culture in the 18th century. Tecospa Indians have godparents for every important rite in life—baptism, confirmation, first communion, marriage, and last communion (Madsen, 1960). A Tecospan godfather plans the baptism and buys the child a new outfit for the ceremony. Through the baptism in the Tecospan culture, the godparents and the child establish a lifelong relationship. From then on, if the biological parents of the child are unable to provide for him or her, the godparents take the child in as one of their own (Madsen, 1960).

References

Bourque, N. L. (1995). Developing people and plants: Life cycle and agricultural festivals in the Andes. *Ethnology, 34,* 75.

Madsen, W. (1960). *The virgin's children: Life in an Aztec village today.* Austin: University of Texas Press.

Wells, S. (2000). *Holiness: Baptism.* New York: Christian Century Foundation.

Parental ethnotheories   Parental ethnotheories are beliefs about the province of parenting that have become known as parental belief systems. These are the attitudes, principles, and practices of parents and other child caretakers regarding the appropriate way to raise a child, and they include such frequent practices as the provision of affection and warmth, agenda for feeding and abolition, and even the agenda for development (e.g., when a child should walk, talk, be potty trained, and choose relationships) (Berry, Poortinga, Segall, & Dasen, 2002). This is a parental style that gives parents legal and moral duty to rear their children, which includes providing for their nourishment and well-being as well as their social, ethical, and personal development. To fulfill this responsibility, parents have to find ways to convey their principles, expectations, and policies (Craighead & Nemeroff, 2001). It is useful to study these beliefs because they provide insight into the cognition and development of adults; help us understand parenting behavior; are one aspect of the context in which children develop; and, when studied across generations, can provide clues about cultural transmission and change (Goldstein, 2000). These values and practices represent the processes of enculturation and socialization that have been studied for some time. The advantage of this newer concept is that it links the earlier literature on "child-rearing" practices more closely to the ecological and cultural contexts in which they arise (Berry et al., 2002). According to their specific goals for children, different cultures provide varied child-nurturing environments and obtain diverse behavioral outcomes. As a result, the behavior of infants, young children, and older individuals varies across cultures. Although it is not argued that these early experiences are completely formative by themselves, there tends to be continuity of socialization over time. The fundamental behavior patterns set in place during early socialization are further elaborated on as the child grows, and they persist into adulthood. Cultures may have markedly different goals and socialization practices (Commons & Miller, 1998). Parental ethnotheories play an important role in the extent to which even young infants are left to themselves between feeding times (as in The Netherlands) or taken from their cribs when showing signs of distress (as in the United States). For Dutch parents, imposing regularity in sleeping patterns is an important issue. If children are not getting enough sleep, they are believed to become fussy; moreover, young children need sleep for their growth and development. This is also emphasized in the Dutch health care system. In the United States, regular sleeping patterns are viewed as something the child will acquire with age, but these are, by and large, not viewed as something that can be induced (Berry et al., 2002).

References

Berry, J. W., Poortinga, Y. H., Segall, M. H., & Dasen, P. R. (2002). *Cross-cultural psychology: Research and applications* (2nd ed.) Cambridge, UK: Cambridge University Press.

Commons, M., & Miller, P. (1998, May). *Emotional learning in infants: A cross-cultural examination.* Paper presented at the American Association for the Advancement of Science, Philadelphia, PA.

Craighead, E., & Nemeroff, C. (2001). *The Corsini encyclopedia of psychology and behavioral science* (3rd ed., pp. 1146–1147). New York: John Wiley.

Goldstein, S. (2000). *Cross-cultural explorations: Activities in culture and psychology.* Boston: Allyn & Bacon.

Paternalistic racism   This implies that the majority race in one country or setting has the right to rule over the minority race for its own good (Halstead 1988). Paternalistic racism is particularly related to Blacks or African Americans and Whites in the United States. It implies that White people have the right to interfere with the lives of Black people for their own good. Furthermore, the majority race has the right to define what is good for the minority race; historically, Whites or Anglo Saxons have been the ones defining what is right for the minority races in the United States (Halstead, 1988). This type of racism refers to the process in which the freedom of the minority race is defined or restricted by the regulations that are created by the majority race. This type of racism involves the initiation of new practices and rules because of the presence of racial minorities in the country. It also involves more precise usage of power by the majority race (Halstead, 1988). Some of the characteristics of paternalistic racism are found in Helms's (1995) White and people of color identity model. At the nonracist identity stage, there is an intellectual commitment to ones' own racial group but not full tolerance of people from other groups. When such an individual helps someone from outside his or her group, it may come across as paternalistic racism (Daniels, 2001). The Ku Klux Klan, which advocates White supremacy and practices overt racism in private, publicly adopted a paternalistic approach toward African Americans. The Klan argued that it was its duty to protect African Americans from foreign influences (McVeigh, 1999).

References

Daniels, J. A. (2001). The conceptualizing of a case of indirect racism using the white racial identity development model. *Journal of Mental health Counseling, 23,* 3.

Halstead, M. (1988). *Education, justice, and cultural diversity: An examination of the Honeyford affair.* London: Falmer.

Helms, J. E. (1995). An update of Helms's White and people of color racial identity models. In J. G. Ponterotto, J. M. Class, L. A. Suzuki, & C. M. Alexander (Eds.), *Handbook of multicultural counseling.* Thousand Oaks, CA: Sage.

McVeigh, R. (1999). The structural incentives for conservative mobilization: Power devaluation and the rise of the Ku Klux Klan, 1915–1925. *Social Forces, 77*(4).

Personal space   Personal space is a distance people keep around their bodies as they come into contact with other people (Manstead & Hewstone, 1995). Its size depends on the comfort level or how well acquainted one is with another person (Myers, 2002). People may feel annoyed or distressed if they believe that a stranger has violated this space. This area decreases in size, however, if the closeness to that person is significant. Hall (1959) coined the term *proxemics,* which researches how a person uses and views personal space. This zone is most common when people are chatting among others and varies from 1½ to 4 feet (Beebe, Beebe, & Redmond, 2002). Like nonverbal communication, personal space has to do with the person's culture and whether that person is familiar with the person with whom he or she is interacting (Jimenez Arias, 1996). Arabs tend to keep a smaller personal space when communicating with others. Western Europeans tend to feel comfortable with a larger personal space, unless the relationship with the other is an intimate one.

References

Beebe, S. A., Beebe, S. J., & Redmond, M. V. (2002). *Interpersonal communication: Relating to others* (3rd ed.). Boston: Allyn & Bacon.

Hall, E. T. (1959). *The silent language.* Garden City, NY: Doubleday.

Jimenez Arias, I. (1996). Proxemics in the ESL classroom. *Forum, 34*(1), 32.

Manstead, A. S. R., & Hewstone, M. (1995). *The Blackwell encyclopedia of social psychology.* Cambridge, UK: Blackwell.

Myers, D. G. (2002). *Social psychology* (7th ed.). New York: McGraw-Hill.

Personalismo   Personalismo consists of the Hispanic or Latino focus on, and orientation toward, having close interpersonal relationships and friendships with others. Developing close personal relationships is very important. There is no direct translation for this word. Basically, it includes such characteristics as being charming, congenial, agreeable, open, and outgoing. Behaviors or qualities that express this cultural norm include loyalty, honesty, and generosity toward one's friends; hospitality toward others; a sense of mutual trust; and a willingness to help others. Personalismo is a Hispanic or Latino value that focuses on relationship formation before a task can be completed. The person who has this trait takes on a leadership role and is described as being charismatic (Hauberg, 1974). Personalismo is the individual preparation needed to earn the trust and respect of the followers. Personalismo means that the leader embodies the traits that earn the respect of his or her community. It calls for an inner self preparation for leadership that emphasizes character formation and personal development (Bordas, 2001). Personalismo is the Spanish word for interpersonal relationships. Hispanics like to think of themselves as being friendly and hospitable, and they will strive to be viewed as simpatico, which is directly related to personalismo. Someone who is simpatico has qualities such as being charming, congenial, agreeable, open, and outgoing—characteristics directly related to personalismo. When Cubans in exile return to Cuba with their U.S.-born children, they unrealistically hope that their children will feel as Cuban as they do—that is, experience the warm feeling of personalismo. For Cubans, personalismo is as important as education. It implies the use of personal interaction among people (Boyd-Webb, 2001).

References

Bordas, J. (2001). Latino leadership: Building a humanistic and diverse society. *Journal of Leadership Studies, 8*(2), 112–136.

Boyd-Webb, N. (2001). *The culturally diverse parent-child and family relations: A guide for social workers and other practitioners.* New York: Columbia University Press.

Hauberg, C. A. (1974). *Puerto Rico and the Puerto Ricans.* New York: Twane.

Philotimo   Philotimo is personal honor—the feeling of self-esteem that governs day-to-day behavior. This creed requires that a male never lose face in public. The emotions surrounding the value of philotimo have a powerful influence on family life (U.S. Department of State, 1993). Philotimo ("love of honor") is a polysemantic, traditional social value that characterizes Greeks more than other nationalities and accounts for a set of human qualities and is the central part of the Greek self-concept and social value. Philotimo involves qualities such as honesty, morality, respect, love, duty, obedience, success, progress, and humaneness as well as living up to one's expectations (Goldstein, 2000).

References

Goldstein, S. (2000). *Cross-cultural explorations: Activities in culture and psychology.* Boston: Allyn & Bacon.

U.S. Department of State, Bureau of Public Affairs. (1993). *Background notes: Greece.* Washington, DC: Author.

Polychronic   Polychronic is defined as being able to "work happily with many things happening at one time, in a nonlinear and emotional way that lets you change your plans at a moment's notice without distress and without worrying about deadlines" (www.quinion.com). Polychronic people can be more productive because they can work on, and maybe complete, more than one task at a time (i.e., language translators being able to listen in one language and speak in another at the same time). For one to be polychronic, organization and good management are necessities. If tasks cannot be performed calmly, chaos may result. Cotte and Ratneshwar (1999) note that "polychronic behavior is a form of behaving with and within time and has previously been examined within the literature on time and temporal perception" (p. 186). Polychronic people are also noted to exclude interpersonal relationships from their time management. Wessel (2003) states, "Polychronic people change plans frequently, consider schedules as goals instead of imperatives, and focus on relationships with people" (p. 16). Polychronic people seem to be highly organized and are able to effectively concurrently manage their personal and business activities. Ihator (2000) notes,

> In polychronic time, many activities, private and official, may be scheduled at the same time. No time priority may be placed on work assignments. Business and social events are allowed to evolve without regard to the strict restriction of timing and scheduling and prior planning. (p. 38)

Being polychronic is associated with certain cultures. High-context societies tend to be polychronic, whereas many African, Latin American, and Arab countries are polychronic (Ihator, 2000). There is also the notion that "polychronic time is female time" (Morehead, 2001, p. 355).

References

Cotte, J., & Ratneshwar, S. (1999). Juggling and hopping: What does it mean to work poly-chronically? *Journal of Managerial Psychology, 14,* 184–205.

Ihator, A. (2000). Understanding the cultural patterns of the world—An imperative in implementing strategic international PR programs. *Public Relations Quarterly, 45,* 38.

Morehead, A. (2001). Synchronizing time for work and family: Preliminary insights from qualitative research with mothers. *Journal of Sociology, 37,* 355.

Wessel, R. (2003, January 9). Is there time to slow down? As the world speeds up, how cultures define the elastic nature of time may affect our environmental health. *Christian Science Monitor,* 16.

Polygamy   "[F]rom the late Greek *polygamia* which means 'polygamy,' in turn from *polygamos* 'often married,' from *poly* 'many' and *gamos* 'marriage'" (Harper, 2001, p. 602). Polygamy refers to marriage in which a person may have several spouses concurrently. Polygamy may take one of two forms: polygyny or polyandry (Gibbs, 2002). In polygyny, a man has two or more wives at the same time. If the wives are sisters, the marriage is referred to as sororal polygyny. In ancient Asian countries, polygyny was practiced in the form of concubinage. Polygyny is important in certain societies because it increases the wealth of the family and consequently the family's social importance. It also affords companionship, and labor can be shared among the wives. Polygyny also provides for the absorption of an excess of marriageable women, especially when the male population has been reduced because of war. Many studies on polygyny suggest that women's attitudes toward this practice vary within and between societies. In many instances, women disapprove of polygynous unions, and jealousy may reduce the potential for cooperation among the wives or between a wife and a husband (Meekers & Franklin, 1995). In contrast, polyandry is the sharing of a single wife by two or more husbands at the same time. When the husbands of a woman are brothers, this is called *adelphic* (or fraternal) polyandry (Gibbs, 2002). Polyandry serves two important purposes. First, it promotes the continuity and conservation of family property, especially land. Under a traditional system of marriage, family land would be divided among each son born to each individual husband. In polyandry, however, each brother has security and a stake in the family land but this property is legally shared, not divided. The second purpose that polyandry serves is an economical one. The poor in some societies cannot afford wives; thus, the costs—and the wife—are shared. Polyandry is far rarer than polygyny (Gibbs, 2002). In the United States, polygamy is often confused with polygyny due to the influence of the Mormon society's erroneous usage of the word polygamy to denote polygynous marriages (Gibbs, 2002). Polygamy among Mormons has provoked an intense antipolygamy campaign supported by both religious and political parties and by the traditional U.S. populace (Stein, 2003).

References

Gibbs, J. L. (2002). Polygamy. In *Encyclopedia America*. Danbury, CT: Grolier.

Harper, D. (2001). Polygamy. In *Encyclopedia America*. Danbury, CT: Grolier.

Meekers, D., & Franklin, N. (1995). Women's perception of polygyny among the Kaguru of Tanzania. *Ethology, 34,* 4.

Stein, S. (2003). *Sarah Barrington Gordon. The Mormon question: Polygamy and constitutional conflict in nineteenth century America.* Chapel Hill: University of North Carolina Press.

Prejudice   The word prejudice was derived in the early 13th century. The term *prejudice* is consequent from the French word *préjudice* and from the Latin word *praejudicium*, which was derived from *prae* + *judicium* (*Collins English Dictionary*, 2000). The typical glossary definition states that prejudice is a negative prejudgment of a group and its individual members. According to the *Merriam-Webster Dictionary*, prejudice as a noun is defined as "injury or damage resulting from some judgment or action of another in disregard of one's rights, or if it is especially detrimental to one's legal rights or claims" ("Prejudice," 2000, p. 907). In addition, it is also defined as (a) a preconceived judgment or opinion and (b) an adverse opinion or leaning formed without just grounds or sufficient knowledge. The term *prejudice* is in accordance with an instance of judgment or opinion and/or an irrational attitude of hostility directed against an individual, a group, or a race ("Prejudice," 2000). The synonym of prejudice is predilection, which states that there is an attitude of mind that predisposes one to favor something. According to the *Collins English Dictionary*, the transitive verb of prejudice states that it is to cause to be prejudiced or to inflict disadvantage on one or to injure by prejudice. Prejudice follows from using the standard of one's own group when comparing the self to someone in another group; hence, "prejudice is a negative attitude toward a person based upon a social comparison in which the individual's own group is taken as the positive point of reference" (Jones, 1972, p. 23). Sources of prejudice may be race (Gallup & Hugick, 1990; Jones, 1972), gender (Eagly & Mladinic, 1994), unequal status (Myers, 2001), religion (Batson, Schoenrade, & Ventis, 1993), and conformity (Agnew, Curry, & Curry, 1994).

References

Agnew, C. R., Curry, D. P., & Curry, V. D. (1994, August). *Will racism theories with significant empirical support stand up?* Paper presented at the annual meeting of the American Psychological Association.

Batson, C. D., Schoenrade, P., & Ventis, W. L. (1993). *Religion and the individual: A social psychological perspective.* New York: Oxford University Press.

Collins English dictionary. (2000). New York: HarperCollins.

Eagly, A., & Mladinic, A. (1994). Are people prejudiced against women? Some answers from research on attitudes, gender stereotypes and judgments of competence. In W. Stroebe & M. Hewstone (Eds.), *European review of social psychology* (Vol. 5). Chichester, UK: Wiley.

Gallup, G., Jr., & Hugick, L. (1990, June). Racial tolerance grows, progress on racial equality less evident. *Gallup Poll Monthly*, 23–32.

Jones, J. M. (1972). *Prejudice and racism.* Cambridge, MA: Addison-Wesley.

Myers, D. G. (2001). *Social psychology* (5th ed.). New York: McGraw-Hill.

Prejudice. (2000). In *Merriam-Webster's dictionary.* Springfield, MA: Merriam-Webster.

Pueblo Indians   The Pueblo Indians are a group of native tribes who populate regions of northeastern Arizona and northwestern New Mexico. Today, the Pueblo Indians are classified into eastern and western divisions. In the eastern division are the New Mexico Pueblo Indians, whereas the western Pueblo Indians comprise the Hopi, Zuni, Acoma, and Laguna who live in western New Mexico. The Pueblo are the descendants of the ancient Anasazi and Mogollon peoples (Salzmann & Salzmann, 1997). For hundreds of years, these people lived in small, scattered villages in Colorado and Utah. By the early 12th century, however, they had left these small villages in favor of larger, more compact pueblos. In the 13th century, a long period of drought affected the Pueblos; failing crops and lack of water forced the Pueblo south. In approximately 1300, they drifted south to the Rio Grande. The Pueblo community is divided into three clans: the corn clan, turkey clan, and turquoise clan. Members of these clans can play an important role in administration, government, and religious ceremonies. The Pueblo economy is based on agriculture, raising livestock, and selling handicrafts. Crops include corn, beans, cotton, melon, squash, and chili peppers. The Pueblo Indians practice monogamy, whether they are married according to Indian customs or civil and church ceremonies (Dutton, 1983). Men generally work the fields, weave, build houses, and conduct ceremonies. Women prepare food, care for children, make baskets and pottery, and transport water. Women also help with gardening and building houses ("Pueblo Indians," 1994). The religion is animism. Some of their ritual myths are of great length and full of poetic imagery. Belief in witchcraft was universal, and witch executions were frequent. The dead were buried in the ground (Mooney, 2003). The Pueblos were, and still are, peaceable, kind, and industrious. Their way of life has been changed by the White man's civilization beyond the addition of a few conveniences in housekeeping and working methods (Mooney, 2003). The majority, however, still hold persistently to their old beliefs and ceremonials.

References

Dutton, B. P. (1983). *American Indians of the Southwest.* Albuquerque: University of New Mexico Press.

Mooney, J. (2003). *The Catholic encyclopedia* (Vol. 13). New York: Appleton.

Pueblo Indians. (1994). In *Encarta encyclopedia.* New York: Encarta.

Salzmann, J. M., & Salzmann, Z. (1997). *Native Americans of the Southwest.* Boulder, CO: Westview.

Puerto Ricans   Puerto Ricans are natives of an autonomous island commonwealth of the United States in the Caribbean Sea that was populated by Boriquen Indians when it was discovered by Christopher Columbus during his second voyage in 1493. The natives were mistakenly named *Tainos* because Columbus assumed that the natives, when saying "Tainos" in their greetings, were referring to their name, when in fact they were offering assurance of harmlessness. The island was inhabited by approximately 30,000 Tainos Indians, who proved to be successful in agriculture, hunting, and fishing under the leadership of the first governor, Ponce de León, after the island was colonized by the Europeans in 1508. Due to forced labor, disease, and miscegenation, the natives became extinct and were promptly replaced by African slaves, who undertook harsh tasks such as sugar cultivation. With the increase in productivity, domestic and international trade began to increase; this contributed to more urbanization that accommodated French and Spaniard immigrates, many of whom proved to be industrious contributors to the economy (Haslip-Viera, 2001; Kinsbruner, 1996; *Webster's Encyclopedic Unabridged Dictionary,* 1989). Because of all the events that took place on the island, a vast racial diversity was found among the population, and many different racial labels were created to give name to it, such as Black, mulatto, and non-White. Regardless of the precise terminology, however, a census reported that the majority of the Puerto Rican population was White from 1899 to 2000 (Duany, 2002). The United States gained sovereignty over the island in 1898 after the Spanish-American War. The United States created a sustained campaign for Puerto Ricans to Americanize their thoughts, views, and attitudes toward life and toward government (Morris, 1995). Puerto Ricans were granted U.S. citizenship in 1917, although residents of the island did not vote in U.S. presidential elections. Puerto Ricans, being citizens, began to immigrate to the mainland, especially New York, due to an increase in population and economic pressure (Fitzpatrick, 1971). Currently, approximately half of all people of Puerto Rican descent do not live on the island but, rather, in the United States. Many, especially those born and raised in the United States, do not use Spanish, the national language, as their primary means of communication. Moreover, many names are used to refer to Puerto Ricans who reside in the U.S. mainland, such as Neo-Rican, Nuyorican, and Boricua (Duany, 2002).

References

Duany, J. (2002). *The Puerto Rican nation on the move.* Chapel Hill: University of North Carolina Press.

Fitzpatrick, J. (1971). *Puerto Rican Americans.* Englewood Cliffs, NJ: Prentice Hall.

Haslip-Viera, G. (2001). *Taino revival.* Princeton, NJ: Wiener.

Kinsbruner, J. (1996). *Not of pure blood.* Durham, NC: Duke University Press.

Morris, N. (1995). *Puerto Rico.* Westport, CT: Praeger.

Webster's encyclopedia unabridged dictionary of the English language. (1989). New York: Dilithium.

Pygmies   In the 14th century, this term was used to name a race of very diminutive men. It was also a way to measure the length of something going from elbow to fist (*Oxford Dictionary of English Etymology,* 1991). Members of any ethnic group whose adult males have an average height of 59 inches (150 cm) are considered pygmies (*New Encyclopedia Britannica,* 2002). Such terminology includes the African Pygmy peoples, the Andaman Islanders of India, the Semang of the Malay Peninsula, and the Aeta from the Philippines. Also, Asian Pygmies are often called *Negritos.* It is believed that pygmy groups evolved from different full-sized ancestors and immigrated to tropical forests such as in Africa. Then, genetic mutations accounted for dwarfisim, which had survival advantages for some individuals, and spread through natural selection. Pygmies exhibit different kinds of dwarfism, such as ateleotic dwarfism, in which the body parts are proportionate to the reduced height, and achondroplastic dwarfism, in which the extremities are shortened and thickened as in true dwarfs. The term *pygmy* is mostly used to refer to the pygmy groups who are residents of tropical Africa. These groups are nomadic hunters and gatherers and do not practice agriculture or cattle raising. They are small groups or bands that do not have a leader; decisions are made by general discussion and agreement among the men of the band. In most marriages, the wife joins the male's band, and marriages are monogamous (*Encyclopedia Americana,* 1995). The best known pygmies are the *Mbuti,* who are the smallest people in the world and live in the Ituri Forest in northeastern Zaire. Many attribute their lack of height to a major deficiency of a substance called interferon growth factor-1, which is one of the secondary growth factors in humans. They call themselves *Bambuti* and are the most populous and culturally purest group of pygmies. Their bands consist of 10 to 25 individual families. Their population is calculated to be 20,000; for every mile, one would find one Mbuti, in contrast with the population in Manhattan, New York, which is 77,000 per square mile. This enormous divergence in permanent settlement would greatly affect a Mbuti band because it is biologically well adapted to its environment, which provides all the band's basic needs. With arrows, spears, and nets, the men of the band hunt treetop-dwelling monkeys and also elephants. The women fish and collect fruits, roots, and insects. When supplies such as water, food, fuel, and medicinal plants are exhausted in an area, the Mbuti band moves to another location. Due to this type of lifestyle, houses are simple beehive-shaped structures consisting of poles covered with leaves, which also have other functions, such as for bedding, serving food, and dressing (Duffy, 1996; *Encyclopedia Americana,* 1995).

References

Duffy, K. (1996). *Children of the forest: Africa's Mbuti Pygmies.* Prospect Heights, IL: Waveland.

Encyclopedia Americana international edition. (1995). Danbury, CT: Grolier.

New encyclopedia Britannica. (2002). Chicago: Encyclopedia Britannica.

Oxford dictionary of English etymology. (1991). Hong Kong: Oxford University Press.

Q

Quashi   This is a corruption of the word *quasi* (Latin) used in the dialect of English-speaking Caribbean islanders. The meaning of quasi is to have some resemblance, usually by having certain attributes of the real thing. A phenomenon may only bear resemblance or approximations to a certain degree but not to the full extent of what it represents (*Webster's New Collegiate Dictionary*, 2002). In Standard English, the word is used in such combinations as "quasi-judicial" or "quasi-legislative," both of which imply that the terms have some attributes of the meanings of the words but not all. Not all words in the dialect are attributed to corrupted Standard English words. For example, *nyam*, which means "eat," has no English root. Quashi is often used in a derogatory sense to describe someone who is behaving in a manner below expectations. By referring to the person as a quashi, the term may imply that the person is silly, stupid, or idiotic. In reference to an event, the word implies that it had no importance or status, or it was unsatisfactory. For example, a disorganized demonstration, concert, or meeting could all be described as quashi events (Hall, 2002).

References

Hall, L. E. (2002). *Working with the Caribbean client*. Unpublished manuscript. Ft. Lauderdale, FL: Nova Southeastern University.

Webster's new collegiate dictionary. (2002). Springfield, MA: Merriam-Webster.

R

Race Race is defined as a group of people of common descent, blood, or heredity or as the formation of an ethic stock by a group of people (*Webster's Encyclopedia Unabridged Dictionary*, 1989). Race is also described as differences in physical traits, ancestry, and culture among *Homo sapiens*. Race differences are expressed not only by the difference in pigmentation of the skin but also by differences in the lips, nose, mouth, and eyelids. Furthermore, there are also differences in the inner organs, muscles, and drug sensitivity. The term *race* was introduced in *Natural History* by Buffon to describe six groups of men. The term was an extension of the Aristotelian conception of species. Although Buffon recognized that all humans belong to a single species, it was a convenient way to distinguish certain geographical groups of men. Sometimes, race has been identified with religion, such as the Jewish "race," and national groupings in periods of intensive nationalism; religion and national affinity, however, are not measures of race. It was believed that all human groups could be explained in terms of a few original races, such as Negro, Mongoloid, and White, but this has been determined to be an invalid hypothesis (Garn, 1969). It has been attempted to capture the concept of race within a framework, but due to its variation this has been difficult to achieve. Populations are always subtly changing to become more similar to other populations so that it is difficult, if not impossible, to differentiate the race of one population and that of another one established nearby. This phenomenon is called "clines" (Montagu, 1964). As a result, the contemporary approach is based on population genetics, in which race is viewed as a breeding population that shares a common history, common locale, and common dangers and is a product of the common environment. There is evidence that races change their genetic makeup even when there is no genetic mixture involved. These changes occur in response to adaptation to the environment (Garn, 1969). The notion of race has become so socially constructed that it has been used to define people's roles in society (Jones, 1997), and with those roles are concomitant prejudices and discriminatory responses. Multicultural psychologists focus on social and cultural variables associated with race rather than on race per se (Betancourt & Lopez, 1993).

References

Betancourt, H., & Lopez, S. R. (1993). The study of culture, ethnicity and race in American psychology. *American Psychologist, 48,* 629–637.

Buffon, G.-L. (1792). *Natural history, general and particular.*

Garn, S. (1969). *Human races.* Springfield, IL: Charles C Thomas.

Jones, J. M. (1997). *Prejudice and racism* (2nd ed.). New York: McGraw-Hill.

Montagu, A. (1964). *The concept of race.* New York: Free Press.

Webster's encyclopedia unabridged dictionary of the English language. (1989). New York: Dilithium.

Racism   Another term used to refer to this is *racialism*, and it is the belief that human beings can be categorized in exclusive biological entities called races. These races exhibit a connection between inherited physical traits and traits of intellect, morality, and other cultural behavioral features assessing humans as superior or inferior to others (*New Encyclopedia Britannica*, 2002). Racist thinking is based on humans' biological differences, which may be real or not but from which derive practices that pour scorn on certain ethnic groups (Memmi, 2002). In the United States and apartheid South Africa, racism dictated that different races should be separated from one another and, consequently, that each ethic group should have its own school, church, and hospital. Moreover, it was considered unnatural for members of two separate races to intermarry. People who practice racism believe that only low-status jobs should go to low-status races, such as Blacks and Indians in the United States and colored in South Africa. They also believe that members of the economically and culturally dominant race are the only ones that should have access to privileges, political power, and high-status jobs. Some lived experiences of the people from the low-status race include insults, disrespect, and acts of disdain. In the United States, the term *race* was coined to establish differences between people of European descent and those who were brought from Africa as slaves against their will. This resulted in the portrayal of Africans and their descendents as lesser human beings because of their status on arrival to the United States (*New Encyclopedia Britannica*, 2002). For the Spanish, it was a way to justify the invasion and domination of people who were proclaimed to be morally culpable, biologically inferior, and depraved. The Nazis used the same idea to justify their expansion of Germany (Memmi, 2000). Racism can be founded not only in fear and frustration but also in aggression, adequacy, and guilt. Anti-Semitism flourished in Germany possibly because the country achieved nationhood later than worldwide empires such as Britain; therefore, the Germans had to find some sort of reassurance, and they found it in the affirmation of their Aryan superiority. Also, one reason why Englishmen were racially tolerant in their own country but racially prejudiced in Africa and Asia may be that in their colonies the British were a dominant minority group and feared a potential rebellion of the native majority (Bibby, 1960).

References

Bibby, C. (1960). *Race, prejudice and education.* New York: Praeger.

Memmi, A. (2000). *Racism.* Minneapolis: University of Minnesota Press.

New encyclopedia Britannica. (2002). Chicago: Encyclopedia Britannica.

Refugee   This term originated in 1685 from the French *refugie*, "to take shelter, protect," derived from the old French *refuge*. It was first applied to French Huguenots, who migrated after the revocation of the Edict of Nantes. Although banishment into exile and the granting of asylum have occurred throughout history, the use of the word refugee as a noun suggested a new social awareness. What made the Huguenots refugees was the fact that they were fleeing from life-threatening danger, where "life" referred to their spiritual and physical existence (Aguayo, Suhrke, & Zolberg, 1989). Like the Hugenots, the Iberian Jews were faced with life-threatening danger because of their religion. The word meant "one seeking asylum" until 1914, when it evolved to mean "one fleeing home." Refugees are people who have fled to another country or have been expelled and cannot return due to fear of persecution. Refugees are not the same as immigrants, who leave their country by choice. There have been refugees throughout history, but in modern times there have been large numbers of refugees. The three largest and most dramatic refugee movements in the post–Cold War era involved 2 million–3 million Iraqi Kurds and Shi'ites who entered Iran and Turkey following Saddam Hussein's genocidal attacks, 2.5 million ex-Yugoslavs expelled from their homes as a result of "ethnic cleansing," and millions of Somalis displaced as a result of starvation and interclan warfare (Loescher, 1993). Refugees may remain outside the country of their nationality due to race, religion, political opinion, social affiliation, or even civil strife, famine, or environmental disasters. The 1960s and 1970s saw a wave of refugees predominantly from Third World countries during which millions of displaced people posed a challenge to international stability (Loescher, 1993). In 1951, the United Nations' Convention Relating to the Status of Refugees was the primary international law but was limited in scope. In 1967, the geographical and temporal limitations of the law were lifted, but the term *refugee* remained narrowly defined. Thus, the Organization of African Unity adopted a broader definition in 1969, including as refugees people forced to leave their places of residence because of external aggression, foreign occupation or domination, or events seriously disturbing public order. In 1984, further progress was made in Central American countries when the Cartagena Declaration was issued, which included as refugees people fleeing generalized violence, international conflicts, or serious disturbances of public peace. None of these documents, however, made provisions for internally displaced refugees because the designation of refugee applied only to those who crossed international borders (Frelick, 2002).

References

Aguayo, S., Suhrke, A., & Zolberg, A. (1989). *Escape from violence: Conflict and the refugee crisis in the developing world.* New York: Oxford University Press.

Frelick, B. (2002). *Encyclopedia Americano.* New York: Grolier.

Loescher, G. (1993). *Beyond charity: International cooperation and global refugee crisis.* New York: Oxford University Press.

Relativism   From a philosophical standpoint, relativism is the position that all points of view are equally valid, and that all truth is relative to the individual and his or her environment. All ethical, religious, political, and aesthetic beliefs are truths that are relative to the cultural identity to the individual (Edel, 1975). Relativism can include moral relativism (ethics are relative to the social construct), situational relativism (right and wrong depend on the particular situation), and cognitive relativism (truth is relative and has no objective standard) (Bidney, 1989).

Anthropology has focused on relativism in relationship to culture—the idea that all cultures are equally worthy of respect and that in studying another culture one needs to suspend judgment, empathize, and try to understand the way that particular culture views the world (Turner, 1986) (see Cultural Relativism). One of the most controversial challenges to the study of social ethics derives from a methodological approach of the social sciences involving cultural relativism: "Cultural relativism is in essence an approach to the question of the nature and role of values in culture" (Herskovits, 1973, p. 33). If values are shared ideas that give rise to beliefs and norms of behavior around which a people or a group organizes its collective life and goals, cultural relativism declares that these values are relative to the cultural ambiance out of which they arise (Ruggiero, 1973). We live in a rapidly changing world society, which is increasingly bringing people of various cultures into closer contact with each other. This interaction can be positive or negative, depending on the level of sensitivity and respect people have for other cultural groups. These two types of behavior are related to the important concepts of ethnocentrism and cultural relativism. Negative attitudes toward other cultures and ethnic groups arise out of ethnocentrism, whereas positive attitudes are the result of a culturally relativist approach. If people are going to be successful in today's multicultural, information age, world society, they need to develop a culturally sensitive frame of reference and mode of operation. Thus, cultural relativism is a necessary optic to perceive the sociocultural reality in today's multicultural world society (Herskovits, 1973).

References

Bidney, D. (1989). *Ethics and the social sciences.* Notre Dame, IN: University of Notre Dame Press.

Edel, A. (1975). *Ethical judgment, the use of science in ethics.* Glencoe, IL: Free Press.

Herskovits, M. J. (1973). *Cultural relativism: Perspectives in cultural pluralism.* New York: Vintage.

Ruggiero, V. R. (1973). *The moral imperative: Ethical issues for discussion and writing.* New York: Knopf.

Turner, J. H. (1986). *The structure of sociological theory.* Belmont, CA: Wadsworth.

Rites of passage   The anthropologist Arnold van Gennep coined the term *rites of passage* in the early 1900s (Teather, 1999, p. 13). The term is used to describe the various transitions an individual goes through during the course of his or her life (Grimes, 1995, p. 1). Rites of passage are thought of as celebratory acts that publicly indicate the passage of a person from one social group to another (Teather, 1999, p. 157). For example, birth, marriage, maturation, and death are different stages that people go through. Rites of passage are not limited to these. They can be any transition or life crisis that an individual experiences (Grimes, 1995, p. 1). These rituals mark the essential divisions between young and old, male and female, living and dead (Christopher, Madhi, & Meade, 1996, p. 5). Rites of passage are also thought of as a journey through one's life. It is said to be a journey through time and space in which there are episodes of "ups and downs," some so severe that they can be compared to a roller coaster (Teather, 1999, p. 1). These religious, biological, social, and psychological processes are defined by the rites, or names, people give them. Many of the rites of passage are demonstrated through activities such as rituals. For example, the ritual of weddings refers to the rite of passage known as marriage. A ritual is a way of welcoming, intensifying, concentrating, and getting past or coping with these transitions. Rituals aid in organizing processes that by themselves may seem random. They also help add significance to the meaning of a passage so that it is not forgotten or gone unnoticed (Grimes, 1995, p. 1). The transitions or passages we experience, although personal, are highly impacted by organizations of our social life, such as home, school, family, work, and religion (Teather, 1999, p. 1). Gennep (1960) described three common stages in these transitions: separation, transition, and incorporation. Separation and incorporation are often perceived as a self-confidence of safe passage proceeding from the old position to the new one ("Rites of Passage," 1996, p. 793). The separation stage typically occurs when an individual goes into a sacred world. The individual's incorporation stage is his or her return to a "profane world" (Teather, 1999, p. 13). The most important stage, the transition stage, occurs when an individual is "in the middle," not a part of any group. This is often referred to as the liminal stage. Gennep's rites of passage theory is a sociocentered theory. The psychoanalyst-centered theory concentrates on one rite, the puberty rite, and regards the others as less important or a by-product of that one rite ("Rites of Passage," 1996, p. 793). Many view the rites of passage optimistically, believing that they represent significant thresholds in the stages of the life cycle. Others, however, believe that they bring forth sources of strength and empowerment on a passage to spiritual completeness. Some people are concerned that certain cultures, such as that of the United States, are ritually deprived (Teather, 1999, p. 104). The rites of passage vary in order, along with which ones individuals experience, from culture to culture. In some cultures, the connections between the stages are passed without the advantage or requirement of ceremonies. In other societies, however, these movements are weighed down by rituals (Grimes, 1995, p. 1).

References

Christopher, N. G., Madhi, L. C., & Meade, M. (1996). *Crossroads: The quest for contemporary rites of passage.* Chicago: Open Court.

Gennep, V. A. (1960). *The rites of passage: A classic study of cultural celebrations.* Chicago: University of Chicago Press.

Grimes, R. (1995). *Marrying & burying: Rites of passage in a man's life.* Boulder, CO: Westview.

Rites of passage. (1996). In *Concise encyclopedia of psychology* (2nd ed.). New York: John Wiley.

Teather, E. K. (Ed.). (1999). *Embodied geographies: Space, bodies and rites of passages.* New York: Taylor & Francis.

Rootwork   This is another name for the large body of African folkloric practices and beliefs with a considerable admixture of American Indian botanical knowledge and European folklore. It is also known as hoodoo. Hoodoo is not voodoo because hoodoo or rootwork is medicinal. It is also called witchcraft. Rootwork is recognition of the preeminence that dried roots play in the making of charms and the casting of spells. Rootwork is said to derive from the success or failure of slave uprisings that influenced the persistence of African magic. Where priests and their sorcery were believed to have defeated the oppressive masters, African-based magic became a visible element in the emerging African American cultural landscape (Voeks, 1993). Symptoms of rootwork include generalized anxiety; gastrointestinal complaints, such as nausea, vomiting, and diarrhea; weakness and dizziness; and the fear of being poisoned or killed. Such fear of death may continue until the root is removed, usually through the work of a root doctor. Rootwork is known as *mal puesto* or *brujeria* in Latin cultures.

Reference

Voeks, R. (1993). African medicine and magic in the Americas. *Geographical Review, 83,* 66–87.

S

Sampling equivalence Sampling equivalence is implicated when designing research that compares cultures on some psychological phenomenon. It involves several steps beyond what is required for research within a single culture. It rarely makes sense to conduct a study in exactly the same way using exactly the same materials for more than one culture. Although studies of each culture cannot be identical, it is important that they be equivalent at some level (Goldstein, 2000). Sampling equivalence is the method of recruiting research participants who are similar on dimensions other than culture. Most research projects involve sampling equivalence of participants from a population of interest (Goldstein, 2000). In a representative sample, each member of the population of interest has equal probability of selection. Murdock and White (1969), in creating the standard sample for cross-cultural research, take up the issue of sampling the diversity of human communities to learn about coherence or decoherence within and between communities. In cross-cultural research, problems arise regarding the definition of a culture: At what level should cultures be defined? Murdock (1967) defined six cultural areas: North America, South America, sub-Saharan Africa, Asia, Australia, and circum Mediterranean. There are also many areas of interest. Selection of samples stratified according to areas is not representative of large cultures but only the communities that are specified. Research results will be obtained only on specific bundles of practices, beliefs, social roles, norms, expressions, forms of organizations, and conflicts (economic, political, legal, religious, expressive, and artistic) that cannot be generalized to the whole culture (Murdock & White, 1969). Sample equivalence will only be achieved by the use of smaller, more precisely defined culture-bearing units and the use of random selection of individuals within the populations of interest (Berry, Poortinga, Segall, & Dasen, 2002).

References

Berry, J. W., Poortinga, Y. H., Segall, M. H., & Dasen, P. R. (2002). *Cross-cultural psychology: Research and applications* (2nd ed.). Cambridge, UK: Cambridge University Press.

Goldstein, S. (2000). *Cross-cultural explorations: Activities in culture and psychology.* Boston: Allyn & Bacon.

Murdock, G. P. (1967). *Ethnographic atlas.* Pittsburgh, PA: University of Pittsburgh Press.

Murdock, G. P., & White, D. (1969). Standard cross-cultural sample: *Ethnology, 8,* 329–369.

Samurai   *Samurai* is the noun form of the verb *samurau* ("to serve") in the Japanese language. Its first meaning was to denote the soldiers on guard duty at the emperor's palace, but it was subsequently changed to refer to all members of the warrior class that owed loyalty to a feudal emperor. In Japanese society, samurai constituted the leading class, followed by farmers, artisans, and traders (Sansom, 2002). Samurai were bound by the code of ethics known as *bushido,* meaning the "way of the warrior," which prescribed their appropriate service and conduct as elite members of society. Many were required to master administrative skills as well as military arts because they served in positions of bureaucratic leadership (Hauser, 2002). In their early history, the samurai valued military strength, such as weapon skills, horsemanship, self-discipline, and bravery. They prized complete obedience and personal honor. If they were dishonored, they considered it a duty to commit suicide (Jeffrey, 2002). The samurai were a very important military group until the development of firearms, which proved far more effective than bow or sword. Additional problems for the samurai developed in the early 1600s because they had little opportunity for military employment. A few entered into government posts; others devoted their efforts to the arts (e.g., literature or philosophy); and still many others sought work in towns, which reduced their social status. Samurai were responsible for the revolution of 1868, in which feudal structure was replaced by constitutional monarchy. Soon thereafter, samurai as a class disappeared (Sansom, 2002).

References

Hauser, W. B. (2002). *Multimedia encyclopedia.* Danbury, CT: Grolier.

Jeffrey, P. (2002). *Samurai.* Chicago: World Book.

Sansom, G. B. (2002). *Encyclopedia Americana.* Danbury, CT: Grolier.

Santería   Santería (or *La Regla Lucumí*) originated in West Africa in what is currently Nigeria and Benin. It is the traditional religion of the Yoruba people. The slave trade brought many of these people to the shores of Cuba, Brazil, Haiti, Trinidad, and Puerto Rico. Along with the bodies being brought over for sale into a life of misery were their souls and their religion (Nuñez, 1992). To the *Santeros* and millions of its practitioners, Santería is simply known as the Religion. In Santería, there are no leaders who are viewed as central to the religion or as objects of worship. The Santeros or Santeras, who are the priests and priestesses, are viewed only as the mouthpieces of the *orishas* (the saints) and as the instructors in the mysteries of Santería. Those who become imbued with a sense of their own importance are said to be *endiosados* (i.e., self-deified) and are harshly criticized by other Santeros (Gonzalez-Whippler & Wetli, 1998). The religion incorporates the use of animal sacrifice and the practice of sacred drumming and dance. Slaves who landed in the Caribbean and Central and South America were nominally converted to Catholicism. They were able to preserve some of their traditions, however, by fusing together various Dahomean, ba Konga, and Yoruban beliefs and rituals and by synchronizing these with elements from the surrounding Catholic culture. In Cuba, this religious tradition has evolved into what is know today as *Santería*, the Way of the Saints. Today, hundreds of thousands of Americans participate in this ancient religion. Some are fully committed priests and priestesses, others are "godchildren" or members of a particular house tradition, and many are clients seeking help with their everyday problems. Many are of Hispanic and Caribbean descent, but as the religion has moved out of the inner cities and into the suburbs, a growing number are of African American and European American heritage. The religions of Africa were re-created in the Americas, and today Santería is moving into mainstream America; further transformation can be expected (Brandon, 1993).

References

Brandon, G. (1993). *Santeria from Africa to the New World: The dead sell memories.* Bloomington: Indiana University Press.

Gonzales-Whippler, M., & Wetli, C. (1998). *Santeria: The religion: Faith, rights, magic.* St. Paul, MN: Llewelyn.

Nuñez, L. (1992). *Santeria, a practical guide to Afro-Caribbean magic.* Putnam, CT: Spring.

Self   The sense of self is vitally important in understanding one's behavior as well as understanding and predicting the behavior of others (Matsumoto, 2000). When the brain receives unfamiliar information, it tries to associate it with data it already has in an effort to better understand the information or even make new personal knowledge that will remain in memory for later use. This process allows a comparison to be made between reality and one's perception of reality (Levinson, Ponzetti, & Jorgensen, 1999). Self construals are nonetheless affected by cultural variables. The notion of the self is significant among the individualistic cultures in the United States, Canada, Australia, and Western Europe. Collectivistic cultures, such as those found in Asia, Africa, and South America, tend to attach significance to the group rather than the individual self. According to Markus and Kitayama (1991), individualistic cultures have an independent self construal in which the sense of self is separate from those with whom they interact (parents, coworkers, and friends). Conversely, collectivistic cultures have an interdependent construal of self. The sense of self is invariably tied to those with whom one interacts and shares a bond, such as family, friends, coworkers, and social or religious groups. Considerable variation exists, however, among people of different ethnicities within a single culture and among individuals within a single ethnic group (Matsumoto, 2000).

References

Levinson, D., Ponzetti, J. J., Jr., & Jorgensen, P. F. (1999). Attribution theory. In *The encyclopedia of human emotions* (Vol. 1, pp. 94–95). New York: Macmillan.

Markus, H., & Kitayama, S. (1991). Culture and self: Implications for cognition, emotion and motivation. *Psychological Review, 98,* 224–253.

Matsumoto, D. (2000). *Culture and psychology* (2nd ed.). Toronto: Wadsworth.

Self-perception   Self-perception is the method by which people try to understand their attitudes and feelings by examining their own behavior and the situations that cause their behavior. This theory examines how behavior can affect attitudes (Magill, 1993). Bem (1972) introduced this theory. According to this theory of self-perception, people understand themselves by making assumptions based on observations of their own actions. Bem's explanation for the self-perception theory proposes that this internalization arises because people look to their behavior to infer their attitudes and traits, especially when the self-presentations are similar with their former self-views or when the individuals are unsure about their self-views on that aspect (Weiner, 2003). One infers his or her own attitudes from one's behaviors just as he or she would when inferring the attitudes of others (Roeckelein, 1998). This theory suggests that displaying a specific public image can produce behaviors that cause people to see what they are doing as correctly corresponding to part of their true self (Weiner, 2003). Some refer to self-perception as self-knowledge. Self-perception comes into play even more when one cannot say that one's behavior was controlled by some external factor (Myers, 2002). There are three parts of self-perception: the ideal self, the personal self, and the social self. The ideal self is the person one would like to become, whereas the personal self is the way one truly sees oneself. The social self is the way in which one believes that others see oneself (Weiner, 2003). Although mainly due to the social self, the three parts of self-perception help explain why people's behavior is not always consistent or predictable. The self-perception theory is more likely to be applicable when the chances of thinking about the attitude object are relatively low (Roeckelein, 1998). This theory suggests that when the individual's internal signs regarding his or her internal position are weak or ambiguous, the person's knowledge of his or her own feelings tends to come from judgments based on external information instead of directly from his or her internal feelings (Magill, 1993).

References

Bem, D. J. (1972). Self perception theory. In L. Berkowitz (Ed.), *Advances in experimental social psychology* (Vol. 6). New York: Academic Press.

Magill, F. (1993). Self perception. In *Survey of social science: Psychology series* (Vol. 5). Pasadena, CA: Salem Press.

Myers, D. (2002). *Social psychology* (7th ed.). New York: McGraw-Hill.

Roeckelein, J. (1998). *The dictionary of theories, laws, & concepts in psychology* (pp. 57–59). Westport, CT: Greenwood.

Weiner, I. (Ed.). (2003). Personality and social psychology. In *The handbook of psychology* (Vol. 5, pp. 363–369). New York: John Wiley.

Self-serving bias   We, as individuals, are inclined to like ourselves and give ourselves the benefit of the doubt. This comes into play with self-serving bias, which is the tendency to observe and think of our own actions in ways that uphold our self-esteem. According to Myers (2002), we readily excuse our failures, accept credit for our successes, and in many ways view ourselves as better than average; in this way, we maintain high self-esteem. The self-serving bias involves attributions that aid people in looking good when compared to others. People tend to increase their self-esteem and public self-presentation with the use of positive internal attributions. This allows them to take credit for their successes. They also use external attributions to clear themselves from responsibility and guilt for their failures (Levinson & Ponzetti, 1999). Self-serving bias is a kind of attribution bias in which one's individual aspirations, attitudes, and motives interrupt a rational and methodical examination of the causes of behavior (Roeckelein, 1998). The *Penguin Dictionary of Psychology* (Reber, 1995) defines self-serving bias as any bias involved in understanding events in the world that functions in a self-serving manner. Attribution biases were first thought of as errors made by the spectator; social psychologists, however, scrutinized the reasons for these attributions and concluded that the biases were heuristic devices. The biases were thought of as "rules of thumb" or "shortcuts" that assisted observers in making attributions promptly and efficiently. Internal and external attributions pertaining to success or failure spawn intense emotions because of the inferences for the self. These strong emotions are partly why self-serving biases are used so frequently. When people credit themselves for a success, they are flooded with feelings of pride, self-respect, increased self-esteem, and an improved sense of competence. When people experience failures and attribute them to their own shortcomings, however, they often experience depression because of their lowered self-esteem and sense of competence. These are the emotions that people strive to avoid, and in eluding these feelings, individuals often use self-serving biases. By using these biases, they can credit the failures to some external factor. These self-enhancing biases increase the recognition people receive, allowing them to feel more gratification, and avert the blame so as to decrease feelings of guilt and responsibility (Levinson, Ponzetti, & Jorgensen, 1999).

References

Levinson, D., Ponzetti, J. J, Jr., & Jorgensen, P. F. (1999). Attribution theory. In *The encyclopedia of human emotions* (Vol. 1). New York: Macmillan.

Myers, D. (2002). *Social psychology* (7th ed.). New York: McGraw-Hill.

Reber, S. E. (Ed.). (1995). *The Penguin dictionary of psychology.* New York: Penguin.

Roeckelein, J. (Ed.). (1998). Attribution theory. In *The dictionary of theories, laws, & concepts in psychology.* Westport, CT: Greenwood.

Shaman   A shaman is a member of certain tribal societies who mediates between the visible and the spirit worlds for purposes of healing, divination, and control over natural events (Harner, 1973). The word shaman is from the Tungusic word *saman,* which means to raise oneself or enter an ecstatic state. It is also defined as a person who casts impressive spells (Stein, 2002) and is assumed to have been given his or her supernatural powers by guardian angels but may have inherited the role or received it at some point in his or her life. Shamans communicate with the spiritual world through visions and vivid dreams that inspire their work (Wheeler, 2003). Shamanism is the belief that the spiritual underworld comes into contact with the "mundane" world at specific points on the terrain—caves, crags, mountain peaks, and promontories. It is in such places that the remnants of strong shamanistic tradition can be seen in the form of rock carvings and paintings. For example, Puberty Rock in Riverside, California, is a site at which a rite of passage for adolescent girls was conducted, and an image of bighorn sheep scratched into a rock in Inscription Canyon in the Mojave Desert is the imagined "spirit helper" of a medicine man. Shamans envisioned spirits and supernatural events, such as curing, rainmaking, and sorcery. Shamans participated in ceremonies during altered states of consciousness (Kirsch, 2000). Shamans are predominantly members of many Indigenous cultures. They are sometimes referred to as "medicine men" or "medicine women" but actually have different styles and practices depending on the cultures they inhabit.

References

Harner, M. (1973). *Hallucinogens and shamanism.* Oxford, UK: Oxford University Press.

Kirsch, J. (2000, September 20). Visions of California's indigenous shamans [West words]. *Los Angeles Times,* p. 1.

Stein, J. (2002, August 22). Lion king. *Cincinnati Post,* p. 3.

Wheeler, C. (2003, August 6). Weaving dreams. *Press Enterprise* (Riverside, CA), p. 4.

Shenjing shuairuo   In Mandarin Chinese, *shenjing* means "nervous system" and *shuairuo* means "weakness." This is a common ailment among Chinese and is experienced as weakness of the nervous system characterized by feelings of physical and mental exhaustion, difficulty concentrating, memory loss, fatigue, and dizziness. Physical symptoms, such as difficulty sleeping, loss of appetite, sexual dysfunction, headaches, and irritability, often accompany the disorder. In the West, this disorder is known as neurasthenia (Gaw, 2001). See Neurasthenia.

Reference

Gaw, A. C. (2001). *Concise guide to cross-cultural psychiatry.* Washington, DC: American Psychiatric Publishing.

Spiritism   Spiritism is the name properly given to the belief that the living can and do communicate with the spirits of the departed and to the various practices by which such communication is attempted. It should be carefully distinguished from spiritualism, the philosophical doctrine that holds, in general, that there is a spiritual order of beings no less real than the material and, in particular, that the soul of man is a spiritual substance. Spiritism, moreover, has taken on a religious character. It claims to prove the preamble of all religions—that is, the existence of a spiritual world—and to establish a worldwide religion in which the adherents of the various traditional faiths, setting their dogmas aside, can unite. If it has formulated no definite creed, and if its representatives differ in their attitudes toward the beliefs of Christianity, this is simply because spiritism is expected to supply a new and fuller revelation that will either substantiate on a rational basis the essential Christian dogmas or show that they are utterly unfounded. The knowledge thus acquired will naturally affect conduct, the more so because it is hoped that the discarnate spirits, in making known their condition, will also indicate the means of attaining salvation or of progressing, by a continuous evolution in the other world, to a higher plane of existence and happiness (*Catholic Encyclopedia*, 1912). It is the belief that the human personality continues to exist after death and can communicate with the living through the agency of a medium or psychic (*Columbia Encyclopedia*, 2003). An integral part of this belief is that the dead can contact the living via séances. Spiritism may be practiced alone or as part of other faiths, such as Umbanda or Palo Mayombe. The spiritist phenomenon remounts to ancient times. History shows that throughout the world, the belief in spirits and the communication with them have always been practiced. There are reports confirming the belief in spiritism in Greece, Egypt, China, and other countries (Kardek & Wood, 1997).

References

Catholic encyclopedia (Vol. 14). (1912). New York: Appleton.

Columbia encyclopedia (6th ed.). (2003). New York: Columbia University Press.

Kardek, A., & Wood, E. A. (1997). *Experimental spiritism: Book on mediums or a guide for mediums & invocators*. White Fish, MT: Kessinger.

Standard English   English is the language spoken by the people of the United Kingdom, the United States, and countries throughout the world that are now or were formerly under British control. Standard English as defined with respect to spelling, grammar, pronunciation, and vocabulary is substantially uniform although not devoid of regional differences. There is well-established usage in the formal and informal speech and writing of the educated that is widely recognized as acceptable wherever English is spoken and understood (*Webster's New Collegiate Dictionary*, 2002). Although English is considered a global language of business, there are variations with regard to what is considered Standard English. This is due to the fact that English varies throughout the world. There is British English, Australian English, Canadian English, American English, Nigerian English, Indian English, New Zealand English, Caribbean English, and Philippine English, to name a few (Gilsdorf, 2002). English also changes as contact with other cultures increases. Words are added or deleted from the language as the culture changes. The term *Negro* is no longer accepted in academic research when describing a Black person. Educators, academicians, and the business community engage in the use of Standard English as defined by their region. In the United States, there are wide variations of dialects of Standard English (Wolfram, Adger, & Christian, 1999). Generally, Standard English is the composite of the language spoken by the educated professional middle class (Gollnick, 2002).

References

Gilsdorf, J. (2002). Standard Englishes and world Englishes: Living with a polymorph business language. *Journal of Business Communication, 39*(3), 364–370.

Gollnick, D. (2002). *Multicultural education in a pluralistic society* (6th ed.). Upper Saddle River, NJ: Prentice Hall.

Webster's new collegiate dictionary. (2002). Springfield, MA: Merriam-Webster.

Wolfram, W., Adger, C., & Christian, D. (1999). *Dialects in schools and communities.* Mahwah, NJ: Lawrence Erlbaum.

Stereotype   A stereotype is a belief about the personal attributes of a group of people. It is making judgment of a specific ethnic culture, gender, or sexual orientation without fully understanding events or situations (Chorlian, 2000). Stereotypes may result when persons are observed and believed to be the sole representatives of their cultural group (Lopez, 2001). Stereotypes can be overgeneralized, inaccurate, and resistant to new information. Any attempt to describe a group other than one's own is seriously challenged by one's inability to move beyond one's own perceptual world. Stereotypes that make sweeping generalizations about groups of people, such as "women are emotional and men are rational," are termed *alpha bias*, whereas those that minimize or ignore differences are termed *beta bias* (Hall & Barongan, 2002). Race, ethnicity, gender, and sexual orientation are among the most frequently used constructs for describing and classifying people. When used in cross-cultural research, these categories present difficulties. One begins to study other groups with limited tools, reach some conclusions, and assume that these are reliable representations of all members of the groups. The constructs thus developed are arranged into a set of beliefs about the specific groups, with various degrees of accuracy and social consensus. Unfortunately, the actual situation may not be as simplistic because not all individuals within a class may think or react in such predictable fashions. These ideas stem primarily from our understanding of our own cultural biases, constructs, and values (Machado, 2000).

References

Chorlian, M. (2000). Discover American history: Armenian Americans. *Cobblestone, 21*(5), 2.

Hall, G. C. N., & Barongan, C. (2002). *Multicultural psychology.* Upper Saddle River, NJ: Prentice Hall.

Lopez, A. (2001). The borderlands of journalism. *Nieman Reports, 55*(2), 13–14.

Machado, A. (2000). Cultural sensitivity and stereotypes: *Journal of Multicultural Nursing & Health, 7*(2), 13–15.

Stereotype threat   Stereotype threat is the risk of confirming a negative stereotype about one's group. Stereotype threats arise in situations in which the stereotype is relevant. The situation strikes one as a test of stereotype-relevant qualities. This threat is to self-identity. It is the fear of fulfilling negative stereotypes. It is a social factor that influences cognitive functioning due to the person's reaction to being the object of stereotype and prejudice. If the threat is experienced during a domain performance such as in a classroom presentation, the emotional reaction to stereotype threat may affect performance (Steele, 1997). It is therefore a situational phenomenon that occurs when targets of stereotypes alleged to have intellectual inferiority are reminded of the possibility of confirming these stereotypes. The experience of stereotype threat may also interfere with intellectual performance, especially when the individuals are highly identified with success and achievement in the given domain. For example, Spencer, Steele, and Quinn (1999) showed that high-achieving females performed significantly worse than males on a standardized math test when the stereotype about their math ability was made salient. Stereotype threats are more likely to be experienced when there is a consistency in reminding individuals of their membership in a stereotyped group (Steele & Aronson, 1995).

References

Spencer, S. J., Steele, C. M., & Quinn, D. (1999). Stereotype threat and women's math performance. *Journal of Experimental Social Psychology, 35,* 4–28.

Steele, C. M. (1997). A threat in the air: How stereotypes shape intellectual identity and performance. *American Psychologist, 52,* 613–629.

Steele, C. M., & Aronson, J. (1995). Stereotype threat and the intellectual test performance of African Americans. *Journal of Personality and Social Psychology, 69,* 797–811.

Susto   This is a folk illness prevalent among some Latinos in the United States and among people in Mexico, Central America, and South America. Susto is also referred to as *espano, pasmo, tripa ida, perdida del alma,* or *chibih.* Susto is an illness attributed to a frightening event that causes the soul to leave the body and results in unhappiness and sickness. Affected individuals also experience strain in their social roles. Symptoms may appear from days to 10 years after the frightening event. It is believed that in extreme cases, susto may result in death (Gaw, 2001). Typical symptoms of susto include appetite disturbances, inadequate or excessive sleep, troubled sleep, disturbing dreams, feelings of sadness, low self-esteem, and lack of motivation to do anything. Somatic symptoms may also accompany susto, including headache, muscle aches, stomachache, and diarrhea. Ritual healings focus on calling the soul back to the body and cleansing the person to restore spiritual balance (Gaw, 2001).

Reference

Gaw, A. C. (2001). *Concise guide to cross-cultural psychiatry.* Washington, DC: American Psychiatric Publishing.

Symbolic culture A symbol is simply understood as an expression that stands for or represents something else, usually a real-world condition. Culture refers to the cumulative deposit of knowledge, experience, beliefs, values, attitudes, meanings, hierarchies, religion, notions of time, roles, partial relations, concepts of the universe, and material objects and possessions acquired by a group of people in the course of generations through individual and group striving. Symbolic culture is communication; some of its symbols include a group's skills, knowledge, attitudes, values, and motives. The meanings of the symbols are learned and deliberately perpetuated in a society through its institutions (Porter, 1994). The term *symbolic culture* derives from a variety of cultural studies. It is generally understood that there is a culture, and it produces symbols. In this understanding, culture is treated like an object; it is simply presumed to exist and to have the same kind of existence as a tree or a rock. These symbols, signs, figures, and so on are the keys to identity, power, and so on (Anton, 1998). According to Wade (1999), the symbolic culture is the culture that is dependent on symbolic relation and consisting of patterns (explicit and implicit) of and for behaviors acquired and transmitted by these symbols and constituting the distinctive achievement of human groups. All these variables are included in their embodiments in artifacts. Wade concluded that the essential core of culture consists of traditional ideas, especially their attached values; these symbolic cultures may be considered as products of action, on the one hand, and as conditioning influences on further action, on the other hand.

References

Anton, H. (1998). *Culture and practical reason.* Chicago: University of Chicago Press.

Porter, A. (1994). *Introduction to psychology* (10th ed.). New York: Harcourt Brace Jovanovich.

Wade, P. (1999). Can culture be copyrighted? *Current Anthropology, 39,* 193–222.

T

Taboo Taboo applies to the sacred or consecrated or to the dangerous, unclean, and forbidden (Freud & Brill, 1960). It is a Polynesian word in origin from *tapu* or *tabu*, which means sacred or defiled. It is the prohibition of an act or the use of an object or word under pain of punishment. A taboo can be placed on an object, person, place, or word that is believed to have inherent power above the ordinary. This power, called *mana*, can only be approached by special priests. To give distinction to special moments in the life cycle, taboos are often declared at births, deaths, initiations, and marriages. Taboos are commonly placed on a clan's ancestral guardian, called the *totem*. The breaking of a taboo usually requires extermination of the offender or some sort of ceremonial purification to remove the taint from the community. Often, the mana of a taboo is so great that the offender will suffer punishment, even death, merely through fear of its powers (Frazer, 1955). Everything that can happen to a person in the way of disaster should be catalogued according to the active principles involved in the universe of his or her particular culture (Douglas, 1966).

References

Douglas, M. (1966). *Purity and danger.* New York: Routledge.

Frazer, J. G. (1995). *Taboo and the perils of the soul* (3rd ed.). New York: Macmillan. (Original work published 1955)

Freud, S., & Brill, A. A. (1960). *Totem and taboo.* New York: Dover. (Original work published 1918)

Taijin kyofusho Taijin kyofusho is used by the Japanese and is also referred to as "anthrophobia." The term *taijin* refers to "interpersonal" and *kyofusho* means phobia or fear. Individuals experiencing this illness report that their body parts or body functions may offend, embarrass, or displease others. Symptoms include fear of embarrassing others by blushing or causing discomfort by one's gaze, facial expression, or body odor. They also fear offending others by speaking one's thoughts aloud. The disorder primarily affects young people in interpersonal situations (Levine & Gaw, 1995).

Reference

Levine, R. E., & Gaw, A. C. (1995). Culture-bound syndromes. *Psychiatry Clinic North America, 18,* 523–536.

Tainos   *Tainos* were Indians of the Caribbean who lived near the sea, which yielded its bounty to these peaceful Indians. The Tainos were the first Native Americans to encounter the Spanish (Alegria, 1993). Taino culture was the most highly developed in the Caribbean when Columbus reached Hispaniola in 1492. Islands throughout the Greater Antilles were dotted with Taino communities nestled in valleys and along the rivers and coastlines, some of which were inhabited by thousands of people (Biscione, 1998). Taino Indians who inhabited the territory called the island *Boriken* or *Borinken*, which means "the great land of the valiant and noble Lord" or "land of the great Lords." Today, this word is used to designate the people and island of Puerto Rico (Morris, 1995). The first New World society that Columbus encountered was one of tremendous creativity and energy. The Tainos had an extraordinary repertoire of expressive forms in sculpture, ceramics, jewelry, weaving, dance, music, and poetry. Their inventiveness and dynamism were also reflected in their social hierarchies and political organization (Biscione, 1998). The Tainos were bronze colored, average in stature, and had dark, flowing, coarse hair. They had large, dark eyes that were slightly oblique. Males and single women were naked, whereas married women wore a cotton skirt called a *nagua*. The Tainos fished and hunted, but their occupation was mainly agriculture. They believed in life after death, and they buried their dead carefully, placing food and water in the tombs so the spirit could use them in its journey (Biscione, 1998). The Spaniards severely mistreated the Indian population, forcing them to work in mines and construction as well as in agriculture. They did not address the rights of the Tainos. Despite their eventual rebellion against the Spaniards, the disappearance of the Tainos was extreme and fast. Unused to slave labor conditions and exposed for the first time to European diseases for which they had no immunity, the Taino population was rapidly decimated (Morris, 1995).

References

Alegria, R. E. (1993). *Taino: Caribbean ancestors.* New York: Monacelli.

Biscione, M. (1998). *Taino: Pre-Columbian art and culture from the Caribbean.* New York: Monacelli.

Morris, N. (1995). *Puerto Rico: Culture, politics and identity.* Westport, CT: Praeger.

Taoism   Taoism (pronounced "Dow-ism") originally started as a philosophy and developed into a religion during the Han dynasty. *Taoism*, also known as Daoism, is the collective term used in the West for two essentially different movements of Chinese philosophy and religion. Philosophical Taoism, whose most famous representatives were Lao-tzu and Chuang-tzu, teaches conformity by the practice of unassertive action and simplicity. This is also known as the concept of Wu Wei (Fischer-Schreiber, 1989). It represents above all a total acceptance of and trust in the force that rules the universe and is often given the simple name of Tao, which means "The Way." The teachings of Tao are set forth in a slender volume called Tao Te Ching (Dow Deh Jeeng) or "The Way of Life." Like the eightfold path of the Buddha, it is basically a guide to living the serene, untroubled life of pain (Janaro, 1997). Taoism resembles Buddhism in many respects. For instance, the latter teaches that suffering is the fundamental rule of life and the way to escape is by detaching oneself. Taoism, however, puts the source of the pain within each of us and teaches that the serene life is achieved when we see beyond our ideas of the world and everything in it as they really are. Hence, instead of becoming separate from life, one should learn to live in harmony with it (Janaro, 1997). True Taoists have always been concerned with worldly affairs and have been engaged in supporting legitimate governments in general. Fundamental Taoism is the belief that the universe operates through the continual interaction of opposites: joy and pain, birth and death, cold and heat, and male and female. In other words, one cannot be celebrated without the other (Brandon, 1970).

References

Brandon, S. (1970). *A dictionary of comparative religion*. New York: Scribner.

Fischer-Schreiber, I. (1989). *The encyclopedia of Eastern philosophy and religion*. Boston: Shambhala.

Janaro, R. (1997). *The art of being human*. New York: Longman.

Third World   This is a 1950s expression coined by French intellectuals searching for a way to lump together the newly independent former European colonies. It was used to describe the more than 100 economically underdeveloped nations in Asia, Africa, South America, and the Caribbean (Elliot, 1991). All Third World countries share certain characteristics: They all suffer from poverty and lack of development, and most have been subjected until recently to colonial exploitation and regard development as their first priority. There is some amount of exception in terms of poverty because some Third World countries, such as Brazil, are on the verge of a major industrial evolution (Arnold, 1994). There are hazards in defining people by what they cannot do or what they do not have. Being Third World connotes poverty-stricken tropical societies composed of dark-skinned people that are the victims of First and Second World nations instead of societies that have won political independence. This has not aided their development. Efforts have been made to define Third World more positively as the membership of some group that is more useful. In political terms, the most significant group is the Non-Aligned Nations (Elliot, 1991). The nonaligned movement covers the entire spectrum of Third World politics. All members of the nonaligned movement are members of the Third World, but not all members of the Third World are nonaligned, such as Brazil, Chile, and Venezuela (Arnold, 1994). Third World countries are sometimes divided into groups according to regional location. There are major divisions within the classification "Third World." The most obvious are

- Latin American countries, which achieved early independence
- Africa, whose more than 50 nations have almost all achieved independence since 1945 and generally are the world's poorest countries
- The new nations of Asia, whose ancient cultures differ radically from those of the recently dominant Western imperial powers
- The numerous small territories, mainly islands in the Caribbean Sea and in the Pacific and Indian Oceans
- China, which in terms of development needs is a Third World country but is already a superpower (Arnold, 1994)

Third World is considered a derogatory term implying less importance or worth. The origin of the word, however, means a third force consciously developed to attempt to prevent the Cold War from escalating, which is a positive description. Unfortunately, the magnitude of development problems set against the declining world economic conditions led both North and South to think increasingly of the Third World as poor and not as a third force (Arnold, 1994).

References

Arnold, G. (1994). *The Third World hand book* (2nd ed.). London: Cassell.

Elliot, J. M. (1991). *Annual editions: Third World 91/92.* Guilford, CT: Dushkin.

Traditional cultures Traditional cultures may be observed as collectivistic cultures in terms of how each individual views himself or herself within the nation and among his or her people. Traditional cultures exist in those countries whose human activities, such as religion, philosophy, moral standards, laws, politics, economics, society, history, literature, and art, have been preserved, learned, and transmitted in a given community or group over a long period of time (Institute for Japanese Culture and Classics, 1999). Customs, beliefs, and practices have been upheld from their ancestors and handed down to the future generation. This type of culture is usually observed among the natives of a land. A traditional culture may also be a society whose members view their lives and the future of their children as being essentially the same (Levinson, 1991). The people of traditional cultures usually live in small rural settlements commonly called villages. Traditional cultures still exist mainly in the rural areas of many countries and continents, including Africa, Middle Eastern countries, and some areas of the Far East. In traditional cultures, food supply usually derives primarily from subsistence farming within a village. In Zambia, some villagers organize their individual fields into larger fields to support the community, whereas groups of women grow their own crops for sale. In extremely traditional societies, the main type of food consists of staples and starch. Meats are sometimes reserved for special occasions or as a sacrifice during religious ritual (Ember & Ember, 2001). Monogamous matrimonial alliances are usually arranged by families; choice, however, is becoming increasingly common. Polygamy in some areas is not common, possibly because of the high risk of diseases, but it is not illegal (Ember & Ember, 2001). Religion plays a vital role in the survival of people of traditional cultures. These cultures are usually polytheistic and seek to always please their gods. In traditional societies, the education opportunity is very limited or does not exist, and the literacy rate is very low. When education exists within a village, it is not transferable outside of the village. Other times, children do not go to school: Boys are given daily outdoor chores until they are old enough to work in the fields with older men, and girls remain at home because traditions hold that they are needed at home (Gall, 1998b). Traditional culture may be observed partially in Westernized or industrialized urban areas and nations. An example of this is African American people in the United States celebrating traditional holidays and events, such as the birthday of Black legend Martin Luther King, Jr. (Gall, 1998a).

References

Ember, M., & Ember, C. (2001). *Countries and their culture* (Vol. 3). New York: Macmillan.

Gall, T. (1998a). *Worldmark encyclopedia of cultures and daily life* (Vol. 2). Cleveland, OH: Eastwood.

Gall, T. (1998b). *Worldmark encyclopedia of cultures and daily life* (Vol. 3). Cleveland, OH: Eastwood.

Institute for Japanese Culture and Classics. (1999). *Cultural identity and modernization of Asian countries.* Tokyo: Kokugakuin University Press.

Levinson, D. (1991). *Encyclopedia of world cultures* (Vol. 9). Boston: Hall.

U

Uncertainty avoidance   This is defined as the lack of tolerance for ambiguity and the need for formal rules. From a cultural perspective, uncertainty is the extent to which the members of a culture feel threatened by uncertain or unknown situations (Holfstede, 1991). Uncertainty avoidance describes the degree to which different cultures develop ways to deal with anxiety and stress of uncertainty. Cultures high on uncertainty avoidance develop rules and rituals that are embedded not only in their daily lives but also in their organization. They may also be considered rule-oriented and have more structured activities, more task-oriented managers, and more conformity in managerial styles than do cultures low in uncertainty avoidance (Matsumoto, 2000). Cultures highest in uncertainty avoidance include Greece, Portugal, Belgium, and Japan, whereas those lowest on this dimension include Sweden, Denmark, and Singapore (Holfstede, 2001). On the basis of studies by Laurent (1978), there are clear distinctions in connotation between countries that are high on uncertainty avoidance and those that are low. He found that countries that are high on this dimension have a higher anxiety level in the population, higher job stress, and a preference for larger organizations as employers; believe that the hierarchical structures of the organization should be clear and respected; and disapprove of competition between employees. Countries low in uncertainty avoidance have a lower anxiety level in the population, lower job stress, and a preference for smaller organizations as employers; believe that the hierarchical structures of organizations can be bypassed for pragmatic reasons; and endorse fair competition between employees.

References

Holfstede, G. (1991). *Cultures and organizations: Software of the mind.* London: McGraw-Hill.

Holfstede, G. (2001). *Culture's consequences* (2nd ed.). Thousand Oaks, CA: Sage.

Laurent, A. (1978). *Matrix organizations and Latin cultures.* Brussels: European Institute for Advanced Studies in Management.

Matsumoto, D. (2000). *Culture and psychology: People around the world.* San Francisco: Wadsworth.

V

Voodoo The word *voodoo* is Dahomean in origin. Among the Fon-speaking people of West Africa, it signified spirit or deity. Voodoo in Haiti consists of the rites, beliefs, and practices of the Vodoun cult, built around the similar religious systems of the Dahomeans and the Nagos (Courlander, 1996). The history of voodoo begins with the arrival of the first group of slaves at Saint-Domingue in the second half of the 17th century (Metraux, 1972). Voodoo, a Haitian import, first entered New Orleans when the slaves adapted Roman Catholic saints to the deities of their own bush religion. French-speaking Haitian immigrants preferred New Orleans, where French was still spoken (Machovec, 1989). The origin of the voodoo rites has two aspects—one that is supernatural and one that is geographical. Voodoo is sometimes spelled *vodou* or *vodu* because *vo* means "introspection" and *du* means "into the unknown" (Rigaud, 1985). Voodoo shows that the brain can sever physiological stresses and increase suggestibility. Loa, African tribal gods, possess humans during voodoo rituals and carry out behaviors expected of the particular deity. During the voodoo ritual, possession occurs along with frantic dancing, incessant drum beating, rum drinking, and cigar smoking. Those who have experienced it report that they first feel a force inside them and then uncontrollable trembling like shivering, loss of motor control, falling, and seizures as the god takes over (Sargant, 1957). American voodoo differs from that of Africa. African voodoo is very tender and very loving, with more quiet self-respect and character. American voodoo is considered to be rough and aggressive (Machovec, 1989). Voodoo is a system of concepts concerning human behavior, the relation of mankind to those who have lived before, and the relation to the natural and supernatural forces of the universe. It relates the living to the dead and to those not yet born. Voodoo encompasses a very complex religion and magic with complicated rituals and symbols that have developed for thousands of years, longer than any other of today's established faiths (Rigaud, 1985). Vodooism in New Orleans is not an African *cultus* but a curious class of Black practices. In New Orleans, among the people of color and among many of the uneducated of other races, the victim of inexplicable illness or misfortune is believed to be the victim of voodooism. The preferred definition for voodoo is a true religion, which attempts to connect the unknown to the known and create order where madness existed before. Voodoo explains unpredictable events by showing them to be consistent with traditional values (Courlander, 1996).

References

Courlander, H. (1996). *Afro-American folklore.* New York: Marlowe.

Machovec, F. J. (1989). *Cults and personality.* Springfield, IL: Charles C Thomas.

Metraux, A. (1972). *Voodoo in Haiti.* New York: Schocken.

Rigaud, M. (1985). *Secrets of voodoo.* San Francisco: City Lights.

Sargant, W. (1957). *Battle for the mind: A physiology of conversion and brainwashing.* Garden City, NJ: Doubleday.

Wacinko   This is a culture-specific disorder (see Culture-Bound Syndromes). The term refers to a response to interpersonal problems and disappointment. The symptoms are mutism, anger, withdrawal, and suicide (Paniagua, 2000). Additional symptoms are immobility, depression, psychosis, and psychomotor retardation (Lewis, 1975). Also, it can be translated as pouting (James, 1996). The wacinko syndrome is found in the American Indians (Paniagua, 2000). It is specifically found in the Oglala Sioux, which has a population of 13,000 people. The indigenous practitioners recognize the syndrome as a distinctive disorder. Non-Indian practitioners may not recognize it, however, even though the symptoms are not culture bound. Most cases are diagnosed as reactive depressive illness (Lewis, 1975). In addition, most patients are misdiagnosed with schizophrenia (James, 1996). Wacinko can be depression and suicide from hormonal problems. Native herbalists, *yuwipi* doctors, conduct treatment for wacinko. Unfortunately, outsiders may not be aware of the behavior patterns of the Oglala Sioux (Lewis, 1975).

References

James, A. (1996). Assessment with Native American families. In *The Prevention Report.* Washington, DC: National Resource Center for Family Centered Practice.

Lewis, T. H. (1975). A syndrome of depression and mutism in the Oglala Sioux. *American Journal of Psychiatry, 132,* 753–755.

Paniagua, F. A. (2000). Culture-bound syndromes, cultural variations, and psychopathology. In I. Cuellar & F. A. Paniagua (Eds.), *Handbook of multicultural mental health: Assessment and treatment of diverse populations* (pp. 140–141). New York: Academic Press.

Western cultures   Western cultures are those that offer and promote individualistic lifestyles. The Western culture began to take form with the mingling of Greco-Roman and Hebraic-Christian cultures in the later days of the Roman Empire (*Webster's Third New International Dictionary,* 1993). This type of culture can be found on the continent of Europe and also in North and South America, Australia, and other countries because portions of the population originated or have ancestors from Europe. Countries that are classified as having a Western culture are not classified based on geographical location; rather, the classification includes all countries that were (a) once colonized by Europeans and (b) have a majority population from Europe, with their political and social structure influenced and modeled by Europeans (Levinson, 1991). This includes Australia, United Kingdom, Spain, France, and Italy. In terms of race, most Westerners are Caucasoid or White. Western cultures tend to posses most, if not all, similar cultural traits in terms of marriage and family:

- Marriage is monogamous: Each married man has only one wife.
- Kinship is bilateral: Each individual considers the relatives of his or her parents equally closely related.
- The family is mainly or exclusively nuclear.
- All the person's relatives comprise a kindred, which consists of an equal number of mother's kinsmen.
- Marriage is neolocal: Newlyweds preferentially set up a new and independent household of their own.
- Newborn children are usually assigned backup parents known as godparents.

Western cultures are usually monotheistic in belief and religion, and Christianity is the predominant religion (Gall, 1998). Etiquette is similar in most Western cultures and changes between generations; norms for appropriate behavior are still important, however, especially in the elite and middle class. Postural norms are also similar in Western cultures; people lean forward to show interest and cross their legs when relaxed, and smiles and nods encourage conversation (Ember & Ember, 2001).

References

Ember, M., & Ember, C. (Eds.). (2001). *Countries and their culture* (Vol. 2). New York: Macmillan.

Gall, T. (1998). *Worldmark encyclopedia of cultures and daily life* (Vol. 4). Cleveland, OH: Eastwood.

Levinson, D. (Ed.). (1991). *Encyclopedia of world cultures* (Vol. 4). New York: Hall.

Webster's third new international dictionary. (1993). Springfield, MA: Merriam-Webster.

Western psychology Psychology is the study of the mind and mental processes pertaining to human and animal behavior (Dorland, 1994, p. 1383). Western refers to characteristics of the region usually designated as the West. Therefore, *Western psychology* is the term used to characterize the type of psychology that is practiced in Western, individualistic, and highly industrialized societies, such as the United States and those of Western Europe. Western psychology is described as "rational, extroverted, and individualistic" in its approaches toward its subjects. In the West, the self is viewed as an independent, autonomous entity; hence, the focus of psychology is the individual. An interesting value in Western psychology is control, which, according to Gerring and Zimbardo (2002), means making behavior happen or not happen. They report that critics have argued that the focus on control in Western psychology represents a cultural bias that emerged from industrialization and colonization by Europeans and from the mentality of conquest of the frontier in the United States. Another bias of Western psychology is that this control focus is more typical of the male perspective due to the sparcity of women in the development of Western psychology (Riger, 1992). Because Western psychology is specific to individualistic and industrialized cultures, it may not be applicable in collectivistic or Third World cultures (Berry, Poortinga, Segall, & Dasen, 2002, p. 456).

References

Berry, J. W., Poortinga, Y. H., Segall, M. H., & Dasen, P. R. (2002). *Cross-cultural psychology: Research and applications* (2nd ed.). Cambridge, UK: Cambridge University Press.

Dorland, N. W. (1994). *Dorland's illustrated medical dictionary* (23rd ed.). Philadelphia: W. B. Saunders.

Gerring, R. J., & Zimbardo, P. G. (2002). *Psychology and life* (16th ed.). Boston: Allyn & Bacon.

Riger, S. (1992). Epistemological debates, feminist voices: Science, social values and the study of women. *American Psychologist, 47,* 730–740.

Whorfian hypothesis   This is also known as the Sapir-Whorf hypothesis, named after the two U.S. linguists who first formulated it (Lee, 1996). First discussed by Sapir in 1929, the hypothesis became popular in the 1950s following posthumous publication of Whorf's writings on the subject (www.wikipedia.org). Lee notes that Whorf's hypothesis is that people are only able to think about ideas that have labels in their spoken language. Carrol and Whorf (1959) note that the Whorf hypothesis states that it is not the way things are actually said but the environmental factors that produce the reason for saying it. What results from this are the many different points of view from many different languages. Whorf fully believed in linguistic determinism—that what one thinks is fully determined by one's language. He also supported linguistic relativity, which states that the differences in language reflect the different views of different people. The Sapir-Whorf hypothesis theorizes that thoughts and behavior are determined (or at least partially influenced) by language (Orwell, 1990). The Sapir-Whorf hypothesis also states that language creates ways of thinking and perceiving (Lee, 1996). Orwell notes that the Sapir-Whorf hypothesis is generally associated with the position that language structures entail a general philosophical system for perceiving, ordering, and acting on reality, and, as such, language has a major influence on thought and culture.

References

Carroll, J., & Whorf, B. (1959). *Language, thought, and relativity: Selected writings.* Cambridge: MIT Press.

Lee, P. (1996). *The Whorf theory complex: A critical reconstruction.* Philadelphia: Benjamins.

Orwell, G. (1990). *1984* (Reissue ed.). New York: Signet.

Windigo, wind ego, or witiko   This is a culture-bound syndrome of neurotic, obsessive cannibalism, now somewhat dishonored. The term *Windigo* (Ojibwa) or *witiko* (Cree) refers to a folk monster that eats human flesh. Windigo was evidently brought about by consuming human flesh in deprived conditions. Afterwards, the cannibal was supposed to be haunted by cravings for human flesh and thoughts of killing and eating humans (Tseng, 2001). Windigo is usually found in Native Americans, particularly the Algonquian Indians. This syndrome developed in the winter when families were isolated by heavy snow for months in their cabins and had insufficient food supplies. The primary symptoms of this form of psychosis were usually poor appetite, nausea, and vomiting. Consequently, the individual would develop an attribute of delusions of being transformed into a windigo monster. Windigo was first introduced as a sickness by J. E. Saindon, a missionary who worked among the Cree in the early 20th century (Gaw, 2001). People who have windigo mental illness increasingly see others around them as being suitable for eating. At the same time, they have an embellished fear of becoming cannibals. Anxiety centers on the belief that the person is being overcome by a mystical monster and becoming a Windigo (cannibal). There is compulsion for suicide or for the person to be the object of violence (Dorland, 1994). The syndrome involves disgust for ordinary food and feelings of depression and anxiety, leading to possession by the witiko spirit (a giant man-eating monster) and often resulting in homicide and cannibalism. It occurs among Canadian Indians and has been construed as a severe form of starvation anxiety. If a cure is not obtained, the witiko sufferer often pleads for death to avert his or her cannibalistic desire (Berry, Poortinga, Segall, & Dasen, 2002). The legend of the wind ego often varies in details, but the main proposal is the same: Lost hunters or people in a state of food crisis (especially during the wintertime) who turn to cannibalism as a last resort will become windigos or be occupied by the Windigo's spirit and then be drawn toward eating people. When this occurs, they become aggressive and antisocial. It is believed that the only way to kill the Windigo and the malicious spirit is to burn the body of its host to ashes. Windigo is usually associated with winter because lack of food is experienced during this time, and cannibalism may occur. Most tales state that the Windigo rides with the winter wind, howling inhuman screams; others state that the Windigo, or at least its heart, is made of ice and cold. Although most tales recount the Windigo as being cannibalistic, dangerous, and violent, the host can still try to live far from civilization, deep in the woods, to prevent anybody from becoming his or her next victim. Some windigo-inhabited people would even commit suicide to prevent hurting anyone else. The legend also states that when speaking of a supernatural being, the word Windigo should be capitalized, but when speaking of a cannibalistic human, wind ego should be lowercased. There was a case in recent history in which, after a long depression during the winter, an Indian developed a craving for human flesh and acted on it. In modern psychology, there is a condition called windigo psychosis. The symptoms include anorexia. There are many other superstitions surrounding the Windigo—as many as there are Indian tribes in the cold forests of Canada. Regardless of the specifics, the Windigo as a culture-specific disorder may result from the conflict between unmet needs and failing ego defenses (Teicher, 1960).

References

Berry, J. W., Poortinga, Y. H., Segall, M. H., & Dasen, P. R. (2002). *Cross-cultural psychology: Research and applications* (2nd ed.). Cambridge, UK: Cambridge University Press.

Dorland, N. W. (1994). *Dorland's illustrated medical dictionary* (23rd ed.). Philadelphia: W. B. Saunders.

Gaw, A. C. (2001). *A concise guide to cross-cultural psychiatry.* Washington, DC: American Psychiatric Publishing.

Teicher, M. I. (1960). Windigo psychosis: A study of a relationship between belief and behavior among Indians of northeastern Canada. In V. F. Ray (Ed.), *Proceedings of the 1960 annual spring meeting of the American Ethnological Society.* Seattle: University of Washington Press.

Tseng, W. (2001). *Handbook of cultural psychiatry.* San Diego, CA: Academic Press.

Xenophobia   *Xenos* is Greek for stranger, and *phobos* is Greek for fear. Thus, the term *xenophobia* refers to the fear for the stranger, the other, the unknown (Allen, 1993). Xenophobia an irrational fear of foreigners, probably justified, always understandable. Wilhelm Heitmeyer, born in 1945 and a professor of socialization at the University of Bielefeld, Germany, formulated what is known as xenophobia (Allen, 1993). It is a vague psychological concept describing a person's disposition to fear or despise other people or groups viewed as outsiders (Dollard, 1938). Allport (1954) describes xenophobia as an antipathy based on faulty and inflexible generalization. Xenophobia is hatred, resistance, and negative prejudice against foreign people and everything that is foreign, unordinary, or not stereotypical (Allen, 1993). This means that people may hate or dislike others who are different in race, religion, sexual orientation, age, or gender (Allen, 1993). Both racism and homophobia are sometimes reduced to xenophobia (Pechnar, 1997). Xenophobia may be directed toward representatives of a particular nation or groups that threaten one's sense of material well-being. These foreigners may be migrant workers or immigrants. Fear of losing one's job due to the presence of these foreigners may be the mitigating force behind xenophobia.

References

Allen, D. (1993). *Fear of strangers: And its consequences.* Grawn, MI: Bennington.

Allport, G. W. (1954). *The nature of prejudice.* Cambridge, MA: Addison-Wesley.

Dollard, J. (1938). Hostility and fear in social life. *Social Forces, 17,* 19–38.

Pechnar, T. (1997). *Escalation of discrimination and xenophobia against minority religions in today's Germany.* Washington, DC: Oval Books.

Y

Ying-yang This term refers to the dualistic Chinese concept that stands for heaven and earth, also known as the sources of all creations. According to traditional beliefs, *ying* and *yang* are forces that generate feelings in man. In nature, however, it is responsible for the weather and the seasons. In addition, it is responsible for all outward or external living conditions that man depends on to work. The words also refer to the way a person lives his or her life through a balanced moral conduct or attitude (Pye, 1994). Although it is believed that the interactions of these two concepts are the cause of the universe, it is also believed that on reaching its extreme stage, each concept or entity turns into the other (Fischer-Schreiber, 1989). Interestingly, this concept helped in the development of the Chinese principle that all things are mutually related and in a constant process of transformation. Originally, the word ying designated the northern slope of a mountain facing the moon or the passive, female aspects of things, whereas yang referred to the slope of a mountain that faced the sun or the male aspects of things (Cattell, 1967). In recent years, however, the term has come to have a great influence on Chinese culture, metaphysics, cosmology, government, art, and decoration (i.e., Feng Shui) (Brandon, 1970). According to Fischer-Schreiber, ying and yang have become very important in traditional Chinese medicine. In other words, the body is healthy only when ying and yang hold each other in balance. Too much ying causes inadequate functioning of organs, whereas too much yang causes an increase in chemical activity.

References

Brandon, S. G. F. (1970). *A dictionary of comparative religion.* New York: Scribner.

Cattell, A. (1967). *A dictionary of esoteric words.* New York: Citadel.

Fischer-Schreiber, I. (1989). *The encyclopedia of Eastern philosophy and religion.* Boston: Shambhala.

Pye, M. (1994). *The Continuum dictionary of religion.* New York: Continuum.

Yoga In Sanskrit, this term is also known as *yoking.* This is a term with many meanings, however. For instance, in its most basic sense it is synonymous with "path," "practice," or "religion." Specifically, it designates a set of exercises practiced with the aim of either physical benefit or spiritual enrichment (Pye, 1994). When used alone, the word is most likely to refer to methods of self-control and meditation as practiced by most yoga schools (Brandon, 1970). Yoga proposes methods of meditation to bring about purification of consciousness by releasing oneself from nature and moving to a more metacognitive state. In the past, the practice was supposed to bring about the acquisition of magical powers (Brandon, 1970). In Hinduism, this term also refers to the harnessing of oneself to god—that is, seeking unity with him. The term refers to numerous paths or schools of philosophy that are specific to the practitioner, however (Fischer-Schreiber, 1989). Hindu paths or schools of philosophy that are more common in the West are Mantra yoga (the science of vibration), Gnana yoga (intellect is challenged to obtain knowledge of heaven), Bhakti yoga (in which discipline or structure lead to physical satisfaction by means of love and devotion), Karma yoga (the belief that work and attainment happen only through action), Raja yoga (the belief that service and self-sacrifice lead to a balance of worldly matters), and Hatha yoga (the belief that straining for mental and physical power leads to a healthy mind-set) (Cattell, 1967).

References

Brandon, S. G. F. (1970). *A dictionary of comparative religion*. New York: Scribner.

Cattell, A. (1967). *A dictionary of esoteric words*. New York: Citadel.

Fischer-Schreiber, I. (1989). *The encyclopedia of Eastern philosophy and religion*. Boston: Shambhala.

Pye, M. (1994). *The Continuum dictionary of religion*. New York: Continuum.

Yonsei *Yon* is a Japanese term that means fourth, and *sei* means generation (Karin, 2003, p. 1). *Yonsei* is the Japanese term used to describe fourth-generation Japanese immigrants either to the United States or to Canada. This generation is characterized by being of mostly mixed ethnicity, with few speaking Japanese or even looking Japanese. *Nikkei* is the term used to describe all those of Japanese heritage living outside of Japan. The generations of Nikkei are expressed not only in terms of those who first landed in Canada or the United States but also in relation to World War II. The fourth generation is the second generation to be born after the war (Hiruki, 2002, p. 1). The Yonsei are today's youngest generation of Nikkei and are the children of the first generation to be born after the war. They are children of the Sansei. According to the Japanese counting system, the fourth generation should be Shisei, but *shi* in the Japanese language means "death," so the alternative counting system was used in which *yon* means four. The children of the Yonsei will be referred to as *Gosei*, a reversion to the original counting system (Kitano & Daniels, 1995).

References

Hiruki, T. (2002). "Sei what?" In *The runker room*. Tokyo: Island.

Karin, K. (2003). *Japanese America: Meeting. Daily notes*. Berkeley: University of California Press.

Kitano, H. H. L., & Daniels, R. (1995). *Japanese Americans: The evolution of a subculture* (2nd ed.). Englewood Cliffs, NJ: Prentice-Hall.

Z

Zar This is a culture-specific disorder, and the term is derived from the word for "visitation," referring to being "visited" by a possessing spirit or demon (Boddy, 1989). It is a ritual among and for women; it is a kind of catharsis for perceived mental, emotional, and physical troubles. It is usually done by a female leader who occupies a "wise woman" role of some sort; it is often done by women of the same village who know each other (Farrah, 1978).

It is a trance ceremony of North Africa and the Middle East and is technically forbidden by Islam (El-Shamy, 1980). It is best described as a "healing cult" that uses drums and dance in the ceremonies. It also functions as a sharing of knowledge and charitable society among the women of these very patriarchal cultures. Most leaders and most participants are women. The majority of the possessing spirits are male; those possessed are generally female; and the sense of possession is usually, although not exclusively, inherited. It is also contagious and may strike at any time. The Zar is basically a dance of spirits or a religious dance. These ceremonies provide a unique form of relief to women in strict patriarchal societies, in which they are not treated as equals. These ceremonies were well established in the Sudan by the 1820s. They are currently outlawed by Sharia's law of 1983. The Zar of today is practiced more as a relaxation technique and as a spiritual healing for stressed or troubled people. The sacrificing of animals may or may not be part of this modern ceremony. The leader of the modern ceremony is called Kodia (Egypt), a Shaykha (Sudan), or an Umiya (Sudan), depending on the region. The leader is also possessed; she has come to terms with her spirit and is therefore able to help others. Heredity is considered an important qualification; leadership is often passed from mother to daughter or through female members of the family. Men cannot inherit it.

The Zar is not an "exorcism," as people often describe it, because the spirit is accommodated and placated; it is not exorcised (El-Shamy, 1980).

References

Boddy, J. (1989). *Wombs and alien spirits: Women, men and the Zar cult of northern Sudan.* Madison: University of Wisconsin Press.

El-Shamy, H. (1980). *Folktales of Egypt.* Chicago: University of Chicago Press.

Farrah, I. (1978). Zar dance. *Arabesque, 3*(6), 111–114; *4*(1).

Zen   This term is an abbreviation of the word *zenna* or *zenno*. It is also the equivalent of the Chinese word *chan*, which refers to the collectedness of mind and meditative state. Currently, it is used to refer to the teachings and practices of Zen Buddhism (Pye, 1994). Zen attempts to eliminate all dualistic relationships, however, such as I and you, subject and object, or true and false (Fischer-Schreiber, 1989). According to Cattell (1967), by doing so, a state of equilibrium or balance is reached. Zen is not something that one studies, however, but something that one lives by. In other words, one achieves it through the actual process of becoming it. Zen, in a sense, is a religion whose teachings and practices are directed toward the realization of the self. In turn, this leads to enlightenment, which is achieved by intensive meditation and self-discipline (Brandon, 1970). It stresses the importance of self-awareness and that intellectual analysis of doctrine and ritual religious practices are futile for the ultimate attainment of liberation. Instead, it claims that without reliance on scriptures, the essence and spirit of Buddhism are transmitted directly. Proponents of Zen believe that man's original nature is that of the Buddha in an unrealized state (Brandon, 1970). Zen teaches that through meditation, one can cut through the illusion of reality and the illusion of the ego to the truth that underlies all things. Through this process of clearing the mind, one can experience sudden Enlightenment, which in turn leads to the state of nirvana, in which human suffering is no longer experienced (Hurst, 1995).

References

Brandon, S. G. F. (1970). *A dictionary of comparative religion.* New York: Scribner.

Cattell, A. (1967). *A dictionary of esoteric words.* New York: Citadel.

Fischer-Schreiber, I. (1989). *The encyclopedia of Eastern philosophy and religion.* Boston: Shambhala.

Hurst, J. (1995). Buddhism in America: The dharma in the land of the red man. In T. Miller (Ed.), *America's alternative religions.* Albany: State University of New York Press.

Pye, M. (1994). *The Continuum dictionary of religion.* New York: Continuum.

About the Author

Lena E. Hall, PhD, is Associate Professor at Nova Southeastern University. She has been conducting seminars, making presentations, and teaching classes on multicultural psychology for approximately two decades. She published a textbook for undergraduate students titled *Issues in Multicultural Psychology*. She is involved in cross-cultural research in substance abuse.